Fo
GRA

POCKET ANNUAL 1997

Bruce Smith

3rd Year of Publication

F1 NEWS

Virgin

Formula 1 Grand Prix Pocket Annual

To Sarah with all my love.

First published in April 1997 by *Virgin Publishing.*

Virgin Publishing Ltd
332 Ladbroke Grove
London
W10 5AH

Typeset by Bruce Smith Books.

Disclaimer

In a book of this type it is inevitable that some errors will creep in. While every effort has been made to ensure that the details given in this annual are correct at the time of going to press, neither the editor nor the publishers can accept any responsibility for errors within.

CONTENTS

Introduction

This third edition of the Formula 1 Grand Prix Pocket Annual is your passport to a Grand Prix season that promises to be the most intriguing for years. With this annual you will have all the facts, information and background to keep you in the know. You'll find driver profiles, team details, race and qualifying comparisons along with detailed track descriptions, all of which make the Formula 1 Grand Prix Pocket Annual the best, most comprehensive, value for money guide.

A driver merry-go-round of changes and the introduction of two new teams to *The Show* are just two of the ingredients in a mix sure to offer more than its fair share of thrills during 1997. The Rothmans-Williams Renault looks to be invincible as a machine but can Jacques Villeneuve maintain and better the standard he set for himself last year? His team-mate Heinz-Harald Frentzen has been heralded as one of the fastest drivers around for a number of years, now we'll find out if he can secure points on a regular basis.

Too many have been writing off the man he replaced, World Champion Damon Hill, who surprised the racing world when he decided to join Tom Walkinshaw at Arrows – the longest serving team never to win a Grand Prix. History will count for nothing in 1997, and if the Yamaha engine in the Arrows can perform, Hill has the expertise to sneak that first win at some point – getting in the points on a regular basis though will make Arrows' year a successful one as the team build.

Ferrari will be a threat and it seems only a matter of time before Michael Schumacher claims his third Drivers' Championship in a Ferrari. If Eddie Irvine can rake in the points, which he is capable of, then a Constructors' Cup may also be in the offing. But the departure of 53-year old designer John Bernard will take its toll on the development of the car – and watch out for a more orange flavoured red on that Ferrari to please new sponsors Marlboro. Is nothing sacred?

After a year of transition, much more will be expected of Benetton. Jean Alesi had his best year in F1 last term and if he can improve another step then he could be leading the challenge to Villeneuve and Schumacher for the championship. His team-mate Gerhard Berger was plagued by the effects of illness last year and, now in his racing twilight years, will be looking for a big improvement in form. They should regain their competitive edge but the loss of Technical Director Ross Brawn to rivals Ferrari will be a big blow.

Four years ago it would have seemed inconceivable that McLaren could go three seasons without a victory. But that's what has happened. Gone also are sponsors Marlboro and maybe that will be a change in their fortunes. In David Coulthard they have a driver who knows what it takes to win a Grand Prix, and in Mika Hakkinen a driver good enough to win his first Grand Prix. The Mercedes powerplant is arguably the most powerful on the circuit and if the chassis can deliver this year then both McLaren drivers could find themselves on the apex of the podium this term.

Inexperience will probably cost Jordan dearly in 1997. Much will be made of Ralf Schumacher – can he emulate brother Michael? Eddie Jordan will hope so but success, if it is to come, will lay in the future. If investment is the Jordan plan then in Giancarlo Fisichella there is a potential gem. Time, as ever, will tell.

Just weeks before the start of the season came the news that Alain Prost had acquired Ligier. As this team work towards becoming a French national racing team – they signed a contract with Peugeot to supply engines in 1998 – they have, in Olivier Panis, a driver on the edge. His win at Monaco in 1996 was his highlight so far, but he is only a position or two from becoming a regular points scorer. The inclusion of Shinji Nakano as co-driver must be to keep engine suppliers Mugen-Honda happy. His one year contract will probably be no more than that unless he excels in 1997.

This season Sauber have no excuses. Last season the Swiss outfit's good chassis was let down by an under-performing engine. This time round though they have Ferrari technology in their powerplants and a more settled Johnny Herbert to gather points. Nicola Larini secured a podium place for Ferrari in 1994, and is highly rated in the F1 world.

Tyrrell have lost the Yamaha engine to Arrows this year, but it was engine reliability that caused them most problems during 1996. With that in mind the switch to the tried-and-tested Ford V8 could be seen as an improvement. Jos Verstappen has joined the talented Mika Salo, and will be looking to improve on last year's eighth position overall. This could be Salo's last year with the team and he will be looking to impress any prospective new employers.

The arrival of Tom Walkinshaw at Arrows could have benefited the Minardi outfit who have picked up the Hart V-8 engine to power their cars for 1997. The arrival of Ukyo Katayama will provide Minardi with much needed sponsorship moneys as he seeks to re-establish the form he showed in 1994 with Tyrrell. He is joined at Minardi by newcomer Jarno Trulli, who comes from F3 with a good reputation.

That leaves us with the two new teams. The Stewart team have worked hard to ensure that everything is right for their debut, even if it was close cut at times. They have the technology and funds and also the backing of a Ford V-10 engine. Rubens Barrichello is a driver of experience who many observers believe to be on the verge of stepping into the big-time. This is balanced with the experience of Jan Magnussen, who has had a long association with Paul Stewart Racing. Much is expected from the public but the team will consider a regular mid-place position a success and any points a triumph.

Lola are not new to F1. They have supplied chassis to teams in the past. They can also point to a succession of titles at other levels including five IndyCar championships. Using a Ford engine for now, they are developing their own powerplant for future use. Ricardo Rosset, coming from Arrows, and Vincenzo Sospiri making his debut have little to offer in experience terms to race and car development, which will probably see the Lola cars bringing up the rear.

Changes '97

There are a number of changes to the FIA Formula 1 Technical Regulations for 1997. Many of these are relatively minor changes, the more significant of which, and the ones likely to create the most interest, are detailed below.

Starting in 1997, all Formula One cars will be fitted with an Accident Data Recorder (ADR). This will store information about what happens to a car during and immediately before an accident. Such information has never previously been available and its study should enable the FIA to make significant advances in driver protection. In effect it will serve the same function as the so-called 'black box' fitted to all aircraft. The device has been designed by the US company Delco Electronics Corporation.

Any specific part of the car influencing its aerodynamic performance must be rigidly secured to the entirely sprung part of the car (rigidly secured means not having any degree of freedom).

Fuel tanks must now be a single rubber bladder conforming to FIA specifications and all the fuel stored on board the car must be situated between the front face of the engine and the driver's back when viewed in lateral projection. However, a maximum of 2 litres of fuel may be kept outside the survival cell, but only that which is necessary for the normal running of the engine. All fuel lines between the fuel tank and the engine must now have a self sealing breakaway valve which separates at a load which is less than 50% of the load required to break the fuel line fitting or to pull it out of the fuel tank. In addition no lines that contain fuel, cooling water or lubricating oil may pass through the cockpit.

Refuelling equipment has now been standardised and teams must use equipment which has been supplied by an FIA designated manufacturer. To prevent accidental opening in the event of an accident, a strong cover must be fitted over the car connector when the car is running on the track.

There are a number of minor changes concerning roll-over structures to help secure the driver's safety and these simply enforce changes made before the start of the 1996 season. In particular, the incorporation of at least two roll-over structures. Dimensional changes have also been made to the driver's survival cell to further protect him and ensure easy ingress and egress.

Thanks '97

I would like to thank all the Formula 1 teams for their co-operation in producing this annual, in particular: Lindsay Morle (Williams), Anne Bradshaw (Arrows), Claudio Berro (Ferrari), Jessica Walker (Benetton), Anna Guerrier (McLaren), Giselle Davies (Jordan), Chris Williams (Prost), Gustav Busing (Sauber), Avenue Communications (Tyrrell), Roberta Leonardi (Minardi), Stuart Sykes (Stewart) and Anne Hale (Lola). Photographs courtesy of ICN.

Many thanks also to Mark Webb who wrote the season's review and edited and proof-read these pages.

Contact '97

If you have access to the Internet and want to stay in contact with F1 throughout the year, and in particular with this annual, then check out the Sky Sports Formula 1 site at:

http//:www.sky.co.uk/sports/formula1/index.htm

If you have any comments or ideas for future editions of this annual you can eMail me at:

Bruce-Smith@msn.com

Using the Annual

The *Formula 1 Grand Prix Pocket Annual* is divided into several clear sections that arrange information, statistics and reviews in relevant sections which are clearly defined in the Contents list on pages 3 and 4.

At the start of each section you may find a small guide or key to specific information and abbreviations used.

Through the Pocket Annual a set of country abbreviations is used and the key to these is listed below. Thus *Jap* signifies a Grand Prix in Japan.

Key to Races

Arg	Argentina	Jap	Japan
Aus	Australia	Mex	Mexico
Aut	Austria	Mon	Monaco
Bel	Belgium	NZ	New Zealand
Bra	Brazil	Pac	Pacific
Can	Canada	Pes	Pescara
Dal	Dallas	Por	Portugal
Esp	Spain	SA	South Africa
Eur	Europe	San	San Marino
Fin	Finland	Swi	Switzerland
Fra	France	USA	United States of
GB	Great Britain		America
Ger	Germany	USAE	United States of
Hol	Holland		America (East)
Hun	Hungary	USAW	United States of
Ita	Italy		America (West)

Grand Prix
Review 1996

At the start of the 1996 season it was as though the drivers had returned from their break to find that some administrative error had placed them in the wrong cars as *seven* of the top drivers changed teams. The big move was Michael Schumacher to Ferrari – a reported $25 million per year enticing him away from Benetton where he had won two Drivers' World Championships. Schumacher made it clear from the start that 1996, and possibly even 1997, was going to be about getting the car and team in the right frame of mind for a real World Championship assault in 1998. Joining him at Ferrari was to be Eddie Irvine, signed from Jordan where he scored 10 points in 1995.

Alesi switched to Benetton after five semi-productive seasons at Ferrari. Gerhard Berger came too! Both signed two year contracts. Johnny Herbert, moving across from Benetton, joined Heinz-Harald Frentzen at Sauber. Martin Brundle made his sixth change in as many years, starting 1996 with the Jordan-Peugeot alongside Rubens Barrichello.

One of the new boys (the others were Rosset and Fisichella) was Jacques Villeneuve at Williams, who came to F1 as the reigning IndyCar champion. As son of Gilles, he had a big reputation to live up to. Everything else at Williams spelled consistency with the FW18 evolving from the FW17 and the new RS8 engine from partners Renault. Even test driver Jean Christophe Bouillon had his contract with Williams renewed for another year.

Coulthard, Hill's promising partner at Williams in 1995, started a two year contract at McLaren. He joined the remarkable Mika Hakkinen who, having suffered a huge practice accident at Adelaide at the end of 1995 which left him in a coma, worked back to fitness, watched carefully by F1 Doctor, Sid Watkins, to get back in a F1 car in February and make the opening event in Melbourne.

Taki Inoue signed for Minardi for the season to join Pedro Lamy at the Italian based team. Inoue was with Arrows in 1995 but his seat was now taken by Ricardo Rosset. Mark Blundell without a F1 drive traversed the Atlantic for the IndyCar ovals.

Arrows' Ricardo Rosset had made a rapid rise through the racing ranks to become the number two driver to Jos Verstappen, starting in F3 and finishing as runner-up in the FIA F3000 International Championship in 1995.

Katayama and Salo manned the Tyrrell and its Yamaha V10 while Panis and Diniz crewed the Ligier team's Mugen-Honda powered cars. Montermini, who in '95 drove for Pacific (who collapsed after the season had finished), joined Badoer at Forti-Ford. The season began with 11 teams, without Pacific and Simtek from the previous year. It would end with only 10 though.

There was much speculation around McLaren. Alain Prost worked as a consultant pre-season with the brand new MP4/11 car, fuelling rumours that he might drive again. The rumours proved to be just that. As the season loomed some newspapers reported details of the technical report which might form the basis of a prosecution of Williams team members and Imola management over the death of Ayrton Senna.

March

Australia! The inaugural Grand Prix at Melbourne saw the introduction of a new qualifying regime. There were no Friday qualifying sessions. Teams were allowed to have two free practice sessions of one hour, limited to 30 laps on Fridays (Thursday at Monaco). On Saturdays the teams had two 45 minute sessions. The qualifying session was limited to twelve laps and there was a cut off point of Pole Position time plus 7% for qualifying – the so-called 107% rule. If a car was outside this it was also outside of the race!

When the **Australian Grand Prix** got underway Villeneuve stormed to a pole position in his debut and came within a whisker of winning. He led the race from team-mate Hill for much of the time but suddenly his engine started losing oil and he ultimately had to lay off the pace and allow Hill to pass him for the win. The Williams team were clearly ahead of the game and Schumacher's two stop strategy showed that his John Barnard designed F310 was running a much lighter fuel load. Irvine out qualified the German at Melbourne by securing third place on the grid, going on to finish on the podium in the same place.

Brundle's season started in spectacular fashion when he wrote off his Jordan 196 and amazingly walked away to restart the race in the spare car. The crash was more of a launch when he combined with Panis and Coulthard and ended up flying through the air with his Jordan rotating around its long axis. The 150,000 crowd and the worldwide audience beyond were astounded by this display of courage. Rosset's ninth placing in Melbourne was an excellent start to his F1 career and, despite suffering a spin at the hands of Pedro Lamy, he ultimately finished two laps down.

Berger was 77 seconds behind but in the points and Alesi eventually retired after a tangle with Eddie Irvine during an overtaking manoeuvre. Hakkinen was further behind. Like McLaren, the Jordan team displayed none of their pre-season speed, and Barrichello was the victim of an expiring Peugeot engine.

The Sauber seemed a little off the pace, and could only manage ninth on the grid and eighth out of 11 finishers. The Tyrrell and Ligier teams both had two cars finish the race. Minardi's excuse was that they were still not running their new car. Lamy's best performance in qualifying didn't translate to the race. After clutch problems, a bump with Rosset at the second race start caused his seat belt to come loose and he had to stop for safety reasons.

Forti fell first victim to the 107% rule and didn't make it to the start, although Luca Badoer was within 0.4 seconds of qualifying. Montermini's qualification was fraught with problems, not least the fact that his car caught fire in the team garage on the Friday night.

The financial troubles that had haunted Arrows in pre-season seemed to be behind them with the announcement that Tom Walkinshaw was to take over, after relinquishing his interest in Ligier. As the teams decamped to South America, rumours of Bernie Ecclestone negotiating for a Grand Prix to be staged in Disney World raised the spectre of drivers in funny costumes.

The **Brazilian Grand Prix** turned out to be a wet one but the home crowd wasn't concerned with the weather when their new hero 'Rubinho' Barrichello had sped to second place on the grid during a sun punctured qualification. The race featured three natives in all but their tale was eventually an unhappy one. Barrichello didn't have a good start and fought initially with Alesi for third place and later with Schumacher. A battle he eventually lost when he spun off on lap 60. Rosset found himself suffering the other side of F1 when he slipped into a wall at high speed on lap 11. Tarso Marques was the third Brazilian to drive at Interlagos, in the Minardi car, bringing sponsorship to the seat otherwise filled by Fisichella. In his first qualifying session the 20-year old installed himself 19th on the grid, only to find himself relegated to last spot when he missed a signal calling him in for weighing during the session. His first race was short lived when he spun out on the very first lap!

Meanwhile Damon Hill was securing his 15th career win. Starting from pole Hill led all the way, set the fastest lap and won the race by over 20 seconds. Hill and Alesi both adopted what turned out to be perfect tactics with single pit stop strategies. Alesi won through his battle with Barrichello and finished second followed by Schumacher, Hakkinen, Salo and Panis. Villeneuve who had secured third place on the starting grid, spun off having been placed under constant pressure by Jean Alesi.

For the second race running Tyrrell and Ligier managed to get both cars to finish and after two races were the only teams with 100% completion records! Mika Salo finished in fifth. Racing with his visor up due to misting, Ukyo Katayama was hit in the eye with a stone and then spun on his second lap. Managing not to stall his engine Katayama rejoined the race at the rear and then came into the pits only to find it occupied by his team-mate. He recovered to ninth place.

April

Formula 1 drivers formally set up the Grand Prix Drivers Association with a formal constitution, offices and elected representatives. The first three elected representatives were Michael Schumacher, Gerhard Berger and Martin Brundle, the two most experienced drivers and the current World champion. The GPDA declared that they want to develop a "balanced relationship" with the FIA, Grand Prix organisers and the teams. The only driver not to join was Jacques Villeneuve.

Qualifying for the **Argentinian Grand Prix** saw Damon Hill pull an extra special final lap to beat Schumacher to pole position during qualifying and

F1 NEWS

£2.40

The UK's biggest selling fortnightly Formula One
Motor Racing magazine brings you more news
from the track, more gossip from the pit lane and
more inside stories from our team of top Grand
Prix journalists. With 64 superb full-colour pages
in every issue, F1 NEWS adds a whole new
meaning to the pole position!

F1 News is available at all leading newsagents.
Subscriptions Tel: 0171 396 8068 Fax: 0171 396 8013

PUTS THE FUN BACK IN
FORMULA ONE

won the race despite having no radio contact in the latter part. Villeneuve moved up after a bad start and made excellent use of the safety car – out after incidents involving Badoer and Diniz – to climb the position ladder and get second spot. Jean Alesi took the fastest lap, beating Michael Schumacher's lap record with a time of 1.29.413. He took third place even though he stalled in the pits to lose 17 seconds. Barrichello took fourth to score Jordan's first points.

There was joy for Forti when Montermini achieved what was to be his only finish of the season, even though he came in three laps down. Argentina was also the high point of the season for Verstappen. Having recorded his best grid position for two seasons – seventh – he had an excellent race to grab what was to be his only point of the season, bringing his all-time tally to 11. Coulthard came in just outside the points while Hakkinen's throttle stuck.

A refuelling valve on Pedro Diniz's car failed to close properly and allowed fuel to escape under braking to cause a flash fire to engulf his car. The marshals extinguished the fire to forestall any injury to the Ligier driver. Marques showed great improvement, qualifying 14th on the grid, five places ahead of senior team-mate Pedro Lamy. Problems occurred on lap 32 though when he clashed with Martin Brundle's Jordan as the in-use safety car left the circuit. The incident caused too much damage for him to continue. Tyrrell's drivers both dropped out, Sauber's Herbert managed ninth but Frentzen span out.

Three weeks later and as the teams gathered for the **European Grand Prix** at Nurburgring, there were rumours connecting Frentzen with Williams as a possible replacement for Damon Hill. The championship leader, Hill, entered the European phase with an 18 point advantage but he wasted his pole position when a poor start left him down in fourth and it probably cost him the chance of a fifth successive Grand Prix victory.

After the second places, Villeneuve secured his first ever Grand Prix win. He started second on the grid but raced into a lead which he effectively maintained despite great pressure from Schumacher, who was less than a second behind in the final stages. It was almost like old times as David Coulthard took third place after a blinding start rocketed him into second place from sixth on the grid. Hakkinen took eighth place after a 10 second penalty for speeding in the pit lane.

Barrichello was in the points again (fifth) and Brundle got his first point of the season. Fisichella returned for Minardi to finish in 13th behind team-mate Lamy in 12th. Alesi hit Salo on lap two and Berger struggled to ninth. The new TWR Arrows achieved 11th through Rosset but Verstappen dropped out. Ligier's Panis bumped Irvine and Diniz came in 10th.

May

At the **San Marino Grand Prix** Schumacher dominated practice and achieved his first pole position of the year using a special qualifying engine

14

for the first time. The Ferrari, reverting to the standard engine for the race, went on to grab second (Schumacher) and fourth (Irvine) on 'home' territory. Hill kept his cool to implement a race strategy which involved staying in touch for the first half with a heavy fuel load. He popped in for a top-up near the end and hung on to win his fourth race in five starts, giving him a 21 points lead in the Drivers' Championship over Villeneuve, who retired with broken rear suspension.

David Coulthard had another incredible start which saw a McLaren leading a Grand Prix for the first time since 1993 until his hydraulic system failed. Hakkinen managed only to get a stop-go penalty for holding up Schumacher. Mika Salo got his best grid position of the year – eighth – and he made an excellent start which saw him move up into fourth spot in the race. An engine failure on lap 24 ruined the weekend. Irvine and Barrichello picked up points again and Berger got his best finish in third and Alesi snatched a point. Lamy achieved his season's best in ninth, even after occurring a pit lane speeding penalty. Forti's Badoer and Montermini used their new FG03 car to try to qualify and Badoer managed it. He went on to finish 10th in the race.

It was announced after the race that the organisers of the San Marino race were to be questioned by FIA officials about the track invasion that took place after the chequered flag was shown to Damon Hill. The race ended with thousands of fans causing chaos as they swarmed on to the track.

Olivier Panis won the **Monaco Grand Prix**, his first and Ligier's first for 15 years. The win made Ligier the team with the longest time between Grand Prix wins. One wonders what went through the mind of Tom Walkinshaw who had left Ligier for Arrows just a few weeks beforehand! Both Jacques Villeneuve and Damon Hill had hoped to win a race that their famous fathers won. Hill had said "I would like to win here because my father won here five times in the sixties".

Schumacher had qualified in pole for the second successive race but made an honest mistake to be one of a procession of drivers to drop out of the race as the heavens opened during the first lap. Hill got one of his best starts of the season and was in the lead by the first corner. By the end of the first lap six cars were 'missing in action'. Montermini had crashed exiting the tunnel in the familiarisation session caused by the wet start, so he did not start. The two Minardi cars collided and went out at Ste Devote, Verstappen bravely opted for slick tyres and spun out, Barrichello spun at Casino followed by Schumacher, who didn't quite make it all the way round Portier.

Katayama and Rosset lasted until the third lap and Diniz spun and stalled after five. By the time the field had been reduced to 13 cars Hill had built up a 13 second lead. Gerhard Berger's race finished, along with his gearbox, on lap 9. Everyone pitted on laps 28 and 29 to change tyres as the rain abated. Martin Brundle was the next to retire, spinning while on cold slicks on lap 30. The victory seemed to be in the bag as Hill lead by 26 seconds – then disaster when an oil pump failed leaving Damon to coast to a stop. This left Alesi in the lead, though he was to retire on lap 60 with suspension failure.

Villeneuve found it hard to come to terms with the street circuit, qualifying 10th – his worst of the season – and he was eventually bundled out of the race by Badoer at the Mirabeau. Badoer was fined US$5000 and handed a two race ban, suspended for three races.

Salo in the penultimate lap ran into the back of Eddie Irvine's stationary car. Nevertheless, with the field already devoid of cars, he was classified in fifth position for only the fourth time in his career.

Mika Hakkinen also crashed into the stationary Ferrari, leaving four cars running. Panis, Coulthard and Herbert were the only three drivers to finish, Frentzen was still running but was a lap down and pulled into the pits. This turned out to be the highlight of Herbert's season when a third place was the Sauber team's best position of the year and their only podium finish. It was also Johnny's only points win of the season.

Aided by some excellent race strategy by the Ligier team – starting with a full tank of fuel in wet conditions and stopping just once – Panis became the 73rd man to win a Grand Prix and the second F3000 champion (after Alesi) to do so. His win took him up to fourth place in the championship.

June

Awful weather at the **Spanish Grand Prix** led to an incident which saw Coulthard, Lamy, Fisichella and Rosset all collided at the start – the second time this season that the Minardis had hit each other! But the rain in Spain provided the wet platform for a brilliant drive from Schumacher who came home as leader of the pack to record his first win for Ferrari. He overtook Alesi and Villeneuve and finished over 45 seconds ahead of Jean Alesi despite suffering with a misfire problem that effectively limited the power of his car for much of the race.

Alesi struggled with a poor set up, but managed to drive a fine race finishing second ahead of a much improved Villeneuve. Sauber (Frentzen), McLaren (Hakkinen) and Ligier (Diniz) all scored points, though all the cars were at least 1 lap down. Fisichella limped round to the pits and retired. Panis, having qualified in a career best eighth position in the Ligier, spun into a wall. Irvine's Ferrari spun out and got stuck on the grass. The two Jordans both retired with differential problems on lap 17 for Brundle and lap 45 for Barrichello.

Apart from Katayama (electrical problems) and Mika Salo (black flag for using the spare car) all the other retirements were due to spins. Hill, Herbert, Berger, and Verstappen included – Hill finally retiring on what was his third spin on a day when he never looked comfortable with his car. Salo had fallen foul of FIA rules. Having qualified 12th, he had engine problems on the formation lap and, having tried to start from the pits and suffered the same

16

problem, he illegally switched to the spare car, which is not allowed after the start of a race and was duly black flagged.

Forti announced a new sponsorship deal with Shannon Racing that looked to provide much needed cash as George Ryton joined as chief designer but neither came soon enough to make a difference and both drivers failed to qualify for the race.

In his home town of Montreal, Villeneuve qualified second for the **Canadian Grand Prix** and had to be content with a similar finish – it might have been a different story had the yellow flags not come out just as he caught up to Herbert's Sauber. Damon Hill this time used a two stop strategy and had to build up a lead as Villeneuve planned only one refuelling stop.

Coulthard and Hakkinen took fourth and fifth for McLaren while Martin Brundle had a great race to finish sixth – the last of the finishers although Herbert and Fisichella retired on the last laps.

The retirement in Montreal for Montermini due to loose ballast sloshing around the cockpit rather summed up Forti's fortunes although Badoer did qualify 20th in Montreal, ahead of Rosset.

Ferrari's fortunes changed drastically – Schumacher's car couldn't be fired up for the formation lap and so the German had to start from the back of the grid before retiring with drive shaft problems. Katayama's kamikaze move on Rosset knocked them both out of the race and earned the Japanese a suspended one race ban for driving 'without due care and attention'. Everyone else broke down! It was one of those days…

Williams dominated in 1996

There were initially mixed messages from the practice sessions at the **French Grand Prix** but the smooth surface of Magny Cours eventually threw up the established top five grid of Hill, Villeneuve, Schumacher and Alesi. Schumacher's engine blew up in Damon Hill's face even before reaching the grid as things went from bad to really bad for the Italian team. Hill must have taken this as an omen as he constructed a peerless drive with Villeneuve chasing and the Benetton twins in third and fourth. The two McLarens confirmed their improved form with Coulthard taking the one point. Coulthard pressed Brundle from lap 15 to lap 22 and Villeneuve and Hakkinen duelled until the first pit stops. Diniz, Barrichello and Panis fought for eighth place. Berger later passed the ailing McLaren (no first and second gear) at the hairpin. Diniz had his third good race in a row, overtaking the Jordans but retiring when in sixth to show perhaps that his Spanish sixth wasn't an aberration.

In his home race Panis qualified ninth but found the Magny Cours race blighted by fuel rig problems that forced him to make three stops. The light load did help him in setting the second fastest lap time though on the way to a final seventh placing. Minardi and Sauber struggled and Arrows' Rosset was happy to get a finish.

This was Williams' 90th win, their 50th with Renault and Renault had managed a 1-2-3-4 at their home Grand Prix. For Hill the win meant that he had now scored more Grand Prix points than his dad.

July

With the arrival of the **British Grand Prix** fuel suppliers Elf announced that they would be leaving F1 at the end of the year. A team of F1 drivers including Damon Hill, John Watts and Martin Brundle had been working on revised designs for Copse and Stowe corners at Silverstone. The Grand Prix Drivers Association representatives Schumacher and Berger had approved the changes which would make the track slightly faster.

Jacques Villeneuve won his second Grand Prix, getting ahead of Hill at the start and leading into the first corner. Behind him Alesi, Hakkinen and Schumacher all managed to pass Hill who was relegated to fifth place. Ferrari's recent run of bad luck continued with Schumacher retiring on lap three, stuck in sixth gear and Irvine retiring on lap five with smoke pouring from the back of his car. Hill's hope of a second home Grand Prix win spun off with him on on lap 26 due to a loose wheel nut and Alesi later retired with overheating brakes. Gerhard Berger and Mika Hakkinen joined Villeneuve on the podium and Barrichello, Coulthard and Brundle completed the top six.

The introduction of a completely revised Hart V8 engine offered more reliability for the Arrows team and allowed Verstappen only its second finish of the season. Ricardo Rosset retired but had his contract renewed until the end of this season. Fisichella got the Minardi to the finish but Lamy suffered gear selection problems which meant a non-finish. Katayama achieved his best grid position of the season in 12th but his engine let him down in the race. Salo hung on for seventh. Frentzen and Herbert struggled against engineering odds to cross the line in eighth and ninth respectively.

Silverstone proved to be the last time Montermini and Badoer were seen on the 1996 circuit – neither went out in a blaze of glory though as the 107% rule proved too much of a barrier. Forti did make it to the British Grand Prix but unpaid engine bills meant that they could not practice. The cars turned out for official qualifying but without any set-up work from the free practice sessions they were never likely to make it to the grid. Forti's management could only hope that they could sort out their finances in time for the German Grand Prix.

Benetton lodged an official protest at the legality of the front wings on the Williams car, claiming that the end plates were not 10mm thick and so contravened FIA rules concerning leading edges. The FIA rejected the protest and also told Benetton not to bother appealing. It smacked of desperation as Williams moved 70 points clear in the Constructors' Championship. Hill's lead, now down to 15 points, now looked less impregnable.

Hockenheim is one of the fastest circuits on the calendar which takes its toll on the cars. The **German Grand Prix** performed its usual job as a Michael Schumacher fan club gathered for his home Grand Prix. Schumi achieved third place on the grid with Berger second. But it was Hill who was first on the grid again. However, when the red lights went out, so did something in his engine and he was left by Berger and a charging Alesi off the grid. After pit stops Hill regained the lead and began to build a gap but it was not enough and he slotted in between the two Benettons after his second pit stop. Hill couldn't race past Berger but lady luck deserted the Austrian, whose engine exploded to give Hill his 20th Grand Prix victory.

Villeneuve had to settle for third place after his qualifying had been hampered by a seized shock absorber reflected by his sixth position on the grid. After some testing tussles with Coulthard and Alesi, Schumacher stayed in touch to finish fourth.

The Mercedes-powered McLaren was fastest on the straight at 212mph and Coulthard came in fifth. Barrichello got a point and Brundle finished in 10th. Frentzen and Herbert were still struggling in the Sauber. Giovanni Lavaggi's source of funding was his passport into a cash-starved Minardi for the final six races of the 1996 season, at the expense of Giancarlo Fisichella. Having failed to qualify in his first race, it was no surprise that the Minardi team appealed over Damon Hill's pole time in an effort to get their money-bringer a race. They failed.

The long-standing wrangle over Guy Ligier's remaining 15% stake in the Ligier team was finally resolved. Flavio Briatore purchased the remaining stock and obtained total control over the French team. This led to speculation that Alain Prost would step in as team boss to lead a French 'super team'. It was reported that heavy backing from the French president and minister for sport played a part in the final sale of the stock. Olivier Panis signed up for another season at Ligier.

August

In qualifying at the **Hungarian Grand Prix**, only 0.13 seconds covered the front three of Schumacher, Hill and Villeneuve. In the race Damon Hill made yet another bad start and slipped back to fourth place behind Schumacher, Villeneuve and Alesi. Jacques Villeneuve then drove brilliantly and managed to get in front of Michael Schumacher after the first round of pit stops. After taking the lead on lap 25 Jacques never looked like losing it. Hill made steady progress to second place and, although he pushed hard at the end he was unable to get past his team-mate.

Gerhard Berger suffered a very similar-looking engine failure to the one that probably cost him victory at Hockenheim, leaving Alesi to take third place. Eddie Irvine and Michael Schumacher both retired to bolster the Ferrari's reputation for unreliability. Mika Hakkinen finished fourth. Ligier again picked up points when Olivier Panis finished fifth and Rubens Barrichello concluded the points finishers in sixth. Brundle crashed out.

Panis had a bad start but his one-stop strategy allowed him to obtain two points, despite finishing a couple of laps down. Rosset gained a career best eighth position. Salo, Diniz and Verstappen were involved in a multiple collision in which Lamy was also clipped, resulting in his later retirement. Katayama finished his fourth race in a row with his best performance of the season in seventh. The Sauber pair were happier with the Cosworth upgrade to their Ford Zetec V10 but both retired.

Lavaggi, who had four races with the now defunct Pacific Ford team in 1995, made his Minardi debut. He was one of the slowest drivers on the circuit but managed to receive a pit lane speeding penalty on lap 27. Classified in 10th position he didn't actually finish the race when he spun out on lap 74, by which time he was already eight laps down on the race leader.

The Williams one-two concluded the Constructor's Championship in their favour to join Ferrari as the only constructors with eight World titles. Williams have achieved all eight since 1980. Hill's lead was now down to 17 points with 40 still to be won.

The **Belgian Grand Prix** promised a very different race from Hungary and so it proved. Michael Schumacher scored his and Ferrari's second win of the year – this was the fourth time in five years that he had finished first at this circuit, and was his third win (he was disqualified in 1994). A new seven-speed gearbox was clearly beneficial especially at the start when Schumacher stormed into the lead and then had a terrific battle with Villeneuve to keep his victory intact.

Spa also seemed to suit Villeneuve. Qualifying first by more than half a second, he looked to be comfortably in the lead until the yellow flags came out around the track and with confusion on the radio, he lost time in the pits.

Mika Hakkinen was impressive in third for a much improved McLaren team. Jean Alesi finished an untroubled fourth, while behind him Berger was pushing Damon Hill for fifth. Hill just held on to the two points and his lead was down to just 13 points with three races left.

Salo and Katayama brought the Tyrrells home in seventh and eighth. Rosset and Lamy were the other finishers. Sauber had a terrible race with both cars going out in a first lap accident, a knock which took out Panis' Ligier and which also put paid to Barrichello later on. Jos Verstappen had a high speed crash (possibly caused by his throttle sticking open) which needed the safety car to slow the race while the stricken Arrows was removed. He was flown to a nearby hospital for precautionary X-rays.

Marlboro's sponsorship of McLaren was officially declared at an end. McLaren are expected to announce a deal with German tobacco firm Reetsma for their West cigarettes brand – more cowboys!

Forti – having lost their battle to finance the rest of their season – also lost out in the courts who decided that Shannon – the newly announced sponsors – had a 51% share of the racing team. Guido Forti managed to regain control though by buying back the shares.

September

The **Italian Grand Prix** offered Hill his first chance to clinch the drivers' title. Jacques Villeneuve had to finish fourth or better to keep alive his chances, while a win for Hill would almost certainly seal the championship. The announcement that Damon would not be driving for Williams in 1997 was hardly the best preparation and Heinz-Harald Frentzen was confirmed as his replacement. It looked as if once again Williams was parting company with its world champion. (Piquet, Mansell and Prost had previously taken the number one with them out of the Williams team.) By the end of the following week, it seemed both Jordan and Stewart had approached Hill.

A pole position looked to have eased the nerve and Hill made a pretty good getaway to push Villeneuve wide for the first corner. Jean Alesi stormed from sixth to first in the same space! Damon Hill, looking forceful, took the lead at the Lesmo section, then fought off an Alesi attack in the Ascari chicane.

Tyres had been stacked in the chicanes this year to stop drivers going over the kerbs and in the end at least eight drivers had their race affected by these new structures. Villeneuve hit the tyres at the Variante Roggia. They rebounded and hit Coulthard's car causing him to spin off with damaged suspension. One lap later Alesi clipped the tyres and Hakkinen had to pit for a new nose cone after hitting a loose one with his front wing.

While Hill was stretching his lead by about half a second a lap, his team mate was dropping back due to damaged steering. Panis was next out (collision damage), then Berger (electrics) and Lavaggi (engine). On lap six Hill hit the tyres and spun out with; Frentzen followed two laps later. Salo and Lamy then went out with engine problems and by lap 12 eight cars were missing. Irvine hit the tyres on lap 24. Diniz soldiered on in sixth.

Alesi and Schumacher fought for the lead until lap 30 when the pit stops ended with the World Champion in the lead. Schumacher got away dispute hitting the tyres on lap 39, set a new lap record on lap 50 and went on to bring Ferrari a victory at Monza for the first time since 1988 and to send the *tifosi* home happy.

Hakkinen recovered from his bent nose to fight his way up to third. Villeneuve could not overcome steering damage and finished seventh, crucially out of the points. Any sort of finish was vital for Verstappen and it came despite him still suffering with a sore neck from Spa. He drove a careful race to finish in a comfortable eighth. Katayama survived for 10th place, Salo suffered at the hands of his Yamaha engine again.

In another look ahead to 1997, Stewart Grand Prix signed a five year sponsorship deal with HSBC reputed to be worth £25 million.

Jacques Villeneuve *had* to win in the **Portuguese Grand Prix** to have any chance of the championship title in a winner takes all last race in Japan. Damon Hill knew that finishing ahead of his team-mate would clinch the title. A podium finish in each race would also do the trick.

Having taken pole from the Canadian by just 0.009, Hill got away quickly while Villeneuve made an unusually poor start and was passed by Jean Alesi and Michael Schumacher. Villeneuve then moved up into third by overtaking Schumacher on the outside while cornering, and he and Schumacher both got past Alesi during the pit stops. Jacques then caught and passed his team-mate during the pit stops and powered away to an outstanding victory. Hill had to accept a second place finish, which he managed despite a clutch problem. Team Williams were 100 points clear in the Constructors' Championship thanks to their sixth 1-2 of the season.

Schumacher pipped Alesi for third. Behind them Irvine and Berger were having the best fight of the race, even colliding on the last lap. Berger recovered first but was then overtaken by Irvine before the chequered flag.

The McLaren cars were running with a chance of a points finish when they touched at the Corkscrew. Coulthard spun off and rejoined, Hakkinen damaged his nose cone and front wing. Both cars pitted, Hakkinen for repairs, Coulthard for a check. They both went out again only for Hakkinen to retire and Coulthard, after five pit-stops in all, to eventually finish 13th.

Lamy suffered disappointment in his home race when an overheating clutch on the formation lap caused the car to stall on the grid and he had to start the race from the pit lane two laps down.

Jordan's Brundle finished ninth but Barrichello spun out. The team pretty much confirmed that they had signed a deal with Ralf Schumacher for the next season. Salo and Katayama finished next to each other as on the grid. Frentzen (seventh) and Johnny Herbert (eighth) kept their grid positions. Panis battled into 10th, Diniz spun in an incident with Rosset (14th). The Minardis brought up the rear.

Damon Hill unexpectedly announced that he had signed for the Arrows team for 1997. Although it will be an all-new team, Arrows' 287 races without a win is a record to challenge even a World Champion. The Arrows team is now owned by TWR who have helped Jaguar win at LeMans and the man behind TWR (Tom Walkinshaw) is credited with signing Schumacher for Benetton and then building a double championship winning car around the driver. Johnny Herbert announced a new two-year deal with Sauber.

Hill had only to score a point in the **Japanese Grand Prix** to become champion. Villeneuve had to win to even have a chance. Despite conceding pole position to his challenger, Hill was first by the first corner and Villeneuve was seventh. It was by far Hill's best start of the season and it quite literally put him in the driving seat! Jean Alesi left the track at high speed, crashed heavily into the barriers but escaped injury.

The race settled and the order of Hill, Berger, Hakkinen, Schumacher, Irvine and Villeneuve looked unlikely to change until Berger tried to out brake Hill at the chicane. He only succeeded in damaging his front wing when he ran over the high kerb. Villeneuve was now fifth, and Martin Brundle up into sixth. On lap 12 Villeneuve passed Irvine going into the chicane.

Villeneuve's first pit stop was a lengthy one due to a car coming down the pit lane as he was ready to exit. A precautionary pit stop for a suspected puncture on lap 32 revealed nothing wrong with the tyre. Five laps later his rear wheel flew off causing him to slide to a halt in the gravel. It meant but one thing – Hill was world champion! Driving from the front he recorded another win. He became the eighth British driver to take the title and the first son of a world champion to do so. His record of 21 wins from 67 starts placed him fourth in the all time wins/starts ratio (behind Fangio, Ascari and Clark). Williams had now won the Drivers' title on five occasions (Jones, Rosberg, Piquet, Mansell, Prost, Hill).

Michael Schumacher did manage to pass Hakkinen during the pit stops to secure third place in the Drivers' Championship and second for Ferrari in the Constructors'. Gerhard Berger fought back up to fourth place, knocking Irvine out of the race on lap 40, for which he was later given a one race suspended ban. Berger also received a fine for pit lane speeding during practice.

Brundle finished fifth, Frentzen sixth and Panis was just outside the points again. Coulthard had a difficult race, stalling on the grid and starting from the back to finish eighth. Barrichello's last race for Jordan was an ordinary one back in ninth.

It was Damon Hill's and Williams' year but the signs were there in 1996 that Ferrari and Benetton could mount a renewed challenge. McLaren too were beginning to emerge from the pack as real contenders. The number one is up for grabs in 1997. Who will be bold enough to take it?

RACE PROCEDURES

There is a strict timetable laid down by the FIA for the build-up and start of each Grand Prix race. This set of procedures ensures that no team is favoured when it comes to circuit time, qualifying, warm up and the actual race. Details of these are given below – all times are local. Note that what follows is a general guide only and liable to change.

Circuit Practice

There are four sessions of free practice. These take place on the Friday and Saturday, except for the Monaco Grand Prix when the Friday practice is held on the Thursday. The two sessions on the Friday last for one hour each and are held from 11.00 to 12.00 and 13.00 to 14.00. The two sessions on the Saturday last for 45 minutes each and are held from 9.00 to 9.45 and 10.15 to 11.00.

The only stipulation for each day of free practice is that it is limited to a maximum of 30 laps – the teams can determine how this is split between the two sessions on each day. It is not necessary to use the full 30 laps but no laps can be carried from one day to another. A spare car may not be used in the free practice session.

Qualifying Session

A single one-hour session is held for qualifying (prior to 1996 there used to be two sessions). This takes place on the Saturday from 13.00 to 14.00. From 1997 each driver will be limited to a maximum of 12 qualifying laps and a lap will count towards the qualifying laps provided the driver has started it before the expiry of the 60 minute clock. The 12 laps are normally performed by teams as three or four lap sessions. This is at the total discretion of teams and drivers – the usual senario is an 'out' warm-up lap where the tyres are brought up to race temperature; two flat-out laps, where drives go all-out for a fast time, and a final 'in-lap' as drivers come back into the pits.

The fastest lap out of those registered will count as the qualifying time. To qualify for a race all drivers must establish a lap time that is within 107 per cent of the time set by the fastest driver in the qualifying session. Drivers outside of this limit will not automatically qualify for the race – the FIA have the right to admit a driver to the race. (A rough guide to 107% times can be found towards the end of the Annual.)

The driver's grid position is determined by his time. Thus the fastest qualifying time earns the driver the first or pole position on the starting grid. A spare car may be used in the qualifying session in case of accident or mechanical problems. Indeed some teams (Ferrari in 1996) even use a special qualifying engine.

Warm-up Session

A 30-minute warm-up session is held on the Sunday of the race and this normally starts four and a half hours before the start of the race. If, after this, rain occurs an extra 15-minute session may be sanctioned to allow teams to make wet-weather changes.

The Race

The race follows a set countdown to the start. Thirty minutes prior to the race the Pit Lane is opened for just 15 minutes. During this window all cars must leave their paddocks and make their way to the starting grid. Fifteen minutes prior to the start of the race the Pit Lane is closed. Any cars not out of the paddocks must now start from the Pit Lane – this effectively places the car at the back of the grid.

Once all cars are formed on the grid a series of time boards are used to display the amount of time remaining to the start of the race. These are carried through the grid and personnel must adhere to their significance.

Ten minutes before the start of the race all personnel except drivers, team members and officials must leave the starting grid. Boards are shown at five minutes, three minutes, one minute and thirty seconds before the start of the race. At the one minute board engines are started and all technicians and team staff are required to leave the grid.

When the count reaches 30 seconds a green flag is displayed and cars on the starting grid advance on a single formation lap. Cars must adhere strictly to their grid position and no over taking is allowed (cars can be disqualified for doing so). Cars return to their grid position and wait for the start. When all cars are stationary on the grid a series of red lights come on one after the other until they are all switched on. When the lights are then switched off (this is done together) the race has commenced.

Stopping the Race

The race may be stopped as a result of accidents or adverse weather conditions. This is done by showing the red flag. If the race is stopped before two laps are completed, cars return to their original grid positions and the race is restarted. A new time will be given for the race start and this is normally as soon as feasibly possible after the original race was stopped. Cars that might have had to start from the Pit Lane now have an opportunity to join the starting grid. In the case of an accident, drivers have the opportunity to use their spare car. If this cannot be made ready in time to join the grid the car will start from the Pit Lane.

If more than two laps, but less that 75 per cent, of the race is completed, the race restarts on a dummy grid, according to positions at the time the race was stopped. The distance of the re-started race is that required to make up the full race distance, less three laps (thus the race is shortened by three complete laps).

If the race is stopped with more than 75 per cent completed, the race is deemed to have been run and positions at the point of the race being stopped are the finishing positions.

Race Distance

A Grand Prix race must not be shorter than 190 miles (305 kms). The number of laps that a race comprises is the smallest number of laps that will exceed this distance. There is also a two hour time limit on a race and should this time limited be exceeded (perhaps due to bad weather conditions) the chequered flag will be shown to the leader at the end of the lap in which the two hour mark is passed – even if the scheduled race distance has not been completed.

Pit Lane

There is a maximum speed assigned to all Pit Lanes that must not be exceeded. The maximum speed varies from circuit to circuit and is between 50-75mph (80-120kph).

Cars starting from the Pit Lane can only join the race after the cars on the starting grid have all passed the exit from the Pit Lane. Cars in the Pit Lane are not able to take part in the formation lap.

Penalties

Minor violations of rules – such as Pit Lane speeding, 'Jump' starts, and dangerous driving (to name three) may be penalised by a Stop-Go penalty. The driver is required to return to his paddock and wait for a 10-second count.

Drivers and teams who do not adhere to the rules face other penalties. For example, a driver drives an extra lap, say in a practice session, will likely get a fine. This is typically US$5-10,000. A driver who is found to have driven recklessly or created a crash that was avoidable might receive a suspended race ban that would be invoked if he repeated the feat in the time frame specified.

Flags and Signals

There are ten flags that can be shown and these are illusrated on the inside back cover of this annual. A flag's significance may be changed depending on whether it is held stationary or waved.

Red Flag: This is only shown at the start/finish line and is used to indicate that the race has been stopped.

White Flag: When held stationary it indicates the presence of a slower vehicle on the track. When waved it indicates that the driver may be seriously obstructed by a slower vehicle ahead of him on the track.

Black Flag: Shown with white number to indicate the driver to whom it applies. The driver indicated must stop at the Pit within one lap and report to the Clerk of the Course. (This will normally be at the driver's pit paddock where a Stop-Go penalty might be indicated or disqualification.)

Black and White (Diagonal) Flag: Used only once per driver as a warning for unsportsmanlike behaviour.

Black with Red Spot Flag: Shown with white number to indicate the driver to whom it applies. The driver indicated has a mechanical failure and must stop at his pit.

Blue Flag: This flag is used to indicate that a faster car is following. When held stationary the driver concerned must give way, when waved the driver must give way urgently. During a race, failure to give way when the Blue flag is waved may result in a penalty. A Blue flag is also used at the exit from the Pit Lane to indicate to the driver exiting that traffic is approaching on the track.

Yellow and Red Striped Flag: When held stationary it indicates that there is oil or water on the track, when waved there is a slippery surface immediately ahead.

Yellow Flag: This flag indicates a hazard ahead and there should be no overtaking. When held stationary it indicates that there is a hazard on the track and drivers should drive well within their limits. When waved, cars must slow down and be prepared to change direction or follow an unusual line. When double waved, cars must slow down and be prepared to stop as the track is partially or wholly blocked.

Green Flag: This is used to signify the end of a danger area that will have been marked by a yellow flag. Effectively it is an all-clear. Also used to signify the start of the warm-up lap.

Chequered Flag: Signifies the end of the race.

GP Results '96

At a Glance

GP	Winner		Pole	
Australian	D.Hill	Williams	J.Villeneuve	Williams
Brazilian	D.Hill	Williams	D.Hill	Williams
Argentinian	D.Hill	Williams	D.Hill	Williams
European	J.Villeneuve	Williams	D.Hill	Williams
San Marino	D.Hill	Williams	M.Schumacher	Ferrari
Monaco	O.Panis	Ligier	M.Schumacher	Ferrari
Spanish	M.Schumacher	Ferrari	D.Hill	Williams
Canadian	D.Hill	Williams	D.Hill	Williams
French	D.Hill	Williams	M.Schumacher	Ferrari
British	J.Villeneuve	Williams	D.Hill	Williams
German	D.Hill	Williams	D.Hill	Williams
Hungarian	J.Villeneuve	Williams	M.Schumacher	Ferrari
Belgian	M.Schumacher	Ferrari	J.Villeneuve	Williams
Italian	M.Schumacher	Ferrari	D.Hill	Williams
Portuguese	J.Villeneuve	Williams	D.Hill	Williams
Japanese	D.Hill	Williams	J.Villeneuve	Williams

Summary

D.Hill (GB)	Williams	8 wins	9 poles
J. Villeneuve (Canada)	Williams	4 wins	3 poles
O.Panis (France)	Ligier	1 win	–
M.Schumacher (Germany)	Ferrari	3 wins	4 poles

Key to Results

r = retired.
fs = failed to start (either from grid or otherwise).
fsr = failed to start after first start red-flagged.
dq = disqualified.
dnq = did not qualify.
dnf = did not finish.
nc = non-classified – driver finished but outside of 107% race band.

Round 1: Australia – Melbourne

Date: 10 March 1996
Track: 5.269 kilometres
Conditions: Sunny and warm

Attendance: 154,000
Length: 305.602 kilometres
Fastest Lap: J. Villeneuve – 1:33.421

Pos	Driver	Car	Laps	Time/Reason	Fastest	mph
1	D. Hill	Williams	58	1.32:50.491	1:33.621	123.494
2	J. Villeneuve	Williams	58	1.32:28.511	1:33.421	122.656
3	E. Irvine	Ferrari	58	1.33:53.062	1:34.533	122.122
4	G. Berger	Benetton	58	1.34:07.528	1:34.757	121.809
5	M. Hakkinen	McLaren	58	1.34:25.562	1:35.843	121.422
6	M. Salo	Tyrrell	57	1.33:03.181	1:35.280	121.089
7	O. Panis	Ligier	57	1.33:14.468	1:34.767	120.844
8	H-H. Frentzen	Sauber	57	1.33:29.436	1:35.596	120.522
9	R. Rosset	Arrows	56	1.33:21.629	1:36.557	118.573
10	P. Diniz	Ligier	56	1.33:25.689	1:37.024	118.487
11	U. Katayama	Tyrrell	55	1.32:51.827	1:36.377	117.078
r	P. Lamy	Minardi	43	seat belt defect	1:38:784	109.758
r	M. Schumacher	Ferrari	33	brakes	1:33:651	119.290
r	G. Fisichella	Minardi	33	clutch	1:38.007	116.796
r	R. Barrichello	Jordan	30	engine	1:35.064	120.882
r	D. Coulthard	McLaren	25	stuck throttle	1:37.764	118.847
r	J. Verstappen	Arrows	16	engine	1:36.649	117.785
r	J. Alesi	Benetton	10	collision	1:35.519	121.816
r	M. Brundle	Jordan	2	spin	1:56.481	101.825
r	J. Herbert	Sauber	1	collision		–

Starting Grid

1.	J. Villeneuve (Can)	1:32.371	2.	D. Hill (GB)	1:32.509
3.	E. Irvine (GB)	1:32.889	4.	M. Schumacher (Ger)	1:33.257
5.	M. Hakkinen (Fin)	1:34.054	6.	J. Alesi (Fra)	1:34.257
7.	G. Berger (Aut)	1:34.344	8.	R. Barrichello (Bra)	1:34.474
9.	H-H. Frentzen (Ger)	1:34.494	10.	M. Salo (Jap)	1:34.832
11.	O. Panis (Fra)	1:35.330	12.	J. Verstappen (Hol)	1:35.338
13.	D. Coulthard (GB)	1:35.351	14.	J. Herbert (GB)	1:35.453
15.	U. Katayama (Jap)	1:35.715	16.	G. Fisichella (Ita)	1:35.898
17.	P. Lamy (Por)	1:36.109	18.	R. Rosset (Bra)	1:36.198
19.	M. Brundle (GB)	1:36.286	20.	P. Diniz (Bra)	1:36.298

Drivers outside 107% rule:

	L. Badoer (Ita)	1:39.202
	A. Montermini (Ita)	1:42.087

Date: 31 March 1996
Track: 4.325 kilometres
Conditions: Cloudy, wet but drying

Attendance: 54,000
Length: 307.075 kilometres
Fastest Lap: D. Hill – 1:21.547

Pos	Driver	Car	Laps	Time/Reason	Fastest	mph
1	D. Hill	Williams	71	1.49:52.976	1:21.547	104.19
2	J. Alesi	Benetton	71	1.50:10.958	1:21.866	103.90
3	M. Schumacher	Ferrari	70	1.50:00.569	1:22:889	102.60
4	M. Hakkinen	McLaren	70	1.50:16.004	1:22.283	102.36
5	M. Salo	Tyrrell	70	1.50:26.315	1:22.483	102.20
6	O. Panis	Ligier	70	1.50:34.031	1:22.743	102.08
7	E. Irvine	Ferrari	70	1.51:11.438	1:23.062	101.51
8	P. Diniz	Ligier	69	1.50:27.806	1:23.576	100.72
9	U. Katayama	Tyrrell	69	1.51:00.929	1:22.722	100.22
10	P. Lamy	Minardi	68	1.50:02.877	1:23.559	99.64
11	L. Badoer	Forti	67	1.50:52.957	1:25.627	97.43
12	M. Brundle	Jordan	64	spin	1:22.043	100.59
r	R. Barrichello	Jordan	59	spin	1:22.359	100.50
r	H-H. Frentzen	Sauber	36	gearbox	1:36.166	95.76
r	D. Coulthard	McLaren	29	spin	1:36.245	93.99
r	J. Herbert	Sauber	28	electrics	1:38.127	92.90
r	J. Villeneuve	Williams	26	spin	1:36.383	96.89
r	G. Berger	Benetton	26	suspension	1:36.998	93.99
r	A. Montermini	Forti	26	spin	1:40.661	89.55
r	R. Rosset	Arrows	24	collision	1:36.981	94.92
r	J. Verstappen	Arrows	19	engine	1:35.435	94.18
r	T. Marques	Minardi	0	spin	–	94.18

Starting Grid

1	D. Hill (GB)	1.18.111	2	R. Barrichello (Bra)	1.19.092
3	J. Villeneuve (Can)	1.19.254	4	M. Schumacher (Ger)	1.19.474
5	J. Alesi (Fra)	1.19.484	6	M. Brundle (GB)	1.19.519
7	E. Irvine (GB)	1.19.591	8	M. Hakkinen (Fin)	1.19.607
9	G. Berger (Aut)	1.19.762	10	H-H. Frentzen (Ger)	1.19.799
11	M. Salo (Jap)	1.20.000	12	J. Herbert (GB)	1.20.144
13	J. Verstappen (Hol)	1.20.157	14	D. Coulthard (GB)	1.20.167
15	O. Panis (Fra)	1.20.426	16	U. Katayama (Jap)	1.20.427
17	R. Rosset (Bra)	1.20.440	18	P. Diniz (Bra)	1.20.873
19	T. Marques (Bra)	1.21.421	20	P. Lamy (Por)	1.21.491
21	L. Badoer (Ita)	1.23.174	22	A. Montermini (Ita)	1.23.454

Drivers outside 107% rule:
    None – all qualified

Date: 7 April 1996
Track: 4.259 kilometres
Conditions: Sunny and warm

Attendance: 75,000
Length: 306.680 kilometres
Fastest Lap: J. Alesi – 1:29.413

Pos	Driver	Car	Laps	Time/Reason	Fastest	mph
1	D. Hill	Williams	72	1.54:55.322	1:29.413	99.43
2	J. Villeneuve	Williams	72	1.55:07.489	1:30.163	99.25
3	J. Alesi	Benetton	72	1.55:10.076	1:29.413	99.21
4	R. Barrichello	Jordan	72	1.55:50.453	1:31.443	98.64
5	E. Irvine	Ferrari	72	1.56:00.313	1:31.372	98.50
6	J. Verstappen	Arrows	72	1.56:04.235	1:31.099	98.44
7	D. Coulthard	McLaren	72	1.56:08.772	1:31.408	98.38
8	O. Panis	Ligier	72	1.56:09.617	1:31.343	98.37
9	J. Herbert	Sauber	71	1.56:20.691	1:31.930	96.85
10	A. Montermini	Forti	69	1.55:36.450	1:34.592	94.72
r	G. Berger	Benetton	56	suspension	1:30.104	97.84
r	M. Schumacher	Ferrari	46	rear wing	1:30.659	96.06
r	P. Lamy	Minardi	39	spin	1:32.958	94.72
r	M. Salo	Tyrrell	36	stuck throttle	1:31.930	93.89
r	M. Brundle	Jordan	34	accident dam.	1:32.668	93.91
r	T. Marques	Minardi	33	spin	1:32.925	93.99
r	H-H. Frentzen	Sauber	32	spin	1:31.005	94.01
r	P. Diniz	Ligier	29	fire	1:32.882	99.56
r	U. Katayama	Tyrrell	28	clutch	1:31.396	100.24
r	L. Badoer	Arrows	24	accident	1:35.893	96.39
r	R. Rosset	Footwork	24	fuel pump	1:33.606	97.87
r	M. Hakkinen	McLaren	19	throttle	1:32.369	101.02

Starting Grid

1	D. Hill (GB)	1:30.346	2.	M. Schumacher (Ger)	1:30.598
3.	J. Villeneuve (Can)	1:30.907	4.	J. Alesi (Fra)	1:31.038
5.	G. Berger (Aut)	1:31.262	6.	R. Barrichello (Bra)	1:31.404
7.	J. Verstappen (Hol)	1:31.615	8.	M. Hakkinen (Fin)	1:31.801
9.	D. Coulthard (GB)	1:32.001	10.	E. Irvine (GB)	1:32.058
11.	H-H. Frentzen (Ger)	1:32.130	12.	O. Panis (Fra)	1:32.177
13.	U. Katayama (Jap)	1:32.407	14.	T. Marques (Bra)	1:32.874
15.	M. Brundle (GB)	1:32.696	16.	M. Salo (Jap)	1:32.903
17.	J. Herbert (GB)	1:33.256	18.	P. Diniz (Bra)	1:33.424
19.	P. Lamy (Por)	1:33.727	20.	R. Rosset (Bra)	1:33.752
21.	L. Badoer (Ita)	1:34.830	22.	A. Montermini (Ita)	1:35.651

Drivers outside 107% rule:
    None – all qualified

Round 4: Europe – Nurburgring

Date: 28 April 1996
Track: 4.556 kilometres
Conditions: Cool and sunny

Length: 305.252 kilometres
Fastest Lap: D. Hill – 1:21.363

Pos	Driver	Car	Laps	Time/Reason	Fastest	mph
1	J. Villeneuve	Williams	67	1.33:26.473	1:22.090	120.03
2	M. Schumacher	Ferrari	67	1.33:27.235	1:21.769	120.04
3	D. Coulthard	McLaren	67	1.33:59.307	1:22.550	119.33
4	D. Hill	Williams	67	1.33:59.984	1:21.363	119.32
5	R. Barrichello	Jordan	67	1.34:00.186	1:22.472	119.31
6	M. Brundle	Jordan	67	1.34:22.040	1:22.815	118.86
7	J. Herbert	Sauber	67	1.34:44.500	1:23.225	118.39
8	M. Hakkinen	McLaren	67	1.34:44.911	1:22.078	118.37
9	G. Berger	Benetton	67	1.34:47.534	1:22.004	118.32
dq	M. Salo	Tyrrell	66	1.33:36.379	1:22.791	118.03
10	P. Diniz	Ligier	66	1.34:36.937	1:23.720	116.77
dq	U. Katayama	Tyrrell	65	1.33:31.599	1:22.602	116.34
11	R. Rosset	Arrows	65	1.33:33.929	1:24.050	116.30
12	P. Lamy	Minardi	65	1.34:03.416	1:24.369	115.69
13	G. Fisichella	Minardi	65	1.34:25.170	1:24.660	115.24
r	H-H. Frentzen	Sauber	59	accident	1:22.697	117.28
r	J. Verstappen	Arrows	38	gearbox	1:23.233	118.32
r	O. Panis	Ligier	6	accident	1:24.168	112.38
r	E. Irvine	Ferrari	6	misfire	1:24.616	111.61
r	J. Alesi	Benetton	1	accident	–	103.98

Starting Grid

1	D. Hill (GB)	1:18.941		2	J. Villeneuve (Can)	1:19.721
3	M. Schumacher (Ger)	1:20.149		4	J. Alesi (Fra)	1:20.711
5	R. Barrichello (Bra)	1:20.818		6	D. Coulthard (GB)	1:20.888
7	E. Irvine (GB)	1:20.931		8	G. Berger (Aut)	1:21.054
9	M. Hakkinen (Fin)	1:21.078		10	H-H. Frentzen (Ger)	1:21.113
11	M. Brundle (GB)	1:21.117		12	J. Herbert (GB)	1:21.210
13	J. Verstappen (Hol)	1:21.367		14	M. Salo (Fin)	1:21.458
15	O. Panis (Fra)	1:21.509		16	U. Katayama (Jap)	1:21.812
17	P. Diniz (Bra)	1:22.733		18	G. Fisichella (Ita)	1:22.921
19	P. Lamy (Por)	1:23.139		20	R. Rosset (Bra)	1:23.620

Drivers outside 107% rule:

A. Montermini (Ita)	Forti	1:25.053
L. Badoer (Ita)	Forti	1:25.840

Round 5: San Marino – Imola

Date: 5 May 1996
Track: 4.892 kilometres
Conditions: Warm and sunny

Attendance: 130,000
Length: 308.196 kilometres
Fastest Lap: D. Hill – 1:28.931

Pos	Driver	Car	Laps	Time/Reason	Fastest	mph
1	D. Hill	Williams	63	1.35:26.156	1:28.931	120.42
2	M. Schumacher	Ferrari	63	1.35:42.616	1:28.966	120.08
3	G. Berger	Benetton	63	1.36.13.047	1:29.667	119.45
4	E. Irvine	Ferrari	63	1.36:27.739	1:29.503	119.14
5	R. Barrichello	Jordan	63	1.36:44.646	1:29.888	118.80
6	J. Alesi	Benetton	62	1.35:43.597	1:29.542	118.15
7	P. Diniz	Ligier	62	1.36:33.333	1:30.852	117.14
8	M. Hakkinen	McLaren	61	1.34:49.164	1:30.192	117.36
9	P. Lamy	Minardi	61	1.36:59.418	1:31.897	114.73
10	L. Badoer	Forti	59	1.36:10.706	1:32.426	111.91
11	J. Villeneuve	Williams	57	1.27:49.134	1:29.226	118.41
r	O. Panis	Ligier	54	gearbox	1:30.184	117.43
r	U. Katayama	Tyrrell	45	lost drive	1:30.772	117.73
r	D. Coulthard	McLaren	44	hydraulics	1:29.480	118.97
r	R. Rosset	Arrows	40	†	1:32.169	115.72
r	J. Verstappen	Arrows	38	†	1:30.479	117.90
r	M. Brundle	Jordan	36	spin	1:30.000	117.55
r	H-H. Frentzen	Sauber	32	brakes	1:31.092	117.94
r	G. Fisichella	Minardi	30	engine	1:31.633	115.71
r	J. Herbert	Sauber	27	misfire	1:30.811	108.65
r	M. Salo	Tyrrell	23	engine	1:29.997	118.90

†both Arrows retired when their team refuelling rig was broken.

Starting Grid

1	M. Schumacher (Ger)	1:26.890	2	D. Hill (GB)	1:27.105
3	J. Villeneuve (Can)	1:27.220	4	D. Coulthard (GB)	1:27.688
5	J. Alesi (Fra)	1:28.009	6	E. Irvine (GB)	1:28.205
7	G. Berger (Aut)	1:28.336	8	M. Salo (Fin)	1:28.423
9	R. Barrichello (Bra)	1:28.632	10	H-H. Frentzen (Ger)	1:28.785
11	M. Hakkinen (Fin)	1:29.079	12	M. Brundle (GB)	1:29.099
13	O. Panis (Fra)	1:29.472	14	J. Verstappen (Hol)	1:29.539
15	J. Herbert (GB)	1:29.541	16	U. Katayama (Jap)	1:29.892
17	P. Diniz (Bra)	1:29.989	18	P. Lamy (Por)	1:30.471
19	G. Fisichella (Ita)	1:30.814	20	R. Rosset (Bra)	1:31.316
21	L. Badoer (Ita)	1:32.037			

Drivers outside 107% rule:
A. Montermini (Ita)   Forti   1:33.689

Date: 19 May 1996
Track: 3.328 kilometres
Conditions: Wet

Attendance: 50,000
Length: 249.6 kilometres
Fastest Lap: J. Alesi – 1:25.205

Pos	Driver	Car	Laps	Time/Reason	Fastest	mph
1	O. Panis	Ligier	75	2.00:45.629	1:25.581	77.06
2	D. Coulthard	McLaren	75	2.00:50.457	1:26.238	77.01
3	J. Herbert	Sauber	75	2.01.23.132	1:26.852	76.66
dnf	H-H. Frentzen	Sauber	74	stopped in pits	1:25.608	76.29
r	M. Salo	Tyrrell	70	accident	1:26.461	76.33
r	M. Hakkinen	McLaren	70	accident	1:26.482	76.33
r	E. Irvine	Ferrari	68	accident	1:26.120	74.23
r	J. Villeneuve	Williams	66	accident	1:26.682	75.91
r	J. Alesi	Benetton	60	suspension	1:25.205	75.07
r	L. Badoer	Forti	60	accident	1:33.305	69.04
r	D. Hill	Williams	40	engine	1:28.523	72.18
r	M. Brundle	Jordan	30	spin	1:35.477	67.82
r	G. Berger	Benetton	9	gearbox sensor	1:49.966	65.92
r	P. Diniz	Ligier	5	transmission	1:53.469	60.66
r	R. Rosset	Arrows	3	accident	1:58.465	59.16
r	U. Katayama	Tyrrell	2	throttle/accid.	1:55.722	59.79
r	M. Schumacher	Ferrari	0	accident	-	-
r	J. Verstappen	Arrows	0	accident	-	-
r	R. Barrichello	Jordan	0	accident	-	-
r	P. Lamy	Minardi	0	accident	-	-
r	G. Fisichella	Minardi	0	accident	-	-
dns	A. Montermini	Forti	0	crash	-	-

Starting Grid

1	M. Schumacher (Ger)	1:20.356	2	D. Hill (GB)	1:20.866
3	J. Alesi (Fra)	1:20.918	4	G. Berger (Aut)	1:21.067
5	D. Coulthard (GB)	1:21.460	6	R. Barrichello (Bra)	1:21.504
7	E. Irvine (GB)	1:21.542	8	M. Hakkinen (Fin)	1:21.688
9	H-H. Frentzen (Ger)	1:21.929	10	J. Villeneuve (Can)	1:21.963
11	M. Salo (Fin)	1:22.235	12	J. Verstappen (Hol)	1:22.327
13	J. Herbert (GB)	1:22.346	14	O. Panis (Fra)	1:22.358
15	U. Katayama (Jap)	1:22.460	16	M. Brundle (GB)	1:22.519
17	P. Diniz (Bra)	1:22.682	18	G. Fisichella (Ita)	1:22.684
19	P. Lamy (Por)	1:23.350	20	R. Rosset (Bra)	1:24.976
21	L. Badoer (Ita)	1:25.059	22	A. Montermini (Ita)	1:25.393

Drivers outside 107% rule:
    None – all qualified

Date: 2 June 1996
Track: 4.727 kilometres
Conditions: Very wet

Attendance: 53,000
Length: 307.114 kilometres
Fastest Lap: M. Schumacher – 1:45.517

Pos	Driver	Car	Laps	Time/Reason	Fastest	mph
1	M. Schumacher	Ferrari	65	1.59:49.307	1:45.517	95.56
2	J. Alesi	Benetton	65	2.00:34.609	1:48.509	94.96
3	J. Villeneuve	Williams	65	2.00:37.695	1:48.707	94.92
4	H-H. Frentzen	Sauber	64	2.00:05.321	1:48.955	93.88
5	M. Hakkinen	McLaren	64	2.00:57.086	1:49.771	92.21
6	P. Diniz	Ligier	63	2.00:33.439	1:50.636	92.05
r	J. Verstappen	Arrows	47	spin	1:48.302	93.79
r	R. Barrichello	Jordan	45	transmission	1:47.735	93.56
r	G. Berger	Benetton	44	spin	1:49.097	93.95
r	J. Herbert	Sauber	20	spin	1:48.846	93.22
r	M. Brundle	Jordan	17	transmission	1:49.026	92.72
r	M. Salo	Tyrrell	16	black flag	1:51.734	84.86
r	D. Hill	Williams	10	accident	1:50.987	91.74
r	U. Katayama	Tyrrell	8	electrics	1:55.118	85.48
r	E. Irvine	Ferrari	1	spin	1:59.611	88.40
r	O. Panis	Ligier	1	accident dam.	–	71.31
r	G. Fisichella	Minardi	1	accident dam.	–	57.60
r	D. Coulthard	McLaren	0	accident	–	–
r	R. Rosset	Arrows	0	accident	–	–
r	P. Lamy	Minardi	0	accident	–	–

Starting Grid

1	D. Hill (GB)	1:20.650	2	J. Villeneuve (Can)	1:21.084
3	M. Schumacher (Ger)	1:21.587	4	J. Alesi (Fra)	1:22.061
5	G. Berger (Aut)	1:22.125	6	E. Irvine (GB)	1:22.333
7	R. Barrichello (Bra)	1:22.379	8	O. Panis (Fra)	1:22.685
9	J. Herbert (GB)	1:23.027	10	M. Hakkinen (Fin)	1:23.070
11	H-H. Frentzen (Ger)	1:23.195	12	M. Salo (Fin)	1:23.224
13	J. Verstappen (Hol)	1:23.371	14	D. Coulthard (GB)	1:23.416
15	M. Brundle (GB)	1:23.438	16	U. Katayama (Jap)	1:24.401
17	P. Diniz (Bra)	1:24.468	18	P. Lamy (Por)	1:25.274
19	G. Fisichella (Ita)	1:25.531	20	R. Rosset (Bra)	1:25.621

Drivers outside 107% rule:

L. Badoer (Ita)	Forti	1:26.615
A. Montermini (Ita)	Forti	1:27.358

Round 8: Canada – Montreal

Date: 16 June 1996
Track: 4.421 kilometres
Conditions: Hot and dry

Attendance: 85,000
Length: 305.049 kilometres
Fastest Lap: J. Villeneuve – 1:21.916

Pos	Driver	Car	Laps	Time/Reason	Fastest	mph
1	D. Hill	Williams	69	1.36:03.465	1:21.957	118.40
2	J. Villeneuve	Williams	69	1.36:07.648	1:21.916	118.31
3	J. Alesi	Benetton	69	1.36:58.121	1:22.824	117.28
4	D. Coulthard	McLaren	69	1.37:07.138	1:22.941	117.10
5	M. Hakkinen	McLaren	68	1.36.19.585	1:23.070	116.36
6	M. Brundle	Jordan	68	1.36:36.934	1:22.958	116.01
r	J. Herbert	Sauber	68	1.36.55.183	1:23.907	115.64
r	G. Fisichella	Minardi	67	1.36.44.064	1:24.349	114.16
r	P. Lamy	Minardi	44	accident	1:24.855	113.52
r	L. Badoer	Forti	44	gearbox	1:26.007	111.55
r	G. Berger	Benetton	42	spin	1:23.102	116.73
r	M. Schumacher	Ferrari	41	driveshaft	1:24.163	114.90
r	O. Panis	Ligier	39	engine	1:23.399	115.68
r	M. Salo	Tyrrell	39	engine	1:23.648	115.27
r	P. Diniz	Ligier	38	engine	1:24.332	114.59
r	R. Barrichello	Jordan	22	clutch	1:23.028	112.41
r	A. Montermini	Forti	22	loose ballast	1:24.621	110.64
r	H-H. Frentzen	Sauber	19	gearbox	1:24.082	115.67
r	J. Verstappen	Arrows	10	engine	1:24.844	113.75
r	R. Rosset	Arrows	6	accident	1:26.347	110.35
r	U. Katayama	Tyrrell	6	accident	1:25.769	110.28
r	E. Irvine	Ferrari	1	suspension	1:33.016	106.32

Starting Grid

1	D. Hill (GB)	1:21.059		2	J. Villeneuve (Can)	1:21.079
3	M. Schumacher (Ger)	1:21.198		4	J. Alesi (Fra)	1:21.529
5	E. Irvine (GB)	1:21.657		6	M. Hakkinen (Fin)	1:21.807
7	G. Berger (Aut)	1:21.926		8	R. Barrichello (Bra)	1:21.982
9	M. Brundle (GB)	1:22.321		10	D. Coulthard (GB)	1:22.332
11	O. Panis (Fra)	1:22.481		12	H-H. Frentzen (Ger)	1:22.875
13	J. Verstappen (Hol)	1:23.067		14	M. Salo (Fin)	1:23.118
15	J. Herbert (GB)	1:23.201		16	G. Fisichella (Ita)	1:23.519
17	U. Katayama (Jap)	1:23.599		18	P. Diniz (Bra)	1:23.959
19	P. Lamy (Por)	1:24.262		20	L. Badoer (Ita)	1:25.012
21	R. Rosset (Bra)	1:25.193		22	A. Montermini (Ita)	1:26.109

Drivers outside 107% rule:
  None – all qualified

Date: 30 June 1996
Track: 4.250 kilometres
Conditions: Cool and cloudy

Attendance: 80,000
Length: 305.814 kilometres
Fastest Lap: J. Villeneuve – 1:18.610

Pos	Driver	Car	Laps	Time/Reason	Fastest	mph
1	D. Hill	Williams	72	1.36:28.795	1:18.938	118.17
2	J. Villeneuve	Williams	72	1.36:36.922	1:18.610	118.01
3	J. Alesi	Benetton	72	1.37:15.237	1:19.378	117.23
4	G. Berger	Benetton	72	1.37:15.654	1:19.206	117.23
5	M. Hakkinen	McLaren	72	1.37:31.569	1:19.632	116.91
6	D. Coulthard	McLaren	71	1.36:30.673	1:19.968	116.49
7	O. Panis	Ligier	71	1.36:48.120	1:18.712	116.14
8	M. Brundle	Jordan	71	1.37:07.503	1:20.414	115.76
9	R. Barrichello	Jordan	71	1.37:24.841	1:20.134	115.41
10	M. Salo	Tyrrell	70	1.36:52.589	1:20.710	114.42
dq	J. Herbert	Sauber	70	1.37:43.573	1:21.262	113.42
11	R. Rosset	Arrows	69	1.37:00.175	1:22.095	112.64
12	P. Lamy	Minardi	69	1.37:47.135	1:22.842	111.74
r	H-H. Frentzen	Sauber	56	sticking throttle	1:21.273	114.79
r	U. Katayama	Tyrrell	33	engine	1:20.989	113.92
r	L. Badoer	Forti	29	engine	1:22.258	112.24
r	P. Diniz	Ligier	28	engine	1:20.997	115.31
r	J. Verstappen	Arrows	10	steering arm	1:21.461	114.65
r	E. Irvine	Ferrari	5	gearbox	1:21.824	105.66
r	G. Fisichella	Minardi	2	fuel pump	1:23.448	105.09
r	A. Montermini	Forti	2	engine	1:24.818	104.05
dns	M. Schumacher	Ferrari	0	engine	–	–

Starting Grid

1	M. Schumacher (Ger)	1:15.989		2	D. Hill (GB)	1:16.058
3	J. Alesi (Fra)	1:16.310		4	G. Berger (Aut)	1:16.592
5	M. Hakkinen (Fin)	1:16.634		6	J. Villeneuve (Can)	1:16.905
7	D. Coulthard (GB)	1:17.007		8	M. Brundle (GB)	1:17.187
9	O. Panis (Fra)	1:17.390		10	R. Barrichello (Bra)	1:17.665
11	P. Diniz (Bra)	1:17.676		12	H-H. Frentzen (Ger)	1:17.739
13	M. Salo (Fin)	1:18.021		14	U. Katayama (Jap)	1:18.242
15	J. Verstappen (Hol)	1:18.324		16	J. Herbert (GB)	1:18.556
17	G. Fisichella (Ita)	1:18.604		18	P. Lamy (Por)	1:19.210
19	R. Rosset (Bra)	1:19.242		20	L. Badoer (Ita)	1:20.647
21	A. Montermini (Ita)	1:20.647		22	E. Irvine (GB) †	1:17.443

Drivers outside 107% rule:
    None – all qualified

† *demoted from 10th*

Date: 14 July 1996
Track: 5.077 kilometres
Conditions: Warm and cloudy

Attendance: 90,000
Length: 309.697 kilometres
Fastest Lap: J. Villeneuve – 1:29.288

Pos	Driver	Car	Laps	Time/Reason	Fastest	mph
1	J. Villeneuve	Williams	61	1.33:00.874	1:29.288	124.02
2	G. Berger	Benetton	61	1.33:19.900	1:29.984	123.59
3	M. Hakkinen	McLaren	61	1.33:51.704	1:30.531	122.89
4	R. Barrichello	Jordan	61	1.34:07.590	1:30.671	122.55
5	D. Coulthard	McLaren	61	1.34:23.381	1:31.282	121.21
6	M. Brundle	Jordan	60	1.33:17.786	1:30.552	121.65
7	M. Salo	Tyrrell	60	1.33.38.262	1:31.765	121.17
8	H-H. Frentzen	Sauber	60	1.33:59.701	1:32.662	120.71
9	J. Herbert	Sauber	60	1.34:00.496	1:32.213	120.69
10	J. Verstappen	Arrows	60	1.34:05.550	1:31.490	120.59
11	G. Fisichella	Minardi	59	1.34:04.161	1:33.707	118.61
r	J. Alesi	Benetton	44	brakes	1:30.553	122.71
r	O. Panis	Ligier	40	handling	1:32.188	117.32
r	P. Diniz	Ligier	38	engine	1:32.508	118.71
r	D. Hill	Williams	26	loose wheel nut	1:30.264	124.09
r	P. Lamy	Minardi	21	gear selection	1:34.372	118.20
r	R. Rosset	Arrows	13	electrics	1:33.382	118.96
r	U. Katayama	Tyrrell	12	engine	1:32.699	118.99
r	E. Irvine	Ferrari	5	engine	1:31.490	120.77
r	M. Schumacher	Ferrari	3	gbx hydraulics	1:30.944	88.78

Starting Grid

1	D. Hill (GB)	1:26.875	2	J. Villeneuve (Can)	1:27.070
3	M. Schumacher (Ger)	1:27.707	4	M. Hakkinen (Fin)	1:27.856
5	J. Alesi (Fra)	1:28.307	6	R. Barrichello (Bra)	1:28.409
7	G.Berger (Aut)	1:28.653	8	M. Brundle (GB)	1:28.946
9	D. Coulthard (GB)	1:28.966	10	E. Irvine (GB)	1:29.186
11	H-H. Frentzen (Ger)	1:29.591	12	U. Katayama (Jap)	1:29.913
13	J. Herbert (GB)	1:29.947	14	M. Salo (Fin)	1:29.949
15	J. Verstappen (Hol)	1:30.102	16	O. Panis (Fra)	1:30.167
17	P. Diniz (Bra)	1:31.076	18	G. Fisichella (Ita)	1:31.365
19	P. Lamy (Por)	1:31.454	20	R. Rosset (Bra)	dq

Drivers outside 107% rule:

A. Montermini (Ita)	Forti	1:35.206
L. Badoer (Ita)	Forti	1:35.304

Round 11: Germany – Hockenheim

Date: 28 July 1996
Track: 6.823 kilometres
Conditions: Hot and humid

Attendance: 100,000
Length: 307.022 kilometres
Fastest Lap: D. Hill – 1:46.504

Pos	Driver	Car	Laps	Time/Reason	Fastest	mph
1	D. Hill	Williams	45	1.21:43.417	1:46.504	140.06
2	J. Alesi	Benetton	45	1.21:54.869	1:47.643	139.74
3	J. Villeneuve	Williams	45	1.22:17.343	1:47.903	139.10
4	M. Schumacher	Ferrari	45	1.22:24.934	1:48.612	138.89
5	D. Coulthard	McLaren	45	1.22:25.613	1:47.856	138.87
6	R. Barrichello	Jordan	45	1.23:25.516	1:49.559	137.21
7	O. Panis	Ligier	45	1.23:27.329	1:48.288	137.16
8	H-H. Frentzen	Sauber	44	1.21:50.766	1:49.773	136.75
9	M. Salo	Tyrrell	44	1.22:22.768	1:50.553	135.86
10	M. Brundle	Jordan	44	1.23.04.252	1:49.176	134.73
11	R. Rosset	Arrows	44	1.23:23.171	1:51.702	134.22
12	P. Lamy	Minardi	43	1.22.08.733	1:51.654	133.15
13	G. Berger	Benetton	42	engine	1:47.682	140.06
r	E. Irvine	Ferrari	34	gearbox	1:48.336	137.89
r	J. Herbert	Sauber	25	gbx electronics	1:50.304	127.25
r	P. Diniz	Ligier	19	engine	1:49.625	137.55
r	U. Katayama	Tyrrell	19	accident	1:50.569	135.72
r	M. Hakkinen	McLaren	13	gearbox	1:48.490	138.74
r	J. Verstappen	Arrows	0	accident	–	–

Starting Grid

1	D. Hill (GB)	1:43.912		2	G.Berger (Aut)	1:44.299
3	M. Schumacher (Ger)	1:44.477		4	M. Hakkinen (Fin)	1:44.644
5	J. Alesi (Fra)	1:44.670		6	J. Villeneuve (Can)	1:44.842
7	D. Coulthard (GB)	1:44.951		8	E. Irvine (GB)	1:45.389
9	R. Barrichello (Bra)	1:45.452		10	M. Brundle (GB)	1:45.876
11	P. Diniz (Bra)	1:46.575		12	O. Panis (Fra)	1:46.746
13	H-H. Frentzen (Ger)	1:46.899		14	J. Herbert (GB)	1:47.711
15	M. Salo (Fin)	1:48.139		16	U. Katayama (Jap)	1:48.381
17	J. Verstappen (Hol)	1:48.512		18	P. Lamy (Por)	1:49.461
19	R. Rosset (Bra)	1:49.551				

Drivers outside 107% rule:
G. Lavaggi (Ita)   Minardi   1:51.357

Date: 11 August 1996   Attendance: 110,000
Track: 3.968 kilometres   Length: 305.536 kilometres
Conditions: Sunny   Fastest Lap: D. Hill – 1:20.093

Pos	Driver	Car	Laps	Time/Reason	Fastest	mph
1	J. Villeneuve	Williams	77	1:46.21.134	1:20.507	107.11
2	D. Hill	Williams	77	1:46.21.905	1:20.093	107.09
3	J. Alesi	Benetton	77	1:47.45.346	1:21.932	105.71
4	M. Hakkinen	McLaren	76	1:46.43.538	1:22.257	105.35
5	O. Panis	Ligier	76	1:47.40.381	1:21.562	104.42
6	R. Barrichello	Jordan	75	1:46.34.466	1:23.181	104.11
7	U. Katayama	Tyrrell	74	1:46.49.846	1:24.040	102.47
8	R. Rosset	Arrows	74	1:47.07.362	1:24.026	102.19
9	M. Schumacher	Ferrari	70	1:37.31.955	1:20.912	106.17
10	G. Lavaggi	Minardi	69	1:41.39.024	1:25.626	100.42
r	G. Berger	Benetton	64	engine	1:21.733	105.89
r	H-H. Frentzen	Sauber	50	engine	1:21.882	103.48
r	J. Herbert	Sauber	35	engine	1:22.343	105.43
r	E. Irvine	Ferrari	31	gearbox	1:22.099	105.43
r	P. Lamy	Minardi	24	suspension	1:25.066	101.81
r	D. Coulthard	McLaren	23	engine	1:22.760	105.75
r	J. Verstappen	Arrows	10	accident	1:24.018	103.30
r	M. Brundle	Jordan	5	accident	1:23.889	102.44
r	P. Diniz	Ligier	1	accident	1:40.435	88.38
r	M. Salo	Tyrrell	0	accident	–	–

Starting Grid

1	M. Schumacher (Ger)	1:17.129	2	D. Hill (GB)	1:17.182
3	J. Villeneuve (Can)	1:17.259	4	E. Irvine (GB)	1:18.617
5	J. Alesi (Fra)	1:18.754	6	G. Berger (Aut)	1:18.794
7	M. Hakkinen (Fin)	1:19.116	8	J. Herbert (GB)	1:19.292
9	D. Coulthard (GB)	1:19.384	10	H-H. Frentzen (Ger)	1:19.436
11	O. Panis (Fra)	1:19.538	12	M. Brundle (GB)	1:19.828
13	R. Barrichello (Bra)	1:19.966	14	U. Katayama (Jap)	1:20.499
15	P. Diniz (Bra)	1:20.665	16	M. Salo (Fin)	1:20.678
17	J. Verstappen (Hol)	1:20.781	18	R. Rosset (Bra)	1:21.590
19	P. Lamy (Por)	1:21.713	20	G. Lavaggi (Ita)	1:22.468

Drivers outside 107% rule:
   None – all qualified

Round 13: Belgium – Spa Francorchamps

Date: 25 August 1996
Track: 6.974 kilometres
Conditions: Cloudy but dry

Attendance: 80,000
Length: 306.856 kilometres
Fastest Lap: G. Berger – 1:53.067

Pos	Driver	Car	Laps	Time/Reason	Fastest	mph
1	M. Schumacher	Ferrari	44	1:28.15.125	1:53.905	129.52
2	J. Villeneuve	Williams	44	1:28.20.727	1:53.587	129.38
3	M. Hakkinen	McLaren	44	1:28.30.835	1:54.198	129.14
4	J. Alesi	Benetton	44	1:28.34.250	1:54.685	129.05
5	D. Hill	Williams	44	1:28.44.304	1:53.441	128.81
6	G. Berger	Benetton	44	1:28.45.021	1:53.067	128.79
7	M. Salo	Tyrrell	44	1:29.15.879	1:55.854	128.05
8	U. Katayama	Tyrrell	44	1:29.55.352	1:57.149	127.11
9	R. Rosset	Arrows	43	1:28.21.974	1:57.809	126.41
10	P. Lamy	Minardi	43	1:28.39.042	1:57.468	126.01
r	D. Coulthard	McLaren	37	accident	1:54.655	127.60
r	M. Brundle	Jordan	34	engine	1:55.616	125.09
r	E. Irvine	Ferrari	29	gearbox	1:55.753	124.95
r	R. Barrichello	Jordan	29	handling	1:56.943	116.69
r	P. Diniz	Ligier	22	misfire	1:58.665	122.31
r	J. Verstappen	Arrows	11	accident	1:56.704	129.86
r	O. Panis	Ligier	0	accident	–	
r	J. Herbert	Sauber	0	accident	–	
r	H-H. Frentzen	Sauber	0	accident	–	

Starting Grid

1	J. Villeneuve (Can)	1:50.574	2	D. Hill (GB)	1:50.980
3	M. Schumacher (Ger)	1:51.778	4	D. Coulthard (GB)	1:51.884
5	G. Berger (Aut)	1:51.960	6	M. Hakkinen (Fin)	1:52.318
7	J. Alesi (Fra)	1:52.354	8	M. Brundle (GB)	1:52.977
9	E. Irvine (GB)	1:53.043	10	R. Barrichello (Bra)	1:53.152
11	H-H. Frentzen (Ger)	1:53.199	12	J. Herbert (GB)	1:53.993
13	M. Salo (Fin)	1:54.095	14	O. Panis (Fra)	1:54.220
15	P. Diniz (Bra)	1:54.700	16	J. Verstappen (Hol)	1:55.150
17	U. Katayama (Jap)	1:55.371	18	R. Rosset (Bra)	1:56.286
19	P. Lamy (Por)	1:56.830			

Drivers outside 107% rule:
G. Lavaggi (Ita)   Minardi   1:58.579

Round 14: Italy – Monza

Date: 8 September 1996
Track: 5.770 kilometres
Conditions: Warm and sunny

Attendance: 100,000
Length: 305.772 kilometres
Fastest Lap: M. Schumacher – 1:26.110

Pos	Driver	Car	Laps	Time/Reason	Fastest	mph
1	M. Schumacher	Ferrari	53	1:17.43.632	1:26.110	146.67
2	J. Alesi	Benetton	53	1:18.01.897	1:26.652	146.09
3	M. Hakkinen	McLaren	53	1:18.50.267	1:26.827	144.60
4	M. Brundle	Jordan	53	1:19.08.849	1:27.831	144.03
5	R. Barrichello	Jordan	53	1:19.09.107	1:27.557	144.03
6	P. Diniz	Ligier	52	1:17.58.927	1:27.905	143.49
7	J. Villeneuve	Williams	52	1:18.14.701	1:27.027	142.95
8	J. Verstappen	Arrows	52	1:18.40.215	1:28.650	142.17
9	J. Herbert	Sauber	51	1:16.29.260	1:28.223	143.42
10	U. Katayama	Tyrrell	51	1:19.12.208	1:28.980	138.50
r	R. Rosset	Arrows	36	steering arm	1:30.579	139.12
r	E. Irvine	Ferrari	23	accident	1:27.687	145.02
r	P. Lamy	Minardi	12	engine	1:31.353	137.38
r	M. Salo	Tyrrell	9	engine	1:29.418	140.17
r	H-H. Frentzen	Sauber	7	accident	1:29.945	139.97
r	D. Hill	Williams	5	accident	1:27.639	143.53
r	G. Lavaggi	Minardi	5	engine	1:33.189	135.73
r	G.Berger	Benetton	4	gearbox	1:29.123	139.63
r	O. Panis	Ligier	2	accident	1:32.657	130.21
r	D. Coulthard	McLaren	1	accident	1:38.080	131.60

Starting Grid

1	D. Hill (GB)	1:24.204	2	J. Villeneuve (Can)	1:24.521
3	M. Schumacher (Ger)	1:24.781	4	M. Hakkinen (Fin)	1:24.939
5	D. Coulthard (GB)	1:24.975	6	J. Alesi (Fra)	1:25.201
7	E. Irvine (GB)	1:25.228	8	G. Berger (Aut)	1:25.470
9	M. Brundle (GB)	1:26.037	10	R. Barrichello (Bra)	1:26.194
11	O. Panis (Fra)	1:26.206	12	J. Herbert (GB)	1:26.345
13	H-H. Frentzen (Ger)	1:26.505	14	P. Diniz (Bra)	1:26.726
15	J. Verstappen (Hol)	1:27.270	16	U. Katayama (Jap)	1:28.234
17	M. Salo (Fin)	1:28.472	18	P. Lamy (Por)	1:28.933
19	R. Rosset (Bra)	1:29.181	20	G. Lavaggi (Ita)	1:29.833

Drivers outside 107% rule:
    None – all qualified

Round 15: Portugal – Estoril

Date: 22 September 1996
Track: 4.360 kilometres
Conditions: Warm and sunny

Attendance: 25,000
Length: 305.200 kilometres
Fastest Lap: J. Villeneuve – 1:22.973

Pos	Driver	Car	Laps	Time/Reason	Fastest	mph
1	J. Villeneuve	Williams	70	1:40.22.915	1:22.873	113.35
2	D. Hill	Williams	70	1:40.42.881	1:23.762	112.98
3	M. Schumacher	Ferrari	70	1:41.16.860	1:24.059	112.35
4	J. Alesi	Benetton	70	1:41.18.024	1:24.331	112.32
5	E. Irvine	Ferrari	70	1:41.50.304	1:25.206	111.73
6	G. Berger	Benetton	70	1:41.56.056	1:24.647	111.63
7	H-H. Frentzen	Sauber	69	1:41.13.769	1:24.869	110.80
8	J. Herbert	Sauber	69	1:41.17.057	1:25.786	110.74
9	M. Brundle	Jordan	69	1:41.21.217	1:25.028	110.66
10	O. Panis	Ligier	69	1:41.34.267	1:25.008	110.42
11	M. Salo	Tyrrell	69	1:41.37.838	1:26.199	110.36
12	U. Katayama	Tyrrell	68	1:41.50.550	1:26.447	109.61
13	D. Coulthard	McLaren	68	1:41.24.157	1:25.362	109.01
14	R. Rosset	Arrows	68	1:40.44.958	1:26.863	108.10
15	G. Lavaggi	Minardi	65	1:40.33.410	1:28.911	105.07
16	P. Lamy	Minardi	65	1:41.05.173	1:27.754	104.52
r	M. Hakkinen	McLaren	52	accident dam.	1:24.747	110.29
r	J. Verstappen	Arrows	47	engine	1:25.913	110.05
r	P. Diniz	Ligier	46	spin	1:25.791	107.94
r	R. Barrichello	Jordan	41	spin	1:24.954	110.89

Starting Grid

1	D. Hill (GB)	1:20.330	2	J. Villeneuve (Can)	1:20.339
3	J. Alesi (Fra)	1:21.088	4	M. Schumacher (Ger)	1:21.236
5	G. Berger (Aut)	1:21.293	6	E. Irvine (GB)	1:21.362
7	M. Hakkinen (Fin)	1:21.640	8	D. Coulthard (GB)	1:22.066
9	R. Barrichello (Bra)	1:22.205	10	M. Brundle (GB)	1:22.324
11	H-H. Frentzen (Ger)	1:22.325	12	J. Herbert (GB)	1:22.655
13	M. Salo (Fin)	1:22.765	14	U. Katayama (Jap)	1:23.013
15	O. Panis (Fra)	1:23.055	16	J. Verstappen (Hol)	1:23.531
17	R. Rosset (Bra)	1:24.230	18	P. Diniz (Bra)	1:24.293
19	P. Lamy (Por)	1:24.510	20	G. Lavaggi (Ita)	1:25.612

Drivers outside 107% rule:
None – all qualified

Round 16: Japan – Suzuka

Date: 13 October 1996   Attendance: 100,000
Track: 5.864 kilometres   Length: 304.726 kilometres
Conditions: Warm and sunny   Fastest Lap: J. Villeneuve – 1:44.043

Pos	Driver	Car	Laps	Time/Reason	Fastest	mph
1	D. Hill	Williams	52	1:32.33.791	1:44.753	122.73
2	M. Schumacher	Ferrari	52	1:32.35.674	1:44.445	122.69
3	M. Hakkinen	McLaren	52	1:32.37.003	1:44.852	122.66
4	G. Berger	Benetton	52	1:33.00.317	1:44.350	122.15
5	M. Brundle	Jordan	52	1:33.40.911	1:45.882	121.27
6	H-H. Frentzen	Sauber	52	1:33.54.977	1:46.407	120.97
7	O. Panis	Ligier	52	1:33.56.301	1:45.347	120.89
8	D. Coulthard	McLaren	52	1:33.59.024	1:45.613	120.88
9	R. Barrichello	Jordan	52	1:34.14.856	1:45.339	120.54
10	J. Herbert	Sauber	52	1:34.15.590	1:45.932	120.52
11	J. Verstappen	Arrows	51	1:33.22.955	1:46.977	119.32
12	P. Lamy	Minardi	50	1:32.59.965	1:49.220	117.46
13	R. Rosset	Arrows	50	1:33.34.388	1:49.263	116.74
r	E. Irvine	Ferrari	39	accident	1:45.798	121.67
r	U. Katayama	Tyrrell	37	engine	1:47.518	118.21
r	J. Villeneuve	Williams	36	lost wheel	1:44.043	121.87
r	M. Salo	Tyrrell	20	engine	1:49.372	118.12
r	P. Diniz	Ligier	13	spin	1:48.495	118.80
r	J. Alesi	Benetton	0	accident	–	–

Starting Grid

1	J. Villeneuve (Can)	1:38.909	2	D. Hill (GB)		1:39.370
3	M. Schumacher (Ger)	1:40.071	4	G. Berger (Aut)		1:40.364
5	M. Hakkinen (Fin)	1:40.458	6	E. Irvine (GB)		1:41.005
7	H-H. Frentzen (Ger)	1:41.277	8	D. Coulthard (GB)		1:41.384
9	J. Alesi (Fra)	1:41.562	10	M. Brundle (GB)		1:41.600
11	R. Barrichello (Bra)	1:41.919	12	O. Panis (Fra)		1:42.206
13	J. Herbert (GB)	1:42.658	14	U. Katayama (Jap)		1:42.711
15	M. Salo (Fin)	1:42.840	16	P. Diniz (Bra)		1:43.196
17	J. Verstappen (Hol)	1:43.383	18	P. Lamy (Por)		1:44.874
19	R. Rosset (Bra)	1:45.412				

Drivers outside 107% rule:
G. Lavaggi (Ita)   Minardi   1:46.795

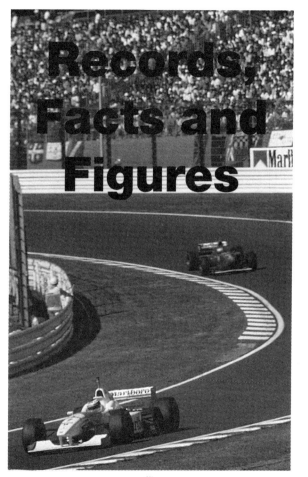

Records, Facts and Figures

DRIVERS – FINISHING POSITIONS – RACE BY RACE '96

Driver	Team	Au	Br	Ar	Eu	SM	Mo	Sp	Ca	Fr	GB	Ge	Hu	Be	It	Po	Ja	Pts
D. Hill	Williams	1	1f	1	4f	1f	r	r	1	1	r	1f	2f	5	r	2	1	97
J. Villeneuve	Williams	2f	r	2	1	11	r	3	2	2f	1f	3	1	2	7	1f	rf	78
M. Schumacher	Ferrari	r	3	r	2	2	r	1f	3	fs	r	4	9	1	1f	3	2	59
J. Alesi	Benetton	r	2	3f	r	r	r	2	r	3	r	2	3	r	r	4	r	47
M. Hakkinen	McLaren	5	4	r	8	4	r	r	5	4	3	3	4	3	r	5	3	31
G. Berger	Benetton	4	r	7	9	3	r	r	4	r	r	r	6	6f	r	6	4	21
D. Coulthard	McLaren	r	r	4	3	r	2	r	r	r	5	r	5	r	5	13	8	18
R. Barrichello	Jordan	r	r	r	5	4	r	r	6	r	4	r	r	r	r	6	r	14
O. Panis	Ligier	7	r	8	r	6	1	r	r	4	r	6	r	r	r	10	7	13
E. Irvine	Ferrari	3	7	5	r	r	r	r	9	r	7	7	5	r	r	r	5	11
M. Brundle	Jordan	r	12	r	6	r	r	6	6	8	8	10	r	4	4	9	6	8
H-H. Frentzen	Sauber	8	5	r	dq	r	4	4	r	r	8	8	r	7	r	11	r	7
M. Salo	Tyrrell	6	6	9	7	5	5	r	r	10	r	9	r	r	9	8	10	5
J. Herbert	Sauber	fs	r	r	10	7	3	r	r	dq	r	9	r	6	6	r	r	4
P. Diniz	Ligier	10	8	r	r	r	7	6	r	r	r	r	r	r	r	r	r	2
J. Verstappen	Arrows	11	9	6	r	r	r	r	r	r	6	r	r	8	r	r	r	1
U. Katayama	Tyrrell	fq	r	r	fq	r	r	fq	r	r	r	r	7	r	8	12	11	
P. Lamy	Minardi	r	10	r	12	r	6	fq	r	r	r	12	r	10	r	16	12	
R. Rosset	Arrows	9	r	r	11	r	r	r	r	11	r	11	8	9	r	14	13	
G. Fisichella	Minardi	fq	r	r	13	8	r	r	8	r	11	–	–	–	–	–	–	
L. Badoer	Forti	fq	11	10	fq	fq	fq	fq	–	–	–	–	–	–	–	–	–	
A. Montermini	Forti	–	10	r	fq	fq	fq	fq	–	–	–	–	–	–	–	–	–	
G. Lavaggi	Minardi	–	–	–	–	–	–	–	–	–	–	dq	10	–	r	15	fq	
T. Marques	Minardi	–	–	–	–	–	–	–	–	–	–	–	–	–	–	–	–	

dq = disqualified. r = retired. fs = failed to start. fq = failed to qualify. f = fastest lap.

Driver	Team	Au	Br	Ar	Eu	SM	Mo	Sp	Ca	Fr	GB	Ge	Hu	Be	It	Po	Ja	Pts
D. Hill	Williams	2	1	1	3	2	2	1	1	2	2	1	2	2	2	1	2	97
J. Villeneuve	Williams	1	3	3	2	3	10	3	2	1	1	2	1	3	3	2	1	78
M. Schumacher	Ferrari	4	4	2	3	1	1	3	3	6	3	3	3	1	1	3	3	59
J. Alesi	Benetton	6	5	7	4	5	3	4	4	3	5	4	5	4	6	3	9	47
M. Hakkinen	McLaren	5	8	9	8	8	8	5	6	4	4	5	6	5	8	5	4	31
G. Berger	Benetton	7	8	5	6	7	4	14	7	7	7	2	2	6	5	8	8	21
D. Coulthard	McLaren	13	14	6	5	4	6	6	10	9	9	6	13	10	10	9	8	18
R. Barrichello	Jordan	8	2	6	6	5	7	8	11	10	16	9	11	14	11	11	11	14
O. Panis	Ligier	11	15	12	15	13	14	8	5	9	16	12	4	9	9	15	12	13
E. Irvine	Ferrari	3	10	10	7	6	16	6	5	10	10	8	10	4	11	6	6	11
M. Brundle	Jordan	19	6	15	10	12	16	15	12	12	11	10	12	11	8	10	10	11
H-H. Frentzen	Sauber	9	6	11	7	9	9	12	8	12	17†	10	8	11	9	11	7	8
M. Salo	Tyrrell	10	11	16	14	8	11	12	14	13	14	14	16	13	17	13	15	7
J. Herbert	Sauber	14	12	17	12	15	13	9	15	16	12	8	8	12	12	12	13	5
P. Diniz	Ligier	20	18	18	15	17	17	17	18	11	17	11	15	15	14	18	16	4
J. Verstappen	Arrows	12	13	7	13	14	12	13	13	15	15	17	17	16	15	16	17	1
U. Katayama	Tyrrell	15	16	13	16	16	15	16	17	14	12	16	14	17	16	17	18	–
P. Lamy	Minardi	17	20	19	18	19	18	18	19	19	18	18	18	19	18	19	18	–
R. Rosset	Arrows	18	17	20	20	20	20	20	21	19	17†	19	18	18	19	17	19	–
G. Fisichella	Minardi	16	–	–	18	18	18	19	16	16	18	19	18	–	–	–	–	–
L. Badoer	Forti	*	–	21	*	21	21	*	20	17	*	*	*	–	–	–	–	–
A. Montermini	Forti	*	22	22	*	*	22	*	22	21	–	*	20	–	–	–	*	–
G. Lavaggi	Minardi	–	–	–	–	–	–	–	–	–	–	–	20	–	–	20	20	–
T. Marques	Minardi	19†	14	–	–	–	–	–	–	–	–	–	–	–	–	–	–	–

= Outside 107% qualifying rule. †=subsequently disqualified and had to start from back of grid.

DRIVERS – POINTS TALLY – RACE BY RACE '96

Driver	Team	Au	Br	Ar	Eu	SM	Mo	Sp	Ca	Fr	GB	Ge	Hu	Be	It	Po	Ja	Pts
D. Hill	Williams	10	10	10	3	10	–	–	10	10	–	10	6	2	–	6	10	97
J. Villeneuve	Williams	6	–	6	10	6	–	–	6	6	10	4	10	6	–	10	6	78
M. Schumacher	Ferrari	–	4	–	6	6	–	10	–	–	–	3	–	10	10	4	–	59
J. Alesi	Benetton	2	6	4	–	1	6	4	4	4	3	6	4	3	6	3	4	47
M. Hakkinen	McLaren	3	3	–	–	–	–	2	2	2	4	–	3	4	4	1	4	31
G. Berger	Benetton	–	–	–	4	4	6	2	3	3	6	6	–	1	–	–	3	21
D. Coulthard	McLaren	–	–	3	2	2	–	–	–	1	2	2	1	–	2	1	–	18
R. Barrichello	Jordan	–	–	–	–	–	–	–	1	–	3	1	2	–	2	2	–	14
O. Panis	Ligier	–	1	1	–	–	10	–	1	–	–	–	–	–	–	–	–	13
E. Irvine	Ferrari	4	–	2	–	1	–	1	–	–	–	–	–	–	–	3	–	11
M. Brundle	Jordan	–	–	–	1	–	–	–	–	–	–	–	–	3	–	2	2	8
H-H. Frentzen	Sauber	1	2	–	–	–	3	–	–	–	1	–	–	–	–	–	–	7
M. Salo	Tyrrell	–	2	–	–	–	1	2	–	–	–	–	–	–	–	–	–	5
J. Herbert	Sauber	–	–	–	–	–	4	–	–	–	–	–	–	–	–	–	–	4
P. Diniz	Ligier	–	–	–	–	–	2	–	–	–	–	–	–	–	–	–	–	2
J. Verstappen	Arrows	–	1	–	–	–	–	–	–	–	–	–	–	–	–	–	–	1

CONSTRUCTORS POINTS WON – RACE BY RACE '96

	Team	Au	Br	Ar	Eu	SM	Mo	Sp	Ca	Fr	GB	Ge	Hu	Be	It	Po	Ja	Pts
1.	Williams Renault	16	10	16	13	10	0	4	16	16	10	14	16	8	0	16	10	175
2.	Ferrari	4	4	2	6	9	0	10	0	2	0	3	0	10	10	4	6	70
3.	Benetton Renault	2	6	4	2	4	0	6	4	4	6	6	5	5	8	3	3	68
4.	McLaren Mercedes	3	3	0	4	2	7	3	3	3	6	0	3	3	4	1	4	49
5.	Jordan Peugeot	0	0	3	1	1	0	0	2	1	4	1	2	0	3	2	2	22
6.	Ligier Mugen Honda	0	1	0	0	0	10	2	1	0	0	0	0	0	0	0	1	15
7.	Sauber Ford	0	0	0	0	0	7	1	0	0	0	2	0	0	1	0	0	11
8.	Tyrrell Yamaha	1	2	0	0	0	2	0	0	0	0	0	0	0	0	0	0	5
9.	Arrows Hart	0	0	1	0	0	0	0	0	0	0	0	0	0	0	0	0	1

CONSTRUCTORS TOTAL LAPS – RACE BY RACE '96

Team	Au	Br	Ar	Eu	SM	Mo	Sp	Ca	Fr	GB	Ge	Hu	Be	It	Po	Ja	Total
Williams Renault	116	97	144	134	120	106	75	138	144	87	90	154	88	57	140	88	1778
McLaren Mercedes	83	99	91	134	105	145	64	137	143	122	58	99	81	54	120	104	1639
Benetton Renault	68	97	128	68	125	69	109	111	144	105	87	141	88	57	140	52	1589
Jordan Peugeot	32	123	106	134	99	30	62	90	142	121	89	80	63	106	110	104	1491
Sauber Ford	57	64	103	126	57	149	84	87	126	120	69	85	0	58	138	104	1427
Ligier Mugen Honda	113	139	101	72	116	80	64	77	94	78	64	77	22	54	115	65	1331
Tyrrell Yamaha	112	139	64	131	68	72	24	45	103	72	63	74	88	60	137	57	1309
Ferrari	91	140	118	73	126	68	66	42	5	8	79	101	73	76	140	91	1297
Arrows Hart	72	43	96	103	78	3	47	16	79	73	44	84	54	88	115	101	1096
Minardi	76	101	39	130	91	0	1	111	71	80	43	93	43	17	130	50	1076
Forti Ford	0	93	93	0	59	60	–	66	31	0	–	–	–	–	–	–	402

DRIVERS – LAPS COMPLETED – RACE BY RACE '96

Driver	Team	Au	Br	Ar	Eu	SM	Mo	Sp	Ca	Fr	GB	Ge	Hu	Be	It	Po	Ja	Total
D. Hill	Williams	58	71	72	67	63	40	10	69	72	26	45	77	44	5	70	52	841
J. Villeneuve	Williams	58	26	72	67	57	66	65	69	72	61	45	77	44	52	70	36	937
M. Schumacher	Ferrari	33	70	46	67	63	60	41	69	0	3	45	70	44	53	70	52	722
J. Alesi	Benetton	10	71	72	1	62	60	65	68	72	44	45	77	44	53	52	0	815
M. Hakkinen	McLaren	58	70	19	67	61	70	64	42	72	61	13	76	44	4	52	52	900
G. Berger	Benetton	58	26	56	67	63	44	9	42	71	61	42	64	44	70	70	52	774
D. Coulthard	McLaren	25	29	72	67	44	75	0	69	71	61	45	23	37	1	68	52	739
R. Barrichello	Jordan	30	59	72	67	63	0	45	22	71	61	45	75	29	53	41	52	785
O. Panis	Ligier	57	70	72	6	54	75	1	39	71	40	45	76	0	1	69	52	729
E. Irvine	Ferrari	58	70	72	6	63	68	1	1	5	5	44	31	29	23	69	39	575
M. Brundle	Jordan	2	64	34	67	36	30	17	68	71	60	44	5	34	53	69	52	706
H-H. Frentzen	Sauber	57	36	36	66	32	74	16	19	56	60	44	50	0	7	69	52	711
M. Salo	Tyrrell	57	70	36	66	23	70	16	39	70	60	44	0	44	9	69	20	693
J. Herbert	Sauber	56	28	71	67	25	75	20	68	70	60	25	35	0	51	69	52	716
P. Diniz	Ligier	56	69	29	66	62	5	63	38	23	38	19	0	22	52	46	13	602
J. Verstappen	Arrows	16	19	72	38	38	0	47	10	10	60	0	10	11	52	47	51	481
U. Katayama	Tyrrell	55	69	28	65	45	2	8	0	33	12	19	74	44	51	68	37	616
P. Lamy	Minardi	43	68	39	65	61	0	0	44	69	21	43	24	43	12	65	50	647
R. Rosset	Arrows	56	24	24	65	40	3	0	6	69	13	44	74	43	36	68	50	615
G. Fisichella	Minardi	33	–	–	65	30	0	1	67	–	59	–	–	–	–	–	–	257
L. Badoer	Forti	0	67	24	0	59	60	0	44	29	0	–	–	–	–	–	–	283
A. Montermini	Forti	0	26	69	0	0	0	0	22	2	0	–	–	–	–	–	–	119
G. Lavaggi	Forti	–	–	–	–	–	–	–	–	–	–	0	69	0	5	65	–	139
T. Marques	Minardi	0	33	–	–	–	–	–	–	–	–	–	–	–	–	–	–	33

FIA DRIVERS' CHAMPIONSHIP PLACINGS 1996

Pos	Driver	Team	Points
1	Damon Hill (GB)	Williams Renault	97
2	Jacques Villeneuve (Can)	Williams Renault	78
3	Michael Schumacher (Ger)	Ferrari	59
4	Jean Alesi (Fra)	Benetton Renault	47
5	Mika Hakkinen (Fin)	McLaren Mercedes	31
6	Gerhard Berger (Aut)	Benetton Renault	21
7	David Coulthard (GB)	McLaren	18
8	Rubens Barrichello (Bra)	Jordan Peugeot	14
9	Olivier Panis (Fra)	Ligier Mugen Honda	13
10	Eddie Irvine (GB)	Ferrari	11
11	Martin Brundle (GB)	Jordan Peugeot	8
12	Heinz-Harald Frentzen (Ger)	Sauber Ford	7
13	Mika Salo (Fin)	Tyrrell Yamaha	5
14	Johnny Herbert (GB)	Sauber Ford	4
15	Pedro Diniz (Bra)	Ligier Mugen Honda	2
16	Jos Verstappen (Hol)	Arrows Hart	1

CONSTRUCTORS' CHAMPIONSHIP PLACINGS 1996

Pos	Team	Points
1	Williams Renault	175
2	Ferrari	70
3	Benetton Renault	68
4	McLaren Mercedes	49
5	Jordan Peugeot	22
6	Ligier Mugen Honda	15
7	Sauber Ford	11
8	Tyrrell Yamaha	5
9	Arrows Hart	1

DRIVERS' WORLD CHAMPIONSHIP
WINNERS 1950-1996

R=Races, W=Wins, P=Poles, F=Fastest laps

Year	Driver	Age	Country	Car	R	W	P	F
1950	Giuseppe Farina	44	Italy	Alfa Romeo	7	3	2	3
1951	Juan-Manuel Fangio	40	Argentina	Alfa Romeo	8	3	4	5
1952	Alberto Ascari	34	Italy	Ferrari	8	6	5	5
1953	Alberto Ascari	35	Italy	Ferrari	9	5	6	4
1954	Juan-Manuel Fangio	43	Argentina	Merc/Maserati	9	6	5	3
1955	Juan-Manuel Fangio	44	Argentina	Mercedes	7	4	3	3
1956	Juan-Manuel Fangio	45	Argentina	Lancia/Ferrari	8	3	5	3
1957	Juan-Manuel Fangio	46	Argentina	Maserati	8	4	4	2
1958	Mike Hawthorn	29	G. Britain	Ferrari	11	1	4	5
1959	Jack Brabham	33	Australia	Cooper	9	2	1	1
1960	Jack Brabham	34	Australia	Cooper	10	5	3	3
1961	Phil Hill	34	USA	Ferrari	8	2	5	2
1962	Graham Hill	33	G. Britain	BRM	9	4	1	3
1963	Jim Clark	27	G. Britain	Lotus	10	7	7	6
1964	John Surtees	30	G. Britain	Ferrari	10	2	2	2
1965	Jim Clark	29	G. Britain	Lotus	10	6	6	6
1966	Jack Brabham	40	Australia	Brabham	9	4	3	1
1967	Denis Hulme	31	N. Zealand	Brabham	11	2	0	2
1968	Graham Hill	39	G. Britain	Lotus	12	3	2	0
1969	Jackie Stewart	30	G. Britain	Matra	11	6	2	5
1970	Jochen Rindt	28	Austria	Lotus	13	5	3	1
1971	Jackie Stewart	32	G. Britain	Tyrrell	11	6	6	3
1972	Emerson Fittipaldi	26	Brazil	Lotus	12	5	3	1
1973	Jackie Stewart	34	Brazil	Tyrrell	15	5	3	1
1974	Emerson Fittipaldi	28	Brazil	McLaren	15	3	2	0
1975	Niki Lauda	26	Austria	Ferrari	14	5	9	2
1976	James Hunt	29	G. Britain	McLaren	16	6	8	2
1977	Niki Lauda	28	Austria	Ferrari	17	3	2	3
1978	Mario Andretti	38	USA	Lotus	16	6	8	3
1979	Jody Scheckter	29	USA	Ferrari	15	3	1	1
1980	Alan Jones	34	Australia	Williams	14	5	3	5
1981	Nelson Piquet	29	Brazil	Brabham	15	3	4	1
1982	Keke Rosberg	34	Finland	Williams	16	1	1	0
1983	Nelson Piquet	31	Brazil	Brabham	15	3	1	4
1984	Niki Lauda	35	Austria	McLaren	16	5	0	5
1985	Alain Prost	30	France	McLaren	16	5	2	5
1986	Alain Prost	31	France	McLaren	16	4	1	2
1987	Nelson Piquet	35	Brazil	Williams	16	3	4	4
1988	Ayrton Senna	28	Brazil	McLaren	16	8	13	3

1989	Alain Prost	34	France	McLaren	16	4	2	5
1990	Ayrton Senna	30	Brazil	McLaren	16	6	10	2
1991	Ayrton Senna	31	Brazil	McLaren	16	7	8	2
1992	Nigel Mansell	39	G. Britain	Williams	16	9	14	8
1993	Alain Prost	38	France	Williams	16	7	13	6
1994	Michael Schumacher	25	Germany	Benetton	16	8	6	8
1995	Michael Schumacher	26	Germany	Benetton	17	9	4	8
1996	Damon Hill	36	G. Britain	Williams	16	8	9	5

DRIVERS' WORLD CHAMPIONSHIP WINS BY NUMBER 1950-96

Titles	Driver	Country	Year
5	Juan-Manuel Fangio	Argentina	1951, 1954, 1955, 1956 & 1957
4	Alain Prost	France	1985, 1986, 1989 & 1993
3	Jack Brabham	Australia	1959, 1960 & 1966
3	Jackie Stewart	Great Britain	1969, 1971 & 1973
3	Niki Lauda	Austria	1975, 1977 & 1984
3	Nelson Piquet	Brazil	1981, 1983 & 1987
3	Ayrton Senna	Brazil	1988, 1990 & 1991
2	Alberto Ascari	Italy	1952 & 1953
2	Graham Hill	Great Britain	1962 & 1968
2	Jim Clark	Great Britain	1963 & 1965
2	Emerson Fittipaldi	Brazil	1972 & 1974
2	Michael Schumacher	Germany	1994 & 1995
1	Giuseppe Farina	Italy	1950
1	Mike Hawthorn	Great Britain	1958
1	Phil Hill	USA	1961
1	John Surtees	Great Britain	1964
1	Denis Hulme	New Zealand	1967
1	Jochen Rindt	Austria	1970
1	James Hunt	Great Britain	1976
1	Mario Andretti	USA	1978
1	Jody Scheckter	USA	1979
1	Alan Jones	Australia	1980
1	Keke Rosberg	Finland	1982
1	Nigel Mansell	Great Britain	1992
1	Damon Hill	Great Britain	1996

1996 DRIVERS ALL-TIME RECORDS

Driver	No	WC	1st	2nd	3rd	4th	5th	6th	P	FL	TP	B
ALESI, Jean	118	0	1	12	13	11	9	3	1	4	189	1
BADOER, Luca	35	0	0	0	0	0	0	0	0	0	0	7
BARRICHELLO, Rubens	64	0	0	1	1	8	4	4	1	1	46	2
BERGER, Gerhard	196	0	9	16	21	23	8	10	11	17	358	1
BRUNDLE, Martin	158	0	0	2	7	8	12	10	0	0	98	2
COULTHARD, David	41	0	1	6	4	3	2	2	5	4	81	1
DINIZ, Pedro	33	0	0	0	0	0	0	2	2	0	0	6
FISICHELLA, Giancarlo	8	0	0	0	0	0	0	0	0	0	0	8
FRENTZEN, Heinz-Harald	48	0	0	0	1	4	3	7	0	0	48	3
HAKKINEN, Mika	79	0	0	3	9	5	7	4	0	0	90	3
HERBERT, Johnny	96	0	2	1	2	8	3	3	0	1	67	1
HILL, Damon	67	1	21	14	5	3	1	1	20	19	326	1
IRVINE, Eddie	48	0	0	0	2	3	4	3	0	0	28	3
KATAYAMA, Ukyo	78	0	0	0	0	0	2	1	0	0	5	5
LAMY, Pedro	28	0	0	0	0	0	0	1	0	0	1	6
LAVAGGI, Giovanni	10	0	0	0	0	0	0	0	0	0	0	10
MARQUES, Tarso	2	0	0	0	0	0	0	0	0	0	0	-
MONTERMINI, Andrea	17	0	0	0	0	0	0	0	0	0	0	8
PANIS, Olivier	49	0	1	2	0	2	3	4	0	0	38	1
ROSSET, Ricardo	16	0	0	0	0	0	0	0	0	0	0	8
SALO, Mika	35	0	0	0	0	0	4	2	0	0	10	5
SCHUMACHER, Michael	85	2	22	14	10	4	2	2	14	25	362	1
VERSTAPPEN, Jos	31	0	0	0	2	0	1	1	0	0	11	3
VILLENEUVE, Jacques	16	0	4	5	2	0	0	0	3	6	78	1

No=Number of Grands Prix. WC=Number of World Championship titles. 1st, 2nd etc= Number of times finished in this position. P=Number of Poles. FL=Number of Fastest Laps. TP=Total number of World Championship Points won to date. B=Best position achieved.

NB: Gerhard Berger did secure an additional point during the 1989 season but this did not count towards the championship and is not included here.

Driver	'94	'95	'96	Driver	'94	'95	'96
Adams	0	–	–	Irvine	6	10	11
Alboreto	1	–	–	Katayama	–	0	0
Alesi	24	42	47	Lagorce	0	–	–
Alliot	0	–	–	Lamy	0	1	0
Badoer	–	0	0	Larni	6	–	–
Barrichello	19	11	14	Lavaggi	–	0	0
Belmondo	0	–	–	Lehto	1	–	–
Beretta	0	–	–	Magnussen	–	0	–
Berger	41	31	21	Mansell	13	0	–
Bernard	4	–	–	Marques	–	–	0
Blundell	8	13	–	Martini	4	0	–
Boullion	–	3	–	Montermini	0	0	0
Brabham	0	–	–	Morbidelli	3	5	–
Brundle	16	7	0	Moreno	–	0	–
Comas	2	–	–	Noda	0	–	–
Coulthard	14	49	18	Panis	9	16	13
Dalamas	0	–	–	Papis	–	0	–
de Cesaris	4	–	–	Ratzenberger	0	–	–
Delatraz	0	0	–	Rosset	–	–	0
Diniz	–	0	0	Salo	–	5	0
Fisichella	–	–	0	Schiattarella	0	0	–
Fittipaldi	6	–	–	Schumacher, M.	92	102	59
Frentzen	7	15	0	Senna	0	–	–
Gachot	0	0	–	Suzuki	–	1	–
Gounon	0	–	–	Tarquini	–	0	–
Hakkinen	26	17	31	Verstappen	10	–	1
Herbert	0	45	0	Villeneuve	–	0	78
Hill, D.	91	69	97	Wendlinger	4	0	–
Inoue	0	0	–	Zanardi	0	–	–

16 Grands Prix in 1994; 17 Grands Prix in 1995; 16 Grands Prix in 1996. – indicates no races. Number indicates points achieved during the season.

1996 DRIVERS BY COMPLETION %

Driver	Races	Com	Ret	DNQ	HP	Pts	Psn	Comp%
Villeneuve	16	13	3	0	1	78	2	81.25
Hill, D.	16	12	4	0	1	97	1	75.00
Hakkinen	16	12	4	0	3	31	5	75.00
Alesi	16	11	5	0	2	47	4	68.75
Schumacher, M.	16	10	6	0	1	59	3	62.50
Berger	16	9	7	0	2	21	6	56.25
Coulthard	16	9	7	0	2	18	7	56.25
Barrichello	16	9	7	0	4	14	8	56.25
Panis	16	9	7	0	1	13	9	56.25
Brundle	16	9	7	0	4	0	–	56.25
Rosset	16	8	8	0	8	0	–	50.00
Lamy	16	8	8	0	9	0	–	50.00
Herbert	16	7	8	0	3	0	–	43.75
Salo	16	7	9	0	5	0	–	43.75
Diniz	16	6	10	0	6	0	–	37.50
Frentzen	16	6	10	0	4	0	–	37.50
Katayama	16	6	10	0	7	0	–	37.50
Lavaggi	6	2	1	3	10	0	–	33.33
Irvine	16	5	11	0	3	11	10	31.25
Verstappen	16	4	12	0	6	1	11	25.00
Fisichella	8	2	6	0	11	0	–	25.00
Badoer	10	2	4	4	10	0	–	20.00
Montermini	10	1	4	5	10	0	–	10.00
Marques	2	0	2	0	–	0	–	0.00

Com= Races Completed; Ret=Races retired in; DNQ=Races did not qualify in; HP=Highest position achieved in a race; Pts=Driver World Championship points; Psn=Position in DWC table; Comp%=Race completion percentage.

WORLD CHAMPIONSHIP DRIVERS WITH 100 POINTS OR MORE

Driver	Points	Driver	Points	Driver	Points
Prost	768.5	Hulme	248	Rosberg	159.5
Senna	610	Fangio	245	Depailler	139
Piquet	481.5	Laffite	228	Gurney	133
Mansell	480	Regazzoni	209	Boutsen	132
Lauda	420.5	Peterson	206	De Angelis	122
M.Schumacher	362	Jones	199	Farina	116.3
Stewart	359	Alesi	189	Hawthorn	112.5
Berger	358	McLaren	188.5	Ascari	107.5
D. Hill	326	Moss	186.5	Rindt	107
Reutemann	298	Alboreto	185.5	Ginther	107
E. Fittipaldi	281	Arnoux	181	Tambay	103
Patrese	281	Ickx	181	G.Villeneuve	101
G. Hill	270	Andretti	180	Pironi	101
Clark	255	Surtees	180		
J. Brabham	253	Hunt	179		
Scheckter	246	Watson	169		

WORLD CHAMPIONSHIP LAST RACE DECIDERS

Year	Grand Prix	Circuit	Drivers
1950	Italian	Monza	Farina (30), Fangio (27), Fagioli (24)
1951	Spanish	Pedralbes	Fangio (31), Ascari (25)
1956	Italian	Monza	Fangio (30), Collins (25)*
1958	Morocco	Casablanca	Hawthorn (42), Moss (41)
1959	USA	Sebring	Brabham (31), Brooks (27), Moss (25.5)
1962	S. African	E. London	G. Hill (42), Clark (30)
1964	Mexican	Mexico City	Surtees (40), G. Hill (39), Clark (32)
1967	Mexican	Mexico City	Hulme (51), Brabham (46)
1968	Mexican	Mexico City	G. Hill (48), Stewart (36), Hulme (33)
1974	USA	Watkins Glen	E. Fittipaldi (55), Regazzoni (52), Scheckter (45)
1976	Japanese	Mount Fuji	Hunt (69), Lauda (68)
1981	USA	Las Vegas	Piquet (50), Reutemann (49), Laffite (46)
1982	USA	Las Vegas	Rosberg (44), Watson (39)†
1983	S. African	Kyalami	Piquet (59), Prost (57), Arnoux (49)
1984	Portuguese	Estoril	Lauda (72), Prost (71.5)
1986	Australian	Adelaide	Prost (72), Mansell (70), Piquet (69)

| 1994 | Australian | Adelaide | M.Schumacher (92), D. Hill (91) |
| 1996 | Japanese | Suzuka | D. Hill (97), J.Villeneuve (78) |

** Finished third in championship after Moss   † Finished joint second with Pironi
Numbers in brackets are final points total.*

DRIVERS WITH FIVE OR MORE GRAND PRIX WINS

Wins	Driver
51	Alain Prost (France)
41	Ayrton Senna (Brazil)
31	Nigel Mansell (Great Britain)
27	Jackie Stewart (Great Britain)
25	Jim Clark (Great Britain) & Niki Lauda (Austria)
24	Juan-Manuel Fangio (Italy)
23	Nelson Piquet (Brazil)
22	Michael Schumacher (Germany)
21	Damon Hill (Great Britain)
16	Stirling Moss (Great Britain)
14	Jack Brabham (Australia), Emerson Fittipaldi (Brazil) & Graham Hill (Great Britain)
13	Alberto Ascari (Italy)
12	Mario Andretti (USA), Alan Jones (Australia) & Carlos Reutemann (Argentina)
10	James Hunt (Great Britain), Ronnie Peterson (Switzerland), Jody Scheckter (USA)
9	Gerhard Berger (Austria)
8	Denis Hulme (New Zealand) & Jacky Ickx (Belgium)
7	Rene Arnoux (France)
6	Tony Brooks (Great Britain), Jacques Laffite (France), Riccardo Patrese (Italy), Jochen Rindt (Austria), John Surtees (Great Britain) & Gilles Villeneuve (Canada)
5	Michele Alboreto (Italy), Giuseppe Farina (Italy), Clay Regazzoni (Switzerland), Keke Rosberg (Finland) & John Watson (Great Britain)

DRIVERS WITH FIVE OR MORE POLE POSITIONS

Poles	Driver
65	Ayrton Senna (Brazil)
33	Jim Clark (Great Britain) & Alain Prost (France)
32	Nigel Mansell (Great Britain)

28	Juan-Manuel Fangio (Italy)
24	Niki Lauda (Austria) & Nelson Piquet (Brazil)
20	Damon Hill (Great Britain)
18	Mario Andretti (USA) & Rene Arnoux (France)
17	Jackie Stewart (Great Britain)
16	Stirling Moss (Great Britain)
14	Giuseppe Farina (Italy), James Hunt (Great Britain), Ronnie Peterson (Switzerland) & Michael Schumacher (Germany)
13	Jack Brabham (Australia), Graham Hill (Great Britain), Jacky Ickx (Belgium)
11	Gerhard Berger (Austria)
10	Jochen Rindt (Austria)
8	Riccardo Patrese (Italy) & John Surtees (Great Britain)
7	Jacques Laffite (France)
6	Emerson Fittipaldi (Brazil), Phil Hill (USA), Jean-Pierre Labouille (France), Alan Jones (Australia), Carlos Reutemann (Argentina)
5	Chris Amon (New Zealand), Giuseppe Farina (Italy), Clay Regazzoni (Switzerland), Keke Rosberg (Finland), Patrick Tambay (France) & David Coulthard (Great Britain)

DRIVERS WITH FIVE OR MORE FASTEST LAPS

No	*Driver*
41	Alain Prost (France)
30	Nigel Mansell (Great Britain)
28	Jim Clark (Great Britain)
25	Niki Lauda (Austria) & Michael Schumacher (Germany)
23	Juan-Manuel Fangio (Italy) & Nelson Piquet (Brazil)
20	Stirling Moss (Great Britain)
19	Ayrton Senna (Brazil) & Damon Hill (Great Britain)
17	Gerhard Berger (Austria)
15	Clay Regazzoni (Switzerland) & Jackie Stewart (Great Britain)
14	Jacky Ickx (Belgium)
13	Alan Jones (Australia) & Riccardo Patrese (Italy)
12	Rene Arnoux (France)
11	Alberto Ascari (Italy) & John Surtees (Great Britain)
10	Mario Andretti (USA), Jack Brabham (Australia) & Graham Hill (Great Britain)
9	Denis Hulme (New Zealand) & Ronnie Peterson (USA)
8	James Hunt (Great Britain)
7	Jacques Laffite (France) & Gilles Villeneuve (Canada)

6	Giuseppe Farina (Italy), Jose Gonzalez (Argentina), Dan Gurney (USA), Mike Hawthorn (Great Britain), Phil Hill (USA), Didier Pironi (France), Jody Scheckter (USA) & Jacques Villeneuve (Canada)
5	Carlos Pace (Brazil) & John Watson (Great Britain)

DRIVERS WHO HAVE COMPLETED 100 GRANDS PRIX OR MORE

No	Driver
256	Riccardo Patrese (Italy)
208	Andrea de Cesaris (Italy)
204	Nelson Piquet (Brazil)
199	Alain Prost (France)
196	Gerhard Berger (Austria)
194	Michele Alboreto (Italy)
187	Nigel Mansell (Great Britain)
176	Graham Hill (Great Britain) & Jacques Laffite (France)
171	Niki Lauda (Austria)
163	Thierry Boutsen (Belgium)
161	Ayrton Senna (Brazil)
158	Martin Brundle (Great Britain)
152	John Watson (Great Britain)
149	Rene Arnoux (France)
147	Derek Warwick (Great Britain)
146	Carlos Reutemann (Argentina)
144	Emerson Fittipaldi (Brazil)
135	Jean-Pierre Jarier (France)
132	Eddie Cheever (USA) & Clay Regazzoni (Switzerland)
128	Mario Andretti (USA)
126	Jack Brabham (Australia)
123	Ronnie Peterson (USA)
119	Pierluigi Martini (Italy)
118	Jean Alesi (France)
116	Jacky Ickx (Belgium) & Alan Jones (Australia)
112	Denis Hulme (New Zealand) & Jody Scheckter (USA)
111	John Surtees (Great Britain)
109	Philippe Alliot (France)
108	Elio de Angelis (Italy)
105	Jochen Mass (Germany)
102	Joakim Bonnier (Switzerland)
101	Bruce McLaren (New Zealand)

DRIVERS WITH MORE THAN 5 POLE POSITIONS IN A SEASON

Poles	Races	Driver	Year(s)
14	16	Mansell	1992
13	16/16	Senna	1988 and 1989
	16	Prost	1993
10	16	Senna	1990
9	15/14	Lauda	1974 and 1975
	15	Peterson	1973
	16	Piquet	1984
	16	Hill, Damon	1996
8	16/16	Senna	1986 and 1991
	16	Hunt	1976
	16	Andretti	1978
	16	Mansell	1987
7	10	Clark	1963
	17	Andretti	1977
	16	Senna	1985
	17	Hill, Damon	1995
6	9/10/11	Clark	1962, 1965 and 1967
	9	Ascari	1953
	11	Stewart	1971
	17	Hunt	1977
	16	Schumacher, M.	1994

DRIVERS WITH 3 OR MORE SUCCESSIVE GRAND PRIX WINS

Wins	Driver	Year	Grand Prix
9	Ascari	1952/53	Bel, Fra, GB, Ger, Hol, Ita, Arg, Hol, Bel
5	Brabham	1960	Hol, Bel, Fra, GB, Por
	Clark	1965	Bel, Fra, GB, Hol, Ger
	Mansell	1992	SA, Mex, Bra, Esp, San
4	Senna	1988	GB, Ger, Hon, Bel
		1991	USA, Bra, San, Mon
	Fangio	1953/54	Ita/Arg, Bel, Fra
	Clark	1963	Bel, Hol, Fra, GB
	Brabham	1966	Fra, GB, Hol, Ger
	Rindt	1970	Hol, Fra, GB, Ger
	Prost	1993	Can, Fra, GB, Ger
	Schumacher	1994	Bra, Pac, San, Mon

3	Fangio	1954	Ger, Sui, Ita
		1957	Arg, Mon, Fra
	Stewart	1969	Hol, Fra, GB
		1971	Fra, GB, Ger
	Lauda	1975	Mon, Bel, Swe
		1975/76	USA/Bra, SA
	Jones	1979	Ger, Aut, Hol
		1980/81	Can, USAE/USAW
	Prost	1984/85	Eur, Por/Bra
		1990	Mex, Fra, GB
	Mansell	1991	Fra, GB, Ger
		1992	Fra, GB, Ger
	Moss	1957/58	Pes, Ita/Arg
	Clark	1967/68	USA, Mex/SA
	Senna	1989	San, Mon, Mex
	D. Hill	1993	Hun, Bel, Ita
		1994	Bel, Ita, Por
		1996	Aus, Bra, Arg
	M.Schumacher	1995	Eur, Pac, Jap

DRIVERS TO WIN THEIR NATIONAL GRAND PRIX

Wins	Driver	Nat	Year(s)
6	Prost	French	1981, 1983, 1988, 1989, 1990, 1993
5	Clark	British	1962, 1963, 1964, 1965, 1967
4	Fangio	Argentine	1954, 1955, 1956, 1957
	Mansell	British	1986, 1987, 1991, 1992
2	Ascari	Italian	1951, 1952
	Moss	British	1955, 1957
	Stewart	British	1969, 1971
	E. Fittipaldi	Brazilian	1973, 1974
	Piquet	Brazilian	1983, 1986
	Senna	Brazilian	1991, 1993
1	Farina	Italian	1950
	Collins	British	1958
	Scarfiotti	Italian	1966
	Pace	Brazilian	1975
	Scheckter	S. African	1975
	Andretti	American	1977
	Hunt	British	1977
	Villeneuve, G.	Canadian	1978
	Jabouille	French	1979
	Watson	British	1981

Arnoux	French	1982
Lauda	Austrian	1984
D. Hill	British	1994
Herbert	British	1995
Schumacher, M.	German	1995

GRANDS PRIX WITH DRIVER FATALITIES

Year	Grand Prix	Venue	Driver	Car	During
1954	Germany	Nurburgring	O. Marimon	Maserati	Practice
1955	Indianapolis	Indianapolis	B. Vukovich		Race
1958	France	Reims	L. Musso	Ferrari	Race
1958	Germany	Nurburgring	P. Collins	Ferrari	Race
1958	Morocco	Casablanca	S. Lewis-Evans	Vanwall	Race
1959	Indianapolis	Indianapolis	J. Unser		Race
			B. Cortner		Race
1960	Belgium	Spa-Fran'	C. Bristow		Race
			A. Stacey		Race
1961	Italy	Monza	Von Trips	Ferrari	Race
1964	Germany	Nurburgring	C. de Beaufor		Practice
1966	Germany	Nurburgring	J. Taylor	Brabham	Race
1967	Monaco	Monaco	L. Bandini	Ferrari	Inj/Race†
1968	France	Rouen	J. Schlesser	Honda	Race
1969	Germany	Nurburgring	G. Mitter		Practice
1970	Holland	Zandvoort	P. Courage	De Tomaso	Race
1970	Italy	Monza	J. Rindt	Lotus	Practice
1973	Holland	Zandvoort	R. Williamson	March	Race
1973	USA	Watkins Glen	F. Cevert	Tyrrell	Practice
1974	USA	Watkins Glen	H. Koinigg	Surtees	Race
1975	Austria	Osterreichring	M. Donohue	M-Penske	Practice
1977	South Africa	Kyalami	T. Pryce	Shadow	Race
1978	Italy	Monza	R. Peterson	Lotus	Inj/Race*
1982	Belgium	Zolder	G. Villeneuve	Ferrari	Practice
1982	Canada	Montreal	R. Paletti	Osella Ford	Race
1994	San Marino	Imola	R. Ratzenberger	Simtek	Practice
			A. Senna	Williams	Race

† Died three days after race from burns.
* Died the next day from injuries received during start of race.

CONSTRUCTORS' CUP BY CAR

Titles	Car	Year(s)
8	Ferrari	1961, 1964, 1975, 1976, 1977, 1979, 1982 & 1983
8	Williams	1980, 1981, 1986, 1987, 1992, 1993, 1994 & 1996
7	Lotus	1963, 1965, 1968, 1970, 1972, 1973 & 1978
7	McLaren	1974, 1984, 1985, 1988, 1989, 1990 & 1991
2	Cooper	1959 & 1960
2	Brabham	1966 & 1967
1	Vanwall	1958
1	BRM	1962
1	Matra	1969
1	Tyrrell	1971
1	Benetton	1995

CONSTRUCTORS' CUP WINNERS

Year	Team	Year	Team	Year	Team
1958	Vanwall	1971	Tyrrell	1984	McLaren
1959	Cooper	1972	Lotus	1985	McLaren
1960	Cooper	1973	Lotus	1986	Williams
1961	Ferrari	1974	McLaren	1987	Williams
1962	BRM	1975	Ferrari	1988	McLaren
1963	Lotus	1976	Ferrari	1989	McLaren
1964	Ferrari	1977	Ferrari	1990	McLaren
1965	Lotus	1978	Lotus	1991	McLaren
1966	Brabham	1979	Ferrari	1992	Williams
1967	Brabham	1980	Williams	1993	Williams
1968	Lotus	1981	Williams	1994	Williams
1969	Matra	1982	Ferrari	1995	Benetton
1970	Lotus	1983	Ferrari	1996	Williams

GRAND PRIX WINS PER CAR TYPE

Wins	Car Type	Wins	Car Type
109	Ferrari	15	Renault
104	McLaren	10	Alfa Romeo
95	Williams	9	Maserati, Matra, Mercedes, Vanwall & Ligier
79	Lotus		
35	Brabham	3	March & Wolf
26	Benetton	2	Honda
23	Tyrrell	1	Eagle, Hesketh, Penske, Porsche & Shadow
17	BRM		
16	Cooper		

GP PARTICIPATED PER CAR TYPE

GP	Car Type	GP	Car Type	GP	Car Type
586	Ferrari	117	Surtees	35	Honda
490	Lotus	113	Jordan	34	Theodore
459	McLaren	112	Alfa Romeo	33	Porsche
401	Tyrrell	104	Fittipaldi &	30	Penske
394	Brabham		Shadow	28	Vanwall
378	Williams	99	ATS	25	Eagle
342	Ligier	98	Ensign	22	Pacific
304	Arrows	78	Dallara	20	Rial
250	Benetton	69	Maserati	19	Lola Haas
230	March	65	Sauber	17	Onyx & Forti
204	Minardi	61	Matra	16	Simtek
197	BRM	54	Zakspeed	15	Parnelli
139	Lola	48	AGS,	12	Mercedes
132	Osella		Larousse &	11	Forti
129	Cooper		Wolf	10	Merzario
123	Renault	40	Gordini	4	Lancia

GP POLE POSITIONS PER CAR TYPE

Poles	Car Type	Poles	Car Type
118	Ferrari	9	Ligier
107	Lotus	8	Mercedes
97	Williams	7	Vanwall
79	McLaren	5	March
39	Brabham	4	Matra
31	Renault	3	Shadow
14	Tyrrell	2	Lancia
13	Benetton	1	Arrows, Honda, Jordan,
12	Alfa Romeo		Lola, Porsche & Wolf
11	BRM & Cooper		
10	Maserati		

GP FASTEST LAPS PER CAR TYPE

Laps	Car Type	Laps	Car Type
121	Ferrari	12	Matra
100	Williams	11	Ligier
71	Lotus	9	Mercedes
69	McLaren	7	March
40	Brabham	6	Vanwall
36	Benetton	4	Surtees
20	Tyrrell	2	Eagle, Honda, Shadow & Wolf
18	Renault	1	Ensign, Gordini, Hesketh, Jordan, Lancia & Parnelli
15	BRM & Maserati		
14	Alfa Romeo		
13	Cooper		

GP WON BY COUNTRY

Country	Wins	Drivers	Country	Wins	Drivers
Great Britain	171	16	Germany	25	3
Brazil	79	4	Sweden	12	3
France	79	12	New Zealand	12	2
Austria	40	3	Belgium	11	2
Italy	39	13	Canada	10	2
Argentina	38	3	South Africa	10	1
USA	33	15	Switzerland	7	2
Australia	26	2	Finland	5	1
			Mexico	2	1

Drivers 1997

Introduction

These pages contain an A-Z of drivers who have been named as teams' major drivers for the 1997 Grand Prix season plus all the drivers who featured in the 1996 Grand Prix season. In addition to this, where possible we have also included teams' test drivers and advisors and any other drivers who might possibly feature during 1997. While every attempt has been made to ensure that this list is as accurate as possible, new drivers may have come to light after this book went to press. Each entry lists a brief résumé of each driver's F1 career to date and then provides a summary of GP details. This is followed by a list of each of the Grand Prix races he has competed in. Numbers in brackets after named Grands Prix signify the number of points scored in the race in question.

Team and Driver Number Allocation 1997

Listed below are the numbers allocated to the teams for the 1997 season and the drivers allocated to the numbers by their team at the time of going to press. Although the team numbers will remain consistent, the numbers allocated to drivers may change, especially when teams are using more than two drivers during the season.

No.	Driver	Country	Team	Car
1	Damon Hill	GB	Arrows	Arrows Yamaha A18
2	Pedro Diniz	Bra	Arrows	Arrows Yamaha A18
3	Jacques Villeneuve	Can	Williams	Williams Renault FW19
4	Heinz-Harald Frentzen	Ger	Williams	Williams Renault FW19
5	Michael Schumacher	Ger	Ferrari	Ferrari F310B
6	Eddie Irvine	GB	Ferrari	Ferrari F310B
7	Jean Alesi	Fra	Benetton	Benetton Renault B197
8	Gerhard Berger	Austria	Benetton	Benetton Renault B197
9	Mika Hakkinen	Swe	McLaren	McLaren Mercedes MP4-12
10	David Coulthard	GB	McLaren	McLaren Mercedes MP4-12
11	Ralf Schumacher	Ger	Jordan	Jordan Peugeot 197
12	Giancarlo Fisichella	Ita	Jordan	Jordan Peugeot 197
14	Olivier Panis	Fra	Prost (Ligier)	Prost Mugen Honda JS45
15	Shinji Nakano	Jap	Prost (Ligier)	Prost Mugen Honda JS45
16	Johnny Herbert	GB	Sauber	Sauber Petronas C16
17	Nicola Larini	Ita	Sauber	Sauber Petronas C16
18	Jos Verstappen	Hol	Tyrrell	Tyrrell Yamaha 025
19	Mika Salo	Swe	Tyrrell	Tyrrell Yamaha 025
20	Ukyo Katayama	Jap	Minardi	Minardi Ford M197
21	Jarno Trulli	Bra	Minardi	Minardi Ford M197
22	Rubens Barrichello	Bra	Stewart	Stewart Ford SF1
23	Jan Magnussen	Den	Stewart	Stewart Ford SF1
24	Ricardo Rosset	Bra	Lola	Lola Ford T97/30
25	Vincenzo Sospiri	Ita	Lola	Lola Ford T97/30

Test Drivers 1997

Test drivers selected by each of the teams at the time of going to press are:

Team	Driver	Ctry
Arrows Yamaha	Jorg Muller	Ger
Benetton Renault	Alexander Wurz	Austria
Ferrari	Gianni Morbidelli	Ita
Jordan Peugeot	(No test driver due to be appointed)	
Lola Ford		
McLaren Mercedes		
Minardi Ford	Tarso Marques	Bra
Prost Mugen Honda		
Sauber Petronas	Norberto Fontana	Arg
Stewart Ford		
Tyrrell Yamaha	Toranosuke Takagi	Jap
Williams Renault	Jean-Christophe Boullion	Fra

1997 Driver Race Summaries

Total profile summaries of the drivers for the 1997 Championship are listed below.

No.	Driver	Age	Races	Wins	Poles	FLaps	Pts
1	Damon Hill	36	67	21	20	19	326
2	Pedro Diniz	26	33	0	0	0	2
3	Jacques Villeneuve	25	16	4	3	6	78
4	Heinz-Harald Frentzen	29	48	0	0	0	29
5	Michael Schumacher	28	85	22	14	25	362
6	Eddie Irvine	31	48	0	0	0	28
7	Jean Alesi	32	118	1	1	4	189
8	Gerhard Berger	37	196	9	11	19	358
9	Mika Hakkinen	28	79	0	0	0	91
10	David Coulthard	25	41	1	5	4	81
11	Ralf Schumacher	21	0	0	0	0	0
12	Giancarlo Fisichella	24	8	0	0	0	0
14	Olivier Panis	30	49	1	0	0	38
15	Shinji Nakano	26	0	0	0	0	0
16	Johnny Herbert	32	96	2	0	0	67
17	Nicola Larini	33	46	0	0	0	6
18	Jos Verstappen	25	31	0	0	0	11
19	Mika Salo	29	35	0	0	0	10
20	Ukyo Katayama	33	78	0	0	0	5
21	Jarno Trulli	22	0	0	0	0	0
22	Rubens Barrichello	24	64	0	1	0	46
23	Jan Magnussen	23	1	0	0	0	0
24	Ricardo Rosset	28	16	0	0	0	0
25	Vincenzo Sospiri	30	0	0	0	0	0

1996: Benetton Renault   *1997: Benetton Renault*

Jean Alesi had his best ever season in Formula 1 during 1996. That statement might surprise a few people but his fourth position in the World Championship was his best ever as was his points tally of 47. Although he wasn't able to add to his Grand Prix victory of 1995, only three other drivers managed to finish more races than the French-Sicilian. In every race he completed Alesi scored points – only World Champion Damon Hill could lay a similar claim on the season. All this came after his switch to Benetton after five semi-productive seasons at Ferrari and when driving in a car that Alesi often admitted was still more suited to the nervous driving style of its previous incumbent, Michael Schumacher.

The season was still typically Alesi though. A tangle with Eddie Irvine in the opening race of the season in Melbourne during an Alesi overtaking manoeuvre ultimately led to the Benetton's retirement. After which he went on to finish second and third in South America with two superb races. A one-stop strategy in Brazil helped him on the way to six points and in Argentina he achieved the first of two races in which he recorded the fastest lap and he may have done better than his third position had he not stalled the car on his second pit-stop.

The European season saw him crash out on his second lap at the Nurburgring after hitting Mika Salo's Tyrrell. Relative disappointment came at San Marino, when he was forced to race with a broken front wheel rim for a time and then received a 10 second stop-go penalty for pit lane speeding. This was followed by a retirement at Monaco where he led after Hill's engine blew and looked a likely winner before the Benetton's rear suspension gave way. That apart, he would have certainly been able to double his Grand Prix victory tally in a race in which he recorded another fastest lap.

For the French Grand Prix Alesi secured his first-ever podium appearance in France when he finished third at Magny-Cours. The French race also saw him qualify third on the grid – his best of the season – utilising an upgrade of the Renault RS8B engine.

Alesi continued to drive to good finishes in the final part of the season and apart from a brake failure that required him to retire at Silverstone, he was never out of the top four for all but the last race of the season and this sequence included runners-up spots in Germany and Italy. The season ended in Suzuka as it had begun in Melbourne with retirement but this time at the very first corner, when another fast start saw him smash into Armco while trying to get past the Ferraris.

During 1996 Alesi demonstrated that he has the ability to be consistent, a fact shown not just by his results but also by his grid positions, many of which were achieved with major changes being tried on his Benetton. The third and fourth rows were a common starting point aided by some unbelievably blinding starts. However, the rumours of discord were continually emanating from the Benetton headquarters throughout the year. Given a more settled camp and car in 1997, Alesi will remain a strong contender. He will need to turn some of those podium positions into race victories to be able to have any chance of achieving his ultimate aim of becoming Drivers' World Champion.

Born: 11/6/64, Avignon, France. Single, one daughter.

Grand Prix 1996 Record

Grand Prix	Grid	Qual Time	Fin	Laps	Race Time	Reason
Australian	6th	1:34.257	–	10		Collision damage
Brazilian	5th	1.19.484	2th	71	1.50:10.958	
Argentinian	4th	1:31.038	3th	72	1.55:10.076	
European	4th	1:20.711	–	1		Accident
San Marino	5th	1:28.009	6th	62	1.35:43.597	+1 lap down
Monaco	3th	1:20.918	–	60		Suspension
Spanish	4th	1:22.061	2th	65	2.00:34.609	
Canadian	4th	1:21.529	3th	69	1.36:58.121	
French	3th	1:16.310	3th	72	1.37:15.237	
British	5th	1:28.307	–	44		Brakes
German	5th	1:44.670	2th	45	1.21:54.869	
Hungarian	5th	1:18.754	3th	77	1:47.45.346	
Belgian	7th	1:52.354	4th	44	1:28.34.250	
Italian	6th	1:25.201	5th	53	1:18.01.897	
Portuguese	3th	1:21.088	4th	70	1:41.18.024	
Japanese	9th	1:41.562	–	0		Accident

1996 Position Summary

Contested:	16	Finished:	11
Pole Positions:	0	Fastest Laps:	2
Points:	47		
1st:	0	2nd:	4
3rd:	4	4th:	2
5th:	0	6th:	1

Grand Prix Career Record

Contested:	118	(1989-1996)
Pole Positions:	1	1994 (Ita)
Fastest Laps:	4	1991 (USA), 1995 (Mon), 1996 (Arg, Mon)
Points:	189	1989 (8), 1990 (13), 1991 (21), 1992 (18), 1993 (16), 1994 (24), 1995 (42), 1996 (47)
1st:	1	1995 (Can)
2nd:	12	1990 (USA, Mon), 1993 (Ita), 1994 (GB), 1995 (Arg, San, GB, Eur), 1996 (Bra, Esp, Ger, Ita)
3rd:	13	1991 (Mon, Ger, Por), 1992 (Esp, Can), 1993 (Mon), 1994 (Bra, Can, Jap), 1996 (Arg, Can, Fra, Hun)

4th:	11		1989 (Fra, Esp), 1991 (Fra, Esp), 1992 (Bra, Aus), 1993 (Por, Aus), 1994 (Esp), 1996 (Bel, Por)
5th:	9		1989 (Ita), 1991 (Hun), 1992 (Ger, Jap), 1994 (Mon), 1995 (Bra, Fra, Por, Pac)
6th:	4		1990 (San), 1991 (Bra), 1994 (Aus), 1996 (San)

Year	Team	No.	Grand Prix
1989	Tyrrell Ford	8	Fra (3), GB, Ger, Hun, Ita (2), Esp (3), Jap, Aus
1990	Tyrrell Ford	15	USA (6), Bra, San (1), Mon (6), Can, Mex, Fra, GB, Ger, Hun, Bel, Ita, Por, Esp, Aus
1991	Ferrari	16	USA, Bra (1), San, Mon (4), Can, Mex, Fra (3), GB, Ger (4), Hun (2), Bel, Ita, Por (4), Esp (3), Jap, Aus
1992	Ferrari	16	SA, Mex, Bra (3), Esp (4), San, Mon, Can (4), Fra, GB, Ger (2), Hun, Bel, Ita, Por, Jap (2), Aus (3)
1993	Ferrari	16	SA, Bra, Eur, San, Esp, Mon (4), Can, Fra, GB, Ger, Hun, Bel, Ita (6), Por (3), Jap, Aus (3)
1994	Ferrari	14	Bra (4), Mon (2), Esp (3), Can (4), Fra, GB (6), Ger, Hun, Bel, Ita, Por, Eur, Jap (4), Aus
1995	Ferrari	17	Bra (2), Arg (6), San (6), Esp, Mon, Can (10), Fra (2), GB (6), Ger, Hun, Bel, Ita, Por (2), Eur (6), Pac (2), Jap, Aus
1996	Benetton Renault	16	Aus, Bra (6), Arg (4), Eur, San (1), Mon, Esp (6), Can (4), Fra (4), GB, Ger (6), Hun (4), Bel (3), Ita (6), Por (3), Jap

BADOER, Luca   Italy

1996: Forti Ford   *1997: –*

Having got back into F1 racing as part of the Minardi team in 1995, Luca Badoer was always going to struggle to take his career forward with what proved to be a hopelessly under-funded Forti team. The team lasted just 10 Grands Prix before the funding ran out and during that time, Badoer only managed to finish twice.

He and his Forti team-mate, Andrea Montermini, both became the first drivers to fail to qualify for a Grand Prix with the introduction of the 107% qualification rule. Perhaps this was not surprising in Badoer's case as he was unable to do any practice laps on the Thursday. The 107% rule also proved troublesome at the European, Spanish and British Grands Prix.

Although he qualified 21st at the Brazilian Grand Prix, the demotion of Marques and Diniz provided Badoer with his best starting position of the season – 19th which the Italian also turned into the team's first finish of the season. Things looked to improve at Imola when Badoer received his new FG03 car which provided him with a qualification over three seconds better than he had previously achieved. The extra power was obviously too much to handle as he amazingly received two pit lane speeding penalties during the race – and motored on to his best finish of the season – 10th, a feat he bettered only three times at Minardi the previous season.

In Monaco an accident with Villeneuve earned Badoer a hefty fine and a two race ban, suspended for three races. But he provided the team with possibly its highlight of the season in Canada when he out-qualified Ricardo Rosset's Arrows car to secure 20th position on the grid. This was the first time a Forti driver had out-qualified a driver from another team! With only a token gesture at Silverstone during Saturday's qualification, Luca Badoer's, and Forti's, season was over.

Born: 25/1/71, Montebelluna, Treviso, Italy.

Grand Prix 1996 Record

Grand Prix	Grid	Qual Time	Fin	Laps	Race Time	Reason
Australian	107%	1:39.202	dnq	-		
Brazilian	21st	1.23.174	11th	67	1.50:52.957	+ 3 laps down
Argentinian	21st	1:34.830	–	24		Accident
European	107%	1:25.840	dnq			
San Marino	21st	1:32.037	10th	59	1.36:10.706	+2 laps down
Monaco	21st	1:25.059	–	60		Accident
Spanish	107%	1:26.615	dnq	-		
Canadian	20th	1:25.012	–	44		Gearbox
French	20th	1:20.647	–	29		Engine
British	107%	1:35.304	dnq			

Did not race at: German, Hungarian, Belgian, Italian, Portuguese, Japanese.

1996 Position Summary

Contested:	6	Finished:	2
Pole Positions:	0	Fastest Laps:	0
Points:	0		
1st-6th:	0		

Grand Prix Record

Contested:	35	(1993-1996)
Pole Positions:	0	
Fastest Laps:	0	
1st - 6th:	0	
Best Finish:	7th	1993 (San), 1995 (Can)

Year	Team	No.	Grand Prix
1993	Lola BMS	12	SA, Bra, San, Esp, Can, Fra, GB, Ger, Hun, Bel, Ita, Por
1995	Minardi Ford	17	Bra, Arg, San, Esp, Mon, Can, Fra, GB, Ger, Hun, Bel, Ita, Por, Eur, Pac, Jap, Aus
1996	Forti Ford	6	Bra, Arg, San, Mon, Can, Fra

BARRICHELLO, Rubens   Brazil

1996: Jordan Peugeot   *1997: Stewart Ford*

The 1996 season looked to promise much for Rubens Barrichello, not least because Eddie Irvine's departure to Ferrari was said to have boosted the Brazilian's confidence – presumably in his own driving ability. Certainly in the early part of the season Barrichello carried an air of confidence about him and it influenced his early results, only to disappear in the second part of the season as he finished what can only be considered a disappointing eighth place in the Drivers' Championship.

An engine failure ended any chance of a points start in Melbourne but when he secured second place on the grid in Interlagos for his home Grand Prix, things looked bright. Supported by a large home crowd, Barrichello lost his front position at the off, but recaptured it from Alesi in the rain only to spin out 12 laps from home points.

Argentina, Europe and San Marino all provided top five finishes and seven of the 14 championship points he would secure during the season. In Argentina he used the safety car to best effect for his team's first points of the season, and a strong race at the Nurburgring saw him finish just 0.2 seconds behind a fourth-placed Damon Hill. Another fifth at Imola might have been bettered had he not suffered at refuelling stops as his team struggled to deliver fuel into his Jordan.

A hat-trick of failures followed. At Monaco, Barrichello secured sixth position on the grid – Jordan's highest ever starting position in the principality – only to spin off into Armco at Rascasse. In Spain and Canada, transmission and clutch problems respectively made for early retirements and seemed to have a confidence-sapping effect, especially in qualifying where he was often on the fifth or sixth row. Points did come though, including three at Silverstone.

Towards the end of the season Rubens' four-year stint at Jordan was nearing its end with the announcement that his seat would be filled by Ralf Schumacher in 1997. Rubens himself didn't have to wait too long for a new drive when he signed a three-year deal with Stewart Grand Prix where the pressure on him to remain high on the grid and consistently in the points will not be as heavy.

Born: 23/5/72, Sao Paulo, Brazil. Single.

Grand Prix 1996 Record

Grand Prix	Grid	Qual Time	Fin	Laps	Race Time	Reason
Australian	8th	1:34.474	–	30		Engine
Brazilian	2nd	1.19.092	–	59		Spin
Argentinian	6th	1:31.404	4th	72	1.55:50.453	
European	5th	1:20.818	5th	67	1.34:00.186	
San Marino	9th	1:28.632	5th	63	1.36:44.646	
Monaco	6th	1:21.504	–	0		Accident
Spanish	7th	1:22.379	–	45		Transmission
Canadian	8th	1:21.982	–	22		Clutch
French	10th	1:17.665	9th	71	1.37:24.841	*+1 lap down*
British	6th	1:28.409	4th	61	1.34:07.590	
German	9th	1:45.452	6th	45	1.23:25.516	
Hungarian	13th	1:19.966	6th	75	1:46.34.466	*+2 laps down*
Belgian	10th	1:53.152	–	29		Handling
Italian	10th	1:26.194	5th	53	1:19.09.107	
Portuguese	9th	1:22.205	–	41		Spin
Japanese	11th	1:41.919	9th	52	1:34.14.856	

1996 Position Summary

Contested:	16	Finished:	9
Pole Positions:	0	Fastest Laps:	0
Points:	14		
1st:	0	2nd:	0
3rd:	0	4th:	2
5th:	3	6th:	2

Grand Prix Record

Contested:	64	(1993-1996)
Pole Positions:	1	1994 (Bel)
Fastest Laps:	1	
Points:	46	1993 (2), 1994 (19), 1995 (11), 1996 (14)
1st:	0	
2nd:	1	1995 (Can)
3rd:	1	1994 (Aus)
4th:	8	1994 (Bra, GB, Ita, Por, Aus), 1995 (Eur), 1996 (Arg, GB)
5th:	4	1993 (Jap), 1996 (Eur, San, Ita)
6th:	4	1995 (Fra, Bel), 1996 (Ger, Hun)

Year	Team	No.	Grand Prix
1993	Jordan Hart	16	SA, Bra, Eur, San, Esp, Mon, Can, Fra, GB, Ger, Hun, Bel, Ita, Por, Jap (2), Aus

1994	Jordan Hart	15	Bra (3), Pac (4), Mon, Esp, Can, Fra, GB (3), Ger, Hun, Bel, Ita (3), Por (3), Eur, Jap, Aus (3)
1995	Jordan Peugeot	17	Bra, Arg, San, Esp, Mon, Can (6), Fra (1), GB, Ger, Hun, Bel (1), Ita, Por, Eur (3), Pac, Jap, Aus
1996	Jordan Peugeot	16	Aus, Bra, Arg (3), Eur (2), San (2), Mon, Esp, Can, Fra, GB (3), Ger (1), Hun (1), Bel, Ita (2), Por, Jap

BERGER, Gerhard   Austria

1996: Benetton Renault   *1997: Benetton Renault*

Gerhard Berger remained the senior driver on the circuit in 1996 and will continue to be so during 1997. He needs to compete in just four more Grands Prix to mark his 200th start – yet it has been two years since he recorded the last of his nine victories.

Last season he found himself hampered in the early part by the de-Schumachering of his Benetton chassis – a problem that resulted in the Austrian having several crashes in the pre-season testing. If that wasn't enough, a bout of pneumonia took its toll in the first half of the racing season proper and it really wasn't until the French Grand Prix that Gerhard looked like the racing Berger we are all familiar with. In those first eight races of the season 4th was the highest on the grid and he managed just three finishes – those coming in Australia, Europe and San Marino – the latter his first podium of the season. A lack of engine reliability hit hard in that early part of the season and was compounded by problems with his car's suspension and gearbox. That said, a fourth place in Melbourne in the spare car was encouraging, only for suspension problems to deny him finishes in South America.

Nurburgring was a near disaster when a new starting system to prevent creeping on the grid seized and at the end of lap one Berger was down from 8th to 19th. A stalled engine in the pits didn't help matters much but at least reliability prevailed to enable him to come home in 9th place, albeit a lap down.

Berger had his best race to date in San Marino, finishing third and securing Benetton's first podium finish of the year. But it marked the start of three retirements, the first in Monaco due to a faulty gearbox sensor and then spins in Spain and Canada.

There was, however, a definite change in his track fortune in the second half of the season – it would be naive to say that ridding himself of the tail effects of his illness didn't have something to do with it. At Magny-Cours, Gerhard's season took a turn for the better – a 4th place on the grid was matched by a similar finish in the first use of a new Renault RS8B engine. His highlight of the season came in the next race at Silverstone where he achieved his best finish of the season in second place. Arguably though, his best racing performance came two weeks later in Germany where, having qualified on the front row of the grid, he looked capable of achieving a win until engine problems meant that he didn't finish the race. The season finished on a consistent note and for a while he looked capable of challenging Damon Hill for victory in the final race of the season but eventually finished fourth.

On reflection the season probably started six months too early for Gerhard Berger but with a stable chassis to suit his needs and the fitness that eluded him for much of the year, he may have the chance to take at least another Grand Prix victory in what must now be considered the twilight of his F1 career.

Born: 27/8/59, Worgl, Austria. Married with two daughters.

Grand Prix 1996 Record

Grand Prix	Grid	Qual Time	Fin	Laps	Race Time	Reason
Australian	7th	1:34.344	4th	58	1.34:07.528	
Brazilian	8th	1.19.762	–	26		Suspension
Argentinian	5th	1:31.262	–	56		Suspension
European	8th	1:21.054	9th	67	1.34:47.534	
San Marino	7th	1:28.336	3rd	63	1.36.13.047	
Monaco	4th	1:21.067	–	9		Gearbox sensor
Spanish	5th	1:22.125	–	44		Spin
Canadian	7th	1:21.926	–	42		Spin
French	4th	1:16.592	4th	72	1.37:15.654	
British	7th	1:28.653	2nd	61	1.33:19.900	
German	2nd	1:44.299	13th	42	+ 3 laps down dnf	Engine
Hungarian	6th	1:18.794	–	64		Engine
Belgian	5th	1:51.960	6th	44	1.28.45.021	
Italian	8th	1:25.470	–	4		Gearbox
Portuguese	5th	1:21.293	6th	70	1:41.56.056	
Japanese	4th	1:40.364	4th	52	1:33.00.317	

1996 Position Summary

Contested:	16	Finished:	9
Pole Positions:	0	Fastest Laps:	1
Points:	21		
1st:	0	2nd:	1
3rd:	1	4th:	3
5th:	0	6th:	2

Grand Prix Record

Contested:	196	(1984-1996)
Pole Positions:	11	1987 (Por, Jap, Aus), 1988 (GB), 1990 (USA, Mex), 1991 (Esp, Jap), 1994 (Ger, Por), 1995 (Bel)

Fastest Laps:	18	1986 (Ger, Aut), 1987 (Por, Esp, Aus), 1988 (Bra, Bel, Por), 1989 (Por), 1990 (Bra, USA, Can), 1991 (San, Aus), 1992 (Mex, Can), 1995 (San), 1996 (Bel)
Points:	358†	1985 (3), 1986 (17), 1987 (36), 1988 (41), 1989 (20), 1990 (43), 1991 (44), 1992 (49), 1993 (12), 1994 (41), 1995 (31), 1996 (21). *† Also secured one extra point in 1989 which did not count towards the championship.*
1st:	9	1986 (Mex), 1987 (Jap, Aus), 1988 (Ita), 1989 (Por), 1991 (Jap), 1992 (Can, Aus), 1994 (Ger)
2nd:	16	1987 (Por), 1988 (Bra, Mon), 1989 (Ita, Esp), 1990 (Bra, San), 1991 (San, GB, Bel), 1992 (Por, Jap), 1994 (Pac, Ita, Aus), 1996 (GB)
3rd:	21	1986 (Mon), 1988 (Mex, Ger), 1990 (Mon, Mex, Ger, Bel, Ita), 1991 (Bra, Aus), 1992 (Hun), 1993 (Hun), 1994 (Mon, Fra), 1995 (Bra, San, Esp, Mon, Ger, Hun), 1996 (San)
4th:	23	1987 (Bra, Mon, USAE, Ita), 1988 (Fra, Hun, Jap), 1990 (Can, Por, Aus), 1991 (Ger, Hun, Ita), 1992 (Mex, Esp, Ita), 1993 (Can), 1994 (Can), 1995 (Por, Pac), 1996 (Aus, Fra, Jap)
5th:	8	1985 (SA), 1986 (Ita), 1988 (San), 1990 (Fra), 1992 (SA, GB), 1993 (Aus), 1994 (Eur)
6th:	10	1985 (Aus), 1986 (Bra, Esp), 1988 (Esp), 1993 (SA, Esp, Ger), 1995 (Arg), 1996 (Bel, Por)

Year	Team	No.	Grand Prix
1984	ATS BMW Turbo	4	Aut, Ita, Eur, Por
1985	Arrows BMW Turbo	16	Bra, Por, San, Mon, Can, USAE, Fra, GB, Ger, Aut, Hol, Ita, Bel, Eur, SA (2), Aus (1)
1986	Benetton BMW Turbo	16	Bra (1), Esp (1), San (4), Mon, Bel, Can, USAE, Fra, GB, Ger, Hun, Aut, Ita (2), Por, Mex (9), Aus
1987	Ferrari Turbo	16	Bra (3), San, Bel, Mon (3), USAE (3), Fra, GB, Ger, Hun, Aut, Ita (3), Por (6), Esp, Mex, Jap (9), Aus (9)
1988	Ferrari Turbo	16	Bra (6), San (2), Mon (6), Mex (4), Can, USAE, Fra (3), GB, Ger (4), Hun (3), Bel, Ita (9), Por, Esp (1), Jap (3), Aus
1989	Ferrari	15	Bra, San, Mex, USA, Can, Fra, GB, Ger, Hun, Bel, Ita (6), Por (9), Esp (6), Jap, Aus

1990	McLaren Honda	16	USA, Bra (6), San (6), Mon (4), Can (3), Mex (4), Fra (2), GB, Ger (4), Hun, Bel (4), Ita (4), Por (3), Esp, Jap, Aus (3)
1991	McLaren Honda	16	USA, Bra (4), San (6), Mon, Can, Mex, Fra, GB (6), Ger (3), Hun (3), Bel (6), Ita (3), Por, Esp, Jap (9), Aus (4)
1992	McLaren Honda	16	SA (2), Mex (3), Bra, Esp (3), San, Mon, Can (10), Fra, GB (2), Ger, Hun (4), Bel, Ita (3), Por (6), Jap (6), Aus (10)
1993	Ferrari	16	SA (1), Bra, Eur, San, Esp (1), Mon, Can (3), Fra, GB, Ger (1), Hun (4), Bel, Ita, Por, Jap, Aus (2)
1994	Ferrari	16	Bra, Pac (6), San, Mon (4), Esp, Can (3), Fra (4), GB, Ger (10), Hun, Bel, Ita (6), Por, Eur (2), Jap, Aus (6)
1995	Ferrari	17	Bra (4), Arg (1), San (4), Esp (4), Mon (4), Can, Fra, GB, Ger (4), Hun (4), Bel, Ita, Por (3), Eur, Pac (3), Jap, Aus
1996	Benetton Renault	16	Aus (3), Bra, Arg, Eur, San (4), Mon, Esp, Can, Fra (3), GB (6), Ger, Hun, Bel (1), Ita, Por (1), Jap (3)

BOULLION, Jean-Christophe   France

1996: (Test Driver: Williams Renault) 1997: (Test Driver: Williams Renault)
Now in his second season as a test driver for the Williams team, Jean-Christophe Boullion's Formula One debut came in 1995 at Monte Carlo, as a replacement for Karl Wendlinger in the Swiss Sauber team. He showed a steady improvement in his first four races, finishing the race distance twice, with a spin and transmission failure accounting for him in Canada and France. In Hockenheim he took the car home in fifth place for his first two world championship points, and with movement up the qualifying grid he added a sixth place in the Italian Grand Prix at Monza. He has shown that he has talent in racing, and will have picked up valuable experience in testing with Damon Hill and David Coulthard. In 1996 he reverted to the single F1 role as the Williams test driver but competed in three rounds of the Renault Spider Trophy racing at Silverstone, Barcelona and Monza.
Born: 27/12/69, Saint-Brieuc, France. Married.

Grand Prix Record
Contested: 11   (1995)
Pole Positions: 0

Fastest Laps:	0		
Points:	3	1995 (3)	
1st:	0		
2nd:	0		
3rd:	0		
4th:	0		
5th:	1	1995 (Ger)	
6th:	1	1995 (Ita)	

Year	Team	No.	Grand Prix
1995	Sauber Ford	11	Mon, Can, Fra, GB, Ger (2), Hun, Bel, Ita (1), Por, Eur, Pac

BRUNDLE, Martin   Great Britain

1996: Jordan Peugeot   *1997:–*

Martin Brundle's move to the Jordan team for the 1996 season was his sixth change of seat in as many years. As such, consistency has been one factor lacking from what are always determined efforts to succeed and despite being one of the most experienced drivers on the circuit with 158 starts, second only to Gerhard Berger.

Qualifying proved to be disappointing throughout the season with placements invariably in the middle of the grid. However, most will remember Brundle's season for his spectacular crash in Melbourne in which he wrote off his new Jordan 196 and amazingly walked away to restart the race in the spare car. The crash was more of a launch when he combined with Panis and Coulthard and ended up flying through the air with his Jordan rotating around its long axis.

Twelfth and sixth were all that he could manage in the first seven races of the year with all but one of the five non-finishes coming from spins. In Brazil the heavy rain provided a succession of spins and tyre changes, leaving him to finish seven laps down on the field leaders. Brazil was not a happy time, not least because he had to return home for his father's funeral. The race ended when Tarso Marques ran into his gearbox.

The European was a success as he secured his first Jordan point by finishing sixth at the Nurburgring, having at one point been as high as third. This coincided with an improvement in the qualifying sessions which resulted in a definite improvement in race situations and Martin only failed to finish in two of the remaining nine races. He also managed to equal the team's best finish of 4th, that coming at Monza in the Italian Grand Prix.

Despite being one of the fastest drivers in F1, Martin Brundle has yet to win a Grand Prix and it is unlikely that he will achieve that particular ambition. However, the end of the 1996 season left him needing just two more points to join an elite group of drivers to have achieved a century of World Championship points. That goal may not be achieved though. During the close season Brundle failed to secure a drive for 1997 and instead he took up a position as a director with the TWR Arrows team and as lead driver for the TWR-led Nissan GT project in the Le Mans 24-hour race. Brundle was part of the Tom Walkinshaw backed team that won Le Mans with Jaguar in 1990. Despite speculation, Brundle stated before the season that he would not be acting as a test driver for the TWR Arrows F1 team – that will remain with Jorg Muller – but he will have an active input away from the track.

Born: 1/6/59, Kings Lynn, England. Married with son and daughter.

Grand Prix 1996 Record

Grand Prix	Grid	Qual Time	Fin	Laps	Race Time	Reason
Australian	19th	1:36.286	–	2		Spin
Brazilian	6th	1.19.519	12th	64	+7 laps down	Spin
Argentinian	15th	1:32.696	–	34		Damage
European	11th	1:21.117	6th	67	1:34:22.040	
San Marino	12th	1:29.099	–	36		Spin
Monaco	16th	1:22.519	–	30		Spin
Spanish	15th	1:23.438	–	17		Transmission
Canadian	9th	1:22.321	6th	68	1.36:36.934	+1 lap down
French	8th	1:17.187	8th	71	1.37:07.503	+1 lap down
British	8th	1:28.946	6th	60	1.33:17.786	+1 lap down
German	10th	1:45.876	10th	44	1.23.04.252	+1 lap down
Hungarian	12th	1:19.828	–	5		Accident
Belgian	8th	1:52.977	–	34		Engine
Italian	9th	1:26.037	4th	53	1:19.08.849	
Portuguese	10th	1:22.324	9th	69	1:41.21.217	+1 lap down
Japanese	10th	1:41.600	5th	52	1:33.40.911	

1996 Position Summary

Contested:	16	Finished:	9
Pole Positions:	0	Fastest Laps:	0
Points:	8		
1st:	0	2nd:	0
3rd:	0	4th:	1
5th:	1	6th:	3

Grand Prix Record

Contested:	158	(1984-1996)
Pole Positions:	0	
Fastest Laps:	0	
Points:	98	1986 (8), 1987 (2), 1989 (4), 1991 (2), 1992 (38), 1993 (13), 1994 (16), 1995 (7), 1996 (8)
1st:	0	
2nd:	2	1992 (Ita), 1994 (Mon)
3rd:	7	1992 (Fra, GB, Jap, Aus), 1993 (San), 1994 (Aus), 1995 (Fra)

4th:	8	1986 (Aus), 1993 (San, Ger, Bel, Por), 1994 (Hun), 1995 (Fra), 1996 (Ita)
5th:	12	1986 (Bra, GB), 1987 (San), 1989 (Jap), 1991 (Jap), 1992 (Mon, Hun), 1993 (Can, Fra, Hun), 1994 (Ita), 1996 (Jap)
6th:	10	1986 (Hun), 1989 (Mon, Ita), 1993 (Mon, Por, Aus), 1994 (Por), 1996 (Eur, Can, GB)

Year	Team	No.	Grand Prix
1984	Tyrrell Ford	7	Bra, SA, Bel, San, Fra, Can, USAE
1985	Tyrrell Ford	7	Bra, Por, San, Mon, Can, USAE, Ger
	Tyrrell Renault Turbo	8	Fra, GB, Hol, Ita, Bel, Eur, SA, Aus
1986	Tyrrell Renault Turbo	16	Bra (2), Esp, San, Mon, Bel, Can, USAE, Fra, GB (2), Ger, Hun (1), Aut, Ita, Por, Mex, Aus (3)
1987	Zakspeed Turbo	16	Bra, San (2), Bel, Mon, USAE, Fra, GB, Ger, Hun, Aut, Ita, Por, Esp, Mex, Jap, Aus
1988	Williams Judd	1	Bel
1989	Brabham Judd	14	Bra, San, Mon (1), Mex, USA, GB, Ger, Hun, Bel, Ita (1), Por, Esp, Jap (2), Aus
1991	Brabham Yamaha	14	USA, Bra, San, Can, Mex, Fra, GB, Ger, Hun, Bel, Ita, Por, Esp, Jap (2)
1992	Benetton Ford	16	SA, Mex, Bra, Esp, San (3), Mon (2), Can, Fra (4), GB (4), Ger (3), Hun (2), Bel (3), Ita (6), Por (3), Jap (4), Aus (4)
1993	Ligier Renault	16	SA, Bra, Eur, San (4), Esp, Mon (1), Can (2), Fra (2), GB, Ger, Hun (2), Bel, Ita, Por (1), Jap, Aus (1)
1994	McLaren Peugeot	16	Bra, Pac, San, Mon (6), Esp, Can, Fra, GB, Ger, Hun (3), Bel, Ita (2), Por (1), Eur, Jap, Aus (4)
1995	Ligier Mugen Honda	11	Esp, Mon, Can, Fra (3), GB, Hun, Bel (4), Ita, Por, Eur, Aus
1996	Jordan Peugeot	16	Aus, Bra, Arg, Eur (1), San, Mon, Esp, Can (1), Fra, GB (1), Ger, Hun, Bel, Ita (3), Por, Jap (2)

COULTHARD, David   Great Britain

1996: McLaren Mercedes   *1997: McLaren Mercedes*

After a blinding introduction to Grand Prix racing with Williams David
Coulthard dealt with the perceived step down to the McLaren brilliantly and

by the end of the season Coulthard was still averaging over two points per race throughout his career.

The 1995 season had been a problematic one for the McLaren design team but gradually the changes implemented came good and as the season progressed Coulthard was becoming increasingly confident in his car. Those early season problems when understeer prevailed manifested themselves in low qualification positions and failure to finish in the first two races of the season. Australia proved to be a bad start to the season when Coulthard was involved in a spectacular crash with Martin Brundle that forced the race to be restarted. For the Scot that meant from the pit lane in the spare car. Brazil proved to be little better as Coulthard spun out following pneumatic problems.

Seventh in Argentina was the prelude to a spate of good results during the mid-season starting with a 3rd place in the European Grand Prix that was especially remembered for Coulthard's blinding start rocketing him into second place from sixth on the grid. A hydraulic failure hindered progress at Imola, despite another rocket start which this time saw the Scot shoot from fourth to first position before the first corner. Coulthard's season highlight came at Monaco though where he finished second and at one stage got within 1.7 seconds of eventual winner Olivier Panis. He achieved his second spot while wearing a helmet borrowed from Michael Schumacher. He briefly led the race at Spa where he and team-mate Hakkinen ran one and two at one point.

His nine finishes from 16 starts was marginally better than the average he managed for Williams in 1995 when his nine finishes came from 17 starts, although that was in a season where he didn't finish lower than 4th. However, six of the finishes in 1996 earned him and his team championship points.

Coulthard remains one of the fastest drivers on the circuit, although he was generally outpaced by team-mate Mika Hakkinen last year, something he will want to put right during 1997. Given a reliable car devoid of some of the early season problems of 1996 he should have the chance to prove his worth and may need to maintain his position at McLaren, having been linked strongly with the new Stewart team, which has strong Scottish links.

Born: 27/3/71, Twynholm, Scotland. Single.

Grand Prix 1996 Record

Grand Prix	Grid	Qual Time	Fin	Laps	Race Time	Reason
Australian	13th	1:35.351	–	25		Stuck throttle
Brazilian	14th	1.20.167	–	29		Spin
Argentinian	9th	1:32.001	7th	72	1.56:08.772	
European	6th	1:20.888	3rd	67	1.33:59.307	
San Marino	4th	1:27.688	–	44		Hydraulics
Monaco	5th	1:21.460	2nd	75	2.00:50.457	
Spanish	14th	1.23.416	–	0		Accident
Canadian	10th	1:22.332	4th	69	1.37:07.138	

French	7th	1:17.007	6th	71	1.36:30.673	*+1 lap down*
British	9th	1:28.966	5th	61	1.34:23.381	
German	7th	1:44.951	5th	45	1.22:25.613	
Hungarian	9th	1:19.384	–	23		Engine
Belgian	4th	1:51.884	–	37		Accident
Italian	5th	1:24.975	–	1		Accident
Portuguese	8th	1:22.066	13th	68	1:41.24.157	*+2 laps down*
Japanese	8th	1:41.384	8th	52	1:33.59.024	

1996 Position Summary

Contested:	16	Finished:	9
Pole Positions:	0	Fastest Laps:	0
Points:	18		
1st:	0	2nd:	1
3rd:	1	4th:	1
5th:	2	6th:	1

Grand Prix Record

Contested:	41	(1994-1996)
Pole Positions:	5	1995 (Arg, Ita, Por, Eur, Pac)
Fastest Laps:	4	1994 (Ger, Por), 1995 (Bel, Por)
Points:	81	1994 (14), 1995 (49), 1996 (18)
1st:	1	1995 (Por)
2nd:	6	1994 (Por), 1995 (Bra, Ger, Hun, Pac), 1996 (Mon)
3rd:	4	1995 (Fra, GB, Eur), 1996 (Eur)
4th:	3	1994 (Bel), 1995 (San), 1996 (Can)
5th:	3	1994 (Can, GB), 1996 (GB, Ger)
6th:	2	1994 (Ita), 1996 (Fra)

Year	Team	No.	Grand Prix
1994	Williams Renault	8	Esp, Can (2), GB (2), Ger, Hun, Bel (3), Ita (1), Por (6)
1995	Williams Renault	17	Bra (6), Arg, San (3), Esp, Mon, Can, Fra (4), GB (4), Ger (6), Hun (6), Bel, Ita, Por (10), Eur (4), Pac (6), Jap, Aus
1996	McLaren Mercedes	16	Aus, Bra, Arg, Eur (4), San, Mon (6), Esp, Can (3), Fra (1), GB (2), Ger (2), Hun, Bel, Ita, Por, Jap

DINIZ, Pedro   Brazil

1996: Ligier Mugen Honda   *1997: Arrows Yamaha*

Pedro Diniz has been much maligned in the past two seasons. Indeed many of
his fellow drivers have been openly critical of his technique and suggested

that he should not be in the sport. No-one has been more critical than Jacques Villeneuve after the Brazilian forgot to use his mirrors and ushered the Canadian into the guard-rails during practice at Monza. The fact remains though that in his second season as an F1 driver, Pedro scored his first two championship points securing 6th positions at Barcelona and Monza.

The season started with a poor showing in Brazil and a horrific-looking fire in Argentina, but slowly the young Brazilian started to improve and towards the end of the season he was matching his team mate Olivier Panis for pace (if not over a race distance, at least for short periods). This seemed to reflect in his performance during qualifying – having started on the grid in the back few rows for the first eight races, Diniz suddenly found himself in 11th starting position in France.

Finishing races though was a problem. Having scored his first ever point in Spain, he managed to finish only once in the remaining nine races – that being his second 6th position – although five of those non-finishes were down to engine problems.

For 1997 Pedro joins world champion Damon Hill at Arrows. Benetton boss Flavio Briatore has said, 'The two most important drivers in the paddock are Michael Schumacher, because he's the best, and Pedro Diniz, because he's richest!' His enormous backing, estimated by some to be $10 million, will certainly help Arrows and also ensure him plenty of race time to work out what some say is an obstructive driving style. Despite the criticism he certainly improved in 1996 and Harvey Postlethwaite, Tyrrell Technical Director, voted him as being the most improved driver of the year. He could continue to surprise more people in 1997.

Born: 22/5/70, Sao Paulo, Brazil. Single.

Grand Prix 1996 Record

Grand Prix	Grid	Qual Time	Fin	Laps	Race Time	Reason
Australian	20th	1:36.298	10th	56	1.33:25.689	*+2 laps down*
Brazilian	18th	1.20.873	8th	69	1.50:27.806	*+2 laps down*
Argentinian	18th	1:33.424	–	29		Fire
European	17th	1.22.733	10th	66	1.34:36.937	*+1 lap down*
San Marino	17th	1:29.989	7th	62	1.36:33.333	*+1 lap down*
Monaco	17th	1:22.682	–	5		Transmission
Spanish	17th	1:24.468	6th	63	2.00:33.439	*+2 laps down*
Canadian	18th	1:23.959	–	38		Engine
French	11th	1:17.676	–	28		Engine
British	17th	1:31.076	–	38		Engine
German	11th	1:46.575	–	19		Engine
Hungarian	15th	1:20.665	–	1		Accident
Belgian	15th	1:54.700	–	22		Misfire
Italian	14th	1:26.726	6th	52	1:17.58.927	*+1 lap down*
Portuguese	18th	1:24.293	–	46		Spin
Japanese	16th	1:43.196	–	13		Spin

1996 Position Summary

Contested:	16	Finished:	6
Pole Positions:	0	Fastest Laps:	0
Points:	18		
1st:	0	2nd:	0
3rd:	0	4th:	0
5th:	0	6th:	2

Grand Prix Record

Contested:	33	(1995-96)
Pole Positions:	0	
Fastest Laps:	0	
Points:	2	1996 (2)
1st:	0	
2nd:	0	
3rd:	0	
4th:	0	
5th:	0	
6th:	2	1996 (Esp, Ita)

Year	Team	No.	Grand Prix
1995	Forti Ford	17	Pra, Arg, San, Esp, Mon, Can, Fra, GB, Ger, Hun, Bel, Ita, Por, Eur, Pac, Jap, Aus
1996	Minardi Ford	16	Aus, Bra, Arg, Eur, San, Mon, Esp (1), Can, Fra, GB, Ger, Hun, Bel, Ita (1), Por, Jap

FISICHELLA, Giancarlo   Italy

1996: Minardi Ford   *1997: Jordan Peugeot*

Having started the season as a test driver for the Italian Minardi team Giancarlo Fisichella got his chance in the cockpit when Taki Inoue, who was originally drafted by Minardi, failed to come up with the sponsorship he had promised to the team. Fisichella took his chance and was arguably one of the finds of the season.

Giancarlo, in a woefully uncompetitive car, invariably out-qualified team-mate Pedro Lamy, who was the mainstay of the team and who took part in every race. His progress was further hindered by financial considerations which saw the money of Giovanni Lavaggi replace him for six races and Brazilian Tarso Marques drive in South America.

In Melbourne he achieved his best grid position, of 16th, which he later matched in Montreal. Clutch problems beset him throughout the weekend and eventually forced him into early retirement. Having missed out on the South American adventure Fisichella returned for the European Grand Prix when

Tarso Marques failed to come up with the money to continue in his drive. He was the last of the 13 cars to cross the finishing line. Engine problems at Imola were disappointing but events at Monaco were more disastrous when he and team-mate Pedro Lamy took each other out of the race at St Devote, the first corner of the race.

Amazingly exactly the same incident occurred at the very next race in Spain. Fisichella managed to solider on for another lap before Katayama's Tyrrell inflicted itself on him. Those two incidents were the undoubted lows of a season compounded by a lack of funds to develop his car. Thankfully things improved drastically in Canada where a season's best of eighth was achieved with a considered drive, even though he finished two laps down and was last across the line.

A fuel pump failure brought a premature end to his drive at Magny-Cours and at Silverstone he again kept the car going to finish last and two laps down. The British Grand Prix proved to be Fisichella's last race of the season as Giovanni Lavaggi was drafted in as part of a sponsorship package to bring much-needed funds to the team.

Fisichella's potential did not go unnoticed and in 1997 he is driving for the Jordan team and is partner to Ralf Schumacher in an intriguing line-up. The Italian declared that his signature on Eddie Jordan's contract was his best ever result. During a mid-season test drive for Benetton he was on par with Jean Alesi's pace and, given a more competitive car in 1997, it will be more than interesting to see how the 1994 Italian Formula 3 Champion performs.

Born: 14/1/73, Roma, Italy. Single.

Grand Prix 1996 Record

Grand Prix	Grid	Qual Time	Fin	Laps	Race Time	Reason
Australian	16th	1:35.898	–	33		Clutch
European	18th	1:22.921	13th	65	1.34:25.170	+2 laps down
San Marino	19th	1:30.814	–	30		Engine
Monaco	18th	1:22.684	–	0		Accident
Spanish	19th	1:25.531	–	1		Accident damage
Canadian	16th	1:23.519	8th	67	1:36.44.064	+2 laps down
French	17th	1:18.604	–	2		Fuel pump
British	18th	1:31.365	11th	59	1.34:04.161	+2 laps down

Did not race at: Argentinian, Brazilian, German, Hungarian, Belgian, Italian, Portuguese, Japanese.

Grand Prix Record

Contested:	8	Finished:	0
Pole Positions:	0	Fastest Laps:	0
Points:	0		
1st-6th:	0		
Best Finish:	8th (1996, Can)		

Year	Team	No.	Grand Prix
1996	Minardi Ford	8	Aus, Eur, San, Mon, Esp, Can, Fra, GB

FONTANA, Norberto   Argentina

1996: (Test Driver : Sauber Ford)   1997: (Test Driver : Sauber Petronas)
Test driver for the Sauber team since 1995, he first made a name for himself
by racing karts in his native Argentina, before switching to Formula Renault
at the age of 17. In 1993 he won the Swiss Formula Ford Championship in his
maiden season. In 1994 he moved to the German Formula Three
Championship and won the title in the following season. He signed as Sauber
test driver in 1994 and for the past two seasons has also competed in Formula
Nippon.
Born: 20/1/73, Arrecifes, Argentina. Single.

Grand Prix Record
Contested:	0
Pole Positions:	0
Fastest Laps:	0
1st-6th:	0

FRENTZEN, Heinz-Harald   Germany

1996: Sauber Ford   1997: Williams Renault
After two years of paddock rumour, Heinz-Harald Frentzen finally signed for
Williams. Three years at Sauber have left many experts regarding the German
as one of the fastest drivers on the circuit – 1997 will see if they are proved
correct.

   Much of H-H's reputation came to the fore in 1995, but 1996 proved to be a
disappointment in a season when he failed to finish higher than 4th and only
completed six of the 16 races he started in. In truth, reliability of the Ford
V10 engine in the Sauber was a major factor here as the gearbox and throttle
provided problems.

   H-H started the season dominating his team mate Johnny Herbert, but rarely
proved more than a minor distraction for the bigger teams. His 4th position at
Monaco might have been a win had he shown more patience and not tried to
get past Eddie Irvine's Ferrari, damaging himself in the process. Fourth was
equalled again at Barcelona. In the second half of the season H-H found
himself under more pressure from Herbert, who challenged him both on the
grid and in the races.

   H-H will be quick in his Williams although the question remains as to how
consistent he will be and how well he can handle the pressure of his position
and from his new team-mate Jacques Villeneuve. He will be seeking his first

win, his first pole position and his first fastest lap. In his 48 races to date his highest position is 3rd, which was achieved at Monza in 1995.

Born: 18/5/67, Mönchengladbach, Germany. Single.

Grand Prix 1996 Record

Grand Prix	Grid	Qual Time	Fin	Laps	Race Time	Reason
Australian	9th	1:34.494	8th	57	1.33:29.436	*+1 lap down*
Brazilian	9th	1.19.799	–	36		Gearbox
Argentinian	11th	1:32.130	–	32		Spin
European	10th	1:21.113	–	59		Accident
San Marino	10th	1:28.785	–	32		Brakes
Monaco	9th	1:21.929	4th †	74		Stopped in pits
Spanish	11th	1:23.195	4th	64	2.00:05.321	*+1 lap down*
Canadian	12th	1:22.875	–	19		Gearbox
French	12th	1:17.739	–	56		Sticking throttle
British	11th	1:29.591	8th	60	1.33:59.701	*+1 lap down*
German	13th	1:46.899	8th	44	1.21:50.766	*+1 lap down*
Hungarian	10th	1:19.436	–	50		Engine
Belgian	11th	1:53.199	–	0		Accident
Italian	13th	1:26.505	–	7		Accident
Portuguese	11th	1:22.325	7th	69	1:41.13.769	*+1 lap down*
Japanese	7th	1:41.277	6th	52	1:33.54.977	

† *did not finish race – stopped in pits but classified 4th.*

1996 Position Summary

Contested:	16	Finished:	6
Pole Positions:	0	Fastest Laps:	0
Points:	7		
1st:	0	2nd:	0
3rd:	0	4th:	2
5th:	0	6th:	1

Grand Prix Record

Contested:	48	(1994-1996)
Pole Positions:	0	
Fastest Laps:	0	
Points:	29	1994 (7), 1995 (15), 1996 (7)
1st:	0	
2nd:	0	
3rd:	1	1995 (Ita)
4th:	4	1994 (Fra), 1995 (Bel), 1996 (Mon, Esp)
5th:	3	1994 (Pac), 1995 (Arg, Hun)
6th:	7	1994 (Eur, Jap), 1995 (San, Mon, GB, Por), 1996 (Jap)

Year	Team	No.	Grand Prix
1994	Sauber Mercedes	15	Bra, Pac (2), San, Esp, Can, Fra (3), GB, Ger, Hun, Bel, Ita, Por, Eur (1), Jap (1), Aus
1995	Sauber Ford	17	Bra, Arg (2), San (1), Esp, Mon (1), Can, Fra, GB (1), Ger, Hun (2), Bel (3), Ita (4), Por (1), Eur, Pac, Jap, Aus
1996	Sauber Ford	16	Aus, Bra, Arg, Eur, San, Mon (3), Esp (3), Can, Fra, GB, Ger, Hun, Bel, Ita, Por, Jap (1)

HAKKINEN, Mika   Finland

1996: McLaren Mercedes   *1997: McLaren Mercedes*

That Mika Hakkinen had his best ever season in 1996 speaks volumes for the type of person he is. Having suffered a huge practice accident at Adelaide at the end of 1995 which left him in a coma and many doubting his ability to make a full recovery let alone race again, the Finn came back better than ever and was simply superb throughout.

He failed to finish just twice and then was only out of the points twice when he finished 8th in both European and San Marino. His tally of 31 points was his best season's haul and a substantial improvement on the 17 he scored in 1995.

Consistency was the key to Mika's season. Apart from a few aberrations he always qualified on the fourth row or above and eased his way back into racing by finishing 5th and 4th in Australia and Brazil respectively. Having failed to finish in Argentina, he was forced to use the spare car at the European and San Marino Grands Prix, finishing 8th in both. From Monaco though Mika scored points at every race bar Estoril and Suzuka where he suffered accident damage.

He achieved his first podium finish of the year at Silverstone with a fine race when finishing 3rd and, after a 4th in Hungary, he finished 3rd in the next three races he completed.

Some observers suggested that his accident at Adelaide had tempered his over-aggressive nature and in some respects this proved to be true. However, the moments of red mist still arose here and there, and at Estoril he ran into team-mate David Coulthard which ultimately saw him retire and do Coulthard's chances no good with the need for an extra pit stop.

Mika remains one of the best drivers on the circuit but after four years in the McLaren hot seat he is still seeking his first win, pole position and fastest lap. 1997 could well be the year and no-one will begrudge him any success when it comes, as it surely must.

Born: 28/9/68, Helsinki, Finland. Single.

Grand Prix 1996 Record

Grand Prix	Grid	Qual Time	Fin	Laps	Race Time	Reason
Australian	5th	1:34.054	5th	58	1.34:25.562	
Brazilian	7th	1:19.607	4th	70	1.50:16.004	*+1 lap down*
Argentinian	8th	1:31.801	–	19		Throttle
European	9th	1:21.078	8th	67	1.34:44.911	
San Marino	11th	1:29.079	8th	61	1.34:49.164	*dnf* - Engine
Monaco	8th	1.21.688	6th	70	*+5 laps down*	Accident
Spanish	10th	1:23.070	5th	64	2.00:57.086	*+1 lap down*
Canadian	6th	1:21.807	5th	68	1.36.19.585	*+1 lap down*
French	5th	1:16.634	5th	72	1.37:31.569	
British	4th	1:27.856	3rd	61	1.33:51.704	
German	4th	1:44.644	–	13		Gearbox
Hungarian	7th	1:19.116	4th	76	1:46.43.538	*+1 lap down*
Belgian	6th	1:52.318	3rd	44	1.28.30.835	
Italian	4th	1:24.939	3rd	53	1:18.50.267	
Portuguese	7th	1:21.640	–	52		Accident damage
Japanese	5th	1:40.458	3rd	52	1:32.37.003	

1996 Position Summary

Contested:	16	Finished:	12
Pole Positions:	0	Fatest Laps:	0
Points:	31		
1st:	0	2nd:	0
3rd:	4	4th:	2
5th:	4	6th:	1

Grand Prix Record

Contested:	79	(1991-1996)
Pole Positions:	0	
Fastest Laps:	0	
Points:	90	1991 (2), 1992 (11), 1993 (4), 1994 (25), 1995 (17), 1996 (31)
1st:	0	
2nd:	3	1994 (Bel), 1995 (Ita, Jap)
3rd:	9	1993 (Jap), 1994 (San, GB, Bel, Por), 1996 (GB, Bel, Ita, Jap)
4th:	5	1992 (Fra, Hun), 1994 (GB), 1996 (Bra, Hun)
5th:	7	1991 (San), 1992 (Por), 1995 (San), 1996 (Aus, Esp, Can, Fra)
6th:	4	1992 (Mex, GB, Bel), 1996 (Mon)

Year	Team	No.	Grand Prix
1991	Lotus Judd	15	USA, Bra, San (2), Mon, Can, Mex, GB, Ger, Hun, Bel, Ita, Por, Esp, Jap, Aus
1992	Lotus Ford	15	SA, Mex (1), Bra, Esp, Mon, Can, Fra (3), GB (1), Ger, Hun (3), Bel (1), Ita, Por (2), Jap, Aus
1993	McLaren Ford	3	Por, Jap (4), Aus
1994	McLaren Peugeot	15	Bra, Pac, San (4), Mon, Esp, Can, Fra, GB (3), Ger, Bel (6), Ita (4), Por (4), Eur (4), Jap, Aus
1995	McLaren Mercedes	15	Bra (3), Arg, San (2), Esp, Mon, Can, Fra, GB, Ger, Hun, Bel, Ita (6), Por, Eur, Jap (6)
1996	McLaren Mercedes	16	Aus (2), Bra (3), Arg, Eur, San, Mon (1), Esp (2), Can (2), Fra (2), GB (4), Ger, Hun (3), Bel (4), Ita (4), Por, Jap (4)

HERBERT, Johnny   Great Britain

1996: Sauber Ford   *1997: Sauber Petronas*

After scoring 45 points and two Grand Prix victories in 1995 with Benetton, Johnny Herbert had to re-adjust to life at the fledgling Swiss Sauber team. As second driver to Heinz-Harald Frentzen, Johnny suffered in the early part of the season due to lack of testing time. However in the second half of the season, with more miles under his belt, Johnny grew in confidence and started to put his team-mate under pressure both in qualifying and in races. Of his eight non-finishes, four were down to car malfunction.

The highlight of his season was undoubtedly at Monaco where a 3rd place grabbed the Sauber team their best position of the year and their only podium finish. It was also Johnny's only points win of the season which had started with two non-finishes. In Australia a crash at the start effectively put him out of the race after Frentzen had taken the spare car after his car failed on the parade lap. In Brazil, Johnny found himself in the spare car only for electrical problems to end his race prematurely.

Ninth was followed by 7th at the Argentine and European races. The podium place at Monaco was achieved in much the same way as his previous season's win at Silverstone and Monza, by driving steadily and sensibly while those about him lost their heads. Failures at San Marino and in Spain and Canada were followed by a disqualification at Magny-Cours due to illegally high turning vanes – this after finishing 11th. The season ended with a trio of mid-grid finishes as the new generation Ford-Cosworth V10 started to show greater reliability.

It was a season of transition throughout for Johnny Herbert who finished the season more assured and confident. Given that he will be the team's number one driver for 1997 with a Ferrari engine to boot, we should see this popular driver with more points finishes.

Born: 27/6/64, Brentwood, Essex, England. Married with two daughters.

Grand Prix 1996 Record

Grand Prix	Grid	Qual Time	Fin	Laps	Race Time	Reason
Australian	14th	1:35.453	dns	-		Collision
Brazilian	12th	1.20.144	–	28		Electrics
Argentinian	17th	1:33.256	9th	71	1.56:20.691	+1 lap down
European	12th	1:21.210	7th	67	1.34:44.500	
San Marino	15th	1:29.541	–	25		Misfire
Monaco	13th	1:22.346	3rd	75	2.01.23.132	
Spanish	9th	1:23.027	–	20		Spin
Canadian	15th	1:23.201	–	68	1.36.55.183	+1 lap down
French	16th	1:18.556	dq †	70	1.37:43.573	+2 laps down
British	13th	1:29.947	9th	60	1.34:00.496	+1 lap down
German	14th	1:47.711	–	25		Gearbox electronics
Hungarian	8th	1:19.292	–	35		Engine
Belgian	12th	1:53.993	–	0		Accident
Italian	12th	1:26.345	9th	51	1:16.29.260	+1 lap – dnf
Portuguese	12th	1:22.655	8th	69	1.41.17.057	+1 lap down
Japanese	13th	1:42.658	10th	52	1:34.15.590	

† *Disqualified for illegally high turning vanes. Had finished 11th.*

1996 Position Summary

Contested:	16		Finished:	7
Pole Positions:	0		Fastest Laps:	0
Points:	4			
1st:	0		2nd:	0
3rd:	1		4th:	0
5th:	0		6th:	0

Grand Prix Record

Contested:	96	(1989-1996)
Pole Positions:	0	
Fastest Laps:	1	1995 (Ita)
Points:	67	1989 (5), 1992 (2), 1993 (11), 1995 (45), 1996 (4)
1st:	2	1995 (GB, Ita)
2nd:	1	1995 (Esp)
3rd:	2	1995 (Jap), 1996 (Mon)
4th:	8	1991 (Bra), 1993 (Bra, Eur, GB) 1995 (Arg, Mon, Ger, Hun)
5th:	3	1989 (USA), 1993 (Bel), 1995 (Eur)

Year	Team	No.	Grand Prix
1989	Benetton Ford	5	Bra (3), San, Mon, Mex, USA (2)
	Tyrrell Ford	1	Bel
1990	Lotus Lamborghini	2	Jap, Aus
1991	Lotus Judd	7	Mex, Fra, GB, Bel, Por, Jap, Aus
1992	Lotus Ford	16	SA (1), Mex, Bra, Esp, San, Mon, Can, Fra (1), GB, Ger, Hun, Bel, Ita, Por, Jap, Aus
1993	Lotus Ford	16	SA, Bra (3), Eur (3), San, Esp, Mon, Can, Fra, GB (3), Ger, Hun, Bel (2), Ita, Por, Jap, Aus
1994	Lotus Mugen Honda	13	Bra, Pac, San, Mon, Esp, Can, Fra, GB, Ger, Hun, Bel, Ita, Por
	Ligier Renault	1	Eur
	Benetton Ford	2	Jap, Aus
1995	Benetton Renault	17	Bra, Arg (3), San, Esp (6), Mon (3), Can, Fra, GB (10), Ger (3), Hun (3), Bel, Ita (10), Por, Eur (2), Pac (1), Jap (4), Aus
1996	Sauber Ford	16	Aus, Bra, Arg, Eur, San, Mon (4), Esp, Can, Fra, GB, Ger, Hun, Bel, Ita, Por, Jap

HILL, Damon OBE   Great Britain

1996: Williams Renault   *1997: Arrows Yamaha*

Damon Hill won the Drivers' World Championship and there could be few who would begrudge him the title after being 'robbed' of it in 1995. He also won it under the most intense pressure. Having been established firm favourite even before the start of the season, most seemed to have given the title to him after his hat-trick of South American wins. If that wasn't enough, he was cruelly rejected by his Williams employers as the season neared its end, leaving him looking not only to secure the title, but also a new drive for 1997.

That Hill and team-mate Jacques Villeneuve had the best car available for their assault was never in dispute and this fact seemed to take some gloss off Damon's triumph. Reliability was the key with the FW17 and Hill drove it like a demon, finishing in the top two in ten of his 12 finishes. A 4th and 5th secured points in his other two finishes. In qualifying he had no equal – in all 16 races Damon was on the front row, nine of them in pole position. Starting though was the one hiccough he had during the year.

Damon's championship account had already been credited with 30 points by the time the season returned to Europe. Having started second on the grid in Melbourne, Villeneuve made a great start from pole and probably would have won bar an oil leak that sprayed Damon with a stream of oil as he followed on his tail. As it was Hill passed and won. Pole positions in Brazil and Argentina were complemented by commanding wins, the latter despite having not eaten for two days because of illness. The hat-trick ensured an 18 points lead over his team-mate.

At the European Grand Prix Damon's pole position was wasted as his poor start left him down the rankings and unable to recover as he finished 4th. But he bounced back well in San Marino securing his fourth win of the season, again in commanding fashion.

Monaco was the race that Damon wanted to win most – to win where his father Graham had secured five victories. The victory seemed to be in the bag as Hill lead by 26 seconds – then disaster when an oil pump failed leaving Damon to coast to a stop. In the least engine-stressful race of the season, the Williams failed! The rain in Spain proved to be a pain for Damon. Hill admitted after that the car set-up was all wrong for the wet conditions he thought would dry out. After a poor start, his third spin finally saw him out of the race.

Canada and France saw him back into his winning ways. In Montreal Damon's one-stop strategy was up against Villeneuve's two-stop race and it was thrilling entertainment with Hill winning by five seconds. At Magny-Cours Damon led for all but three of the laps due to his pitting. At Silverstone a loose wheel nut ended his pursuit of a second British Grand Prix win.

After a win in Germany the jitters seemed to set in as Damon finished 2nd and 5th in Hungary and Belgium. The announcement that Damon would not be driving for Williams in 1997 was hardly the best preparation for the Italian Grand Prix. A pole position on the grid looked to have eased the nerves but on the 5th lap Hill touched the newly erected tyre barriers and spun out of the race. Thankfully for Hill, Villeneuve had his problems and failed to score any championship points to close the game.

The penultimate race at Estoril saw Hill in position to clinch the title should he beat team-mate Villeneuve – the only driver who could catch him. Damon clinched pole from the Canadian by just 0.009. In the race proper the rookie got ahead of Damon after their final set of pit-stops. Damon finished second and the six points were vital leaving him needing just a point from the final race to secure the championship – for Villeneuve nothing but a win would do.

It was the perfect race for the Englishman. Despite conceding pole position to his challenger he made his best start of the season to rocket into the lead and dominate it from the front. When Villeneuve lost a wheel in the final third of the race it was Damon's championship, which was secured in the best possible style – with a win.

For 1997 Damon is with Arrows and it may be too much of a tall order to expect him to add to his tally of wins, pole positions and fastest laps. He should be able to secure more points though but reliability of the new Yamaha engine and the introduction of Bridgestone tyres will be factors.

More interestingly it will be intriguing to see how the World Champion does racing in a pack of drivers during 1997. In 1996 Damon was superb while leading from the front but there is the suspicion that he will make mistakes in traffic. 1997 will be interesting for Damon and his supporters.

Born: 17/9/60, Hampstead, London, England. Married with two daughters and one son.

Grand Prix 1996 Record

Grand Prix	Grid	Qual Time	Fin	Laps	Race Time	Reason
Australian	2nd	1:32.509	1st	58	1.32:50.491	
Brazilian	1st	1.18.111	1st	71	1.49:52.976	
Argentinian	1st	1:30.346	1st	72	1.54:55.322	
European	1st	1:18.941	4th	67	1.33:59.984	
San Marino	2nd	1:27.105	1st	63	1.35:26.156	
Monaco	2nd	1:20.866	–	40		Engine
Spanish	1st	1:20.650	–	10		Accident
Canadian	1st	1:21.059	1st	69	1.36:03.465	
French	2nd	1:16.058	1st	72	1.36:28.795	
British	1st	1:26.875	–	26		Loose wheel nut
German	1st	1:43.912	1st	45	1.21:43.417	
Hungarian	2nd	1:17.182	2nd	77	1.46.21.905	
Belgian	2nd	1:50.980	5th	44	1.28.44.304	
Italian	1st	1:24.204	–	5		Accident
Portuguese	1st	1:20.330	2nd	70	1.40.42.881	
Japanese	2nd	1:39.370	1st	52	1.32.33.791	

1996 Position Summary

Contested:	16	Finished:	12
Pole Positions:	9	Fastest Laps:	5
Points	97		
1st:	8	2nd:	2
3rd:	0	4th:	1
5th:	1	6th:	0

Grand Prix Record

Contested:	67	(1992-1996)
Pole Positions:	20	1993 (Fra, Por), 1994 (Fra, GB), 1995 (Bra, Mon, Fra, GB, Ger, Hun, Aus), 1996 (Bra, Arg, Eur, Esp, Can, GB, Ger, Ita, Por)
Fastest Laps:	19	1993 (GB, Ita, Por, Aus), 1994 (San, Fra, GB, Bel, Ita, Jap), 1995 (Esp, Hun, GB, Aus), 1996 (Bra, Eur, San, Ger, Hun)
Points:	326	1993 (69), 1994 (91), 1995 (69), 1996 (97)

1st:	21	1993 (Hun, Bel, Ita), 1994 (Esp, GB, Bel, Ita, Por, Jap), 1995 (Arg, San, Hun, Aus), 1996 (Aus, Bra, Arg, San, Can, Fra, Ger, Jap)
2nd:	14	1993 (Bra, Eur, Mon, Fra) 1994 (Bra, Can, Fra, Hun, Eur), 1995 (Mon, Fra, Bel), 1996 (Hun, Por)
3rd:	5	1993 (Can, Por, Aus), 1995 (Por, Pac)
4th:	3	1993 (Jap), 1995 (Esp), 1996 (Eur)
5th:	1	1996 (Bel)
6th:	1	1994 (San)

Year	Team	No.	Grand Prix
1992	Brabham Judd	2	GB, Hun
1993	Williams Renault	16	SA, Bra (6), Eur (6), San, Esp, Mon (6), Can (6), Fra (6), GB, Ger, Hun (10), Bel (10, Ita (10, Por (4), Jap (3), Aus (4)
1994	Williams Renault	16	Bra (6), Pac, San (1), Mon, Esp (10), Can (6), Fra (6), GB (10), Ger, Hun (6), Bel (10), Ita (10), Por (10), Eur (6), Jap (10), Aus
1995	Williams Renault	17	Bra, Arg (10), San (10), Esp (3), Mon (6), Can, Fra (6), GB, Ger, Hun (10), Bel (6), Ita, Por (4), Eur, Pac (4), Jap, Aus (10)
1996	Williams Renault	16	Aus (10), Bra (10), Arg (10), Eur (3), San (10), Mon, Esp, Can (10), Fra (10), GB, Ger (10), Hun (6), Bel (2), Ita, Por (6), Jap (10)

IRVINE, Eddie   Great Britain

1996: Ferrari   *1997: Ferrari*

Despite only finishing five of his 16 races, Eddie Irvine had arguably his best season in F1. Certainly his 11 championship points was one more than he gained for the Jordan team in the previous year. It was a curious year for the likeable Irishman. When recruited by Ferrari it was made clear that he was joining the team as number two to the then reigning double world champion Michael Schumacher. The Ferrari team effort was geared towards Schumacher which left Eddie with virtually no testing time in the lead up to the season and even after it had started. It was then a huge surprise when he out qualified the team number one at Melbourne in the first race of the season by securing third place on the grid. It set the tone for the race and Irvine held his own to finish on the podium in the same place, while Schumacher suffered a brake failure and failed to finish.

In many respects that was Eddie's season highlight as he never came close to the podium again although he managed to chalk up the points here and there. A 7th placing in Brazil was still satisfying in many respects as the weather created problems for the difficult-to-handle Ferrari. Two points in Argentina might have been more had Eddie not suffered wing damage as part of an accident involving Badoer and Diniz. A misfiring engine meant a retirement on lap six at the European Grand Prix which was followed by a 4th placing and three more points in San Marino where oversteer problems were corrected.

It proved to be a false dawn though as a succession of nine retirements, many of them down to failures in the gearbox hydraulics, took their toll in race conditions. Qualifying was different during this sequence with a good deal of consistency seeing Eddie grab positions on the third to fifth rows. An illegal turning vane was the only other blot in the copybook – when it was found to be too high he was punished by a demotion from 10th to last spot on the French grid. Estoril proved to be the only remaining high spot. Sixth on the grid was improved in the race to a final 5th position and another two championship points. In the final race of the season in Japan, Eddie again qualified 6th despite continuing gearbox problems only to come together with Berger and finish the race on the sidelines.

Despite the car problems and the lack of testing time, Eddie Irvine soldiered on throughout the season. His biggest fan was none other than Michael Schumacher who said of Eddie, 'Of all my team-mates, he is the one who comes closest to me in performance.' Certainly Eddie will be looking to improve again in 1997 and, if the problems that haunted him in 1996 are resolved, he almost certainly will. This will undoubtedly be as second fiddle to Schumacher even though the German has openly declared that he will be going all out to help his team-mate progress during 1997.

Born: 10/11/65, Newtownards, Northern Ireland. Single.

Grand Prix 1996 Record

Grand Prix	Grid	Qual Time	Fin	Laps	Race Time	Reason
Australian	3rd	1:32.889	3rd	58	1.33:53.062	
Brazilian	10th	1.19.591	7th	70	1.51:11.438	+1 lap down
Argentinian	10th	1:32.058	5th	72	1.56:00.313	
European	7th	1:20.931	–	6		Misfire
San Marino	6th	1:28.205	4th	63	1.36:27.739	
Monaco	7th	1:21.542	–	68		Accident
Spanish	6th	1:22.333	–	1		Spin
Canadian	5th	1:21.657	–	1		Suspension
French	22nd †	1:17.443	–	5		Gearbox
British	10th	1:29.186	–	5		Engine
German	8th	1:45.389	–	34		Gearbox
Hungarian	4th	1:18.617	–	31		Gearbox
Belgian	9th	1:53.043	–	29		Gearbox

Italian	7th	1:25.228	–	23			Accident
Portuguese	6th	1:21.362	5th	70	1:41.50.304		
Japanese	6th	1:41.005	–	39			Accident

† *Orginally qualified 10th but demoted to 22nd after turning vanes found to be illegal.*

1996 Position Summary

Contested:	16	Finished:	5
Pole Positions:	0	Fastest Laps:	0
Points:	11		
1st:	0	2nd:	0
3rd:	1	4th:	1
5th:	2	6th:	0

Grand Prix Record

Contested:	48	(1993-1996)
Pole Positions:	0	
Fastest Laps:	0	
Points:	28	1993 (1), 1994 (6), 1995 (10), 1996 (11)
1st:	0	
2nd:	0	
3rd:	2	1995 (Can), 1996 (Aus)
4th:	3	1994 (Eur), 1995 (Jap), 1996 (San)
5th:	4	1994 (Jap), 1995 (Esp), 1996 (Arg, Por)
6th:	3	1993 (Jap), 1994 (Esp), 1995 (Eur)

Year	Team	No.	Grand Prix
1993	Jordan Hart	2	Jap (1), Aus
1994	Jordan Hart	13	Bra, Esp (1), Can, Fra, GB, Ger, Hun, Bel, Ita, Por, Eur (3), Jap (2), Aus
1995	Jordan Peugeot	17	Bra, Arg, San, Esp (2), Mon, Can (4), Fra, GB, Ger, Hun, Bel, Ita, Por, Eur (1), Pac, Jap (3), Aus
1996	Ferrari	16	Aus (4), Bra, Arg (2), Eur, San (3), Mon, Esp, Can, Fra, GB, Ger, Hun, Bel, Ita, Por (2), Jap

KATAYAMA, Ukyo   Japan

1996: Tyrrell Yamaha   *1997: Minardi Ford*

Having retired at one race during the 1996 season, Ukyo Katayama found himself hit and knocked off the front bonnet of one of the circuit cars as he made his way to the supposed safety of the area behind the barriers. This one incident rather summed up Katayama's season. Having failed to finish nine of his 16 races he was outpaced by team-mate Mika Salo for the second successive season. Having scored five championship points in 1994 he has failed to find the top six since then. During 1996 he only once managed to qualify in the top dozen and his 7th place in Hungary was his best performance of the season.

Not all the blame can be placed at Ukyo's door though. Despite a number of silly accidents his car did seem to be far less reliable than Mika Salo's, with problems occurring in the electrics and engine. Indeed at Monaco a stuck throttle caused one of his accidents. Unfortunately he has developed a reputation of being accident-prone and will need to work hard to dispel this at his new Minardi team in 1997.

The season started with both luck and misfortune for Ukyo. He managed to stall his engine at the start and was only able to join the race after it was restarted. Then as the race progressed he found his 024 Tyrrell overheating and had to lay off the pace to finish in 11th position. This was bettered in the next race in Brazil and amazingly so really. Racing with his visor up due to misting, Ukyo was hit in the eye with a stone and then spun on his second lap. Managing not to stall his engine Katayama rejoined the race at the rear and then came into the pits only to find it occupied by his team-mate. Ninth was a miracle really!

A faulty clutch brought the Argentine Grand Prix to a premature end and, despite finishing 12th at the European, he was disqualified after receiving a push start off the starting grid, having stalled on the line. Accidents and engine problems haunted Ukyo for the next seven races as he failed to stay the course. In amongst this succession of disasters he managed his best grid position of the season, 12th at Silverstone.

The season started to show more promise with four finishes in the last four races. The best of these was the first at the Hungaroring where he drove a solid race despite suffering the overheating problems that had beset him in Melbourne. Nevertheless he kept on the pace for his highest finish of the year. At Spa, a circuit Ukyo likes, he had another solid drive to finish 8th. At Monza, Katayama looked on course to equal his Spa performance but a collision with Panis meant lost time when a new nose cone was fitted. Estoril provided his last finish of the season, a disappointing 12th not aided by nearly stalling on the grid – a factor which lost him four places. The final race of the season at Suzuka was a major disappointment for Ukyo on his home country track when an engine failure occurred, but not after he had collided with Verstappen and, for the second time in three races, reported in for a new nose cone. These events were compounded by a 10 second stop-go penalty for blocking Villeneuve.

It was to be the last race in a Tyrrell for Katayama. His 64 races in four years had been largely disappointing. For the 1997 season he moves to Italian team Minardi where he will take his much needed sponsorship money – in the region of US$4-$5 million from cigarette company Mild Seven. With a new management team in place, backed by Benetton boss Flavio Briatore and with a change to Hart engines, the small Italian team has potential. Whether Ukyo

Katayama can improve on his past two seasons and achieve the sort of results that brought him to recognition in 1994 remains to be seen.

Born: 29/5/63, Tokyo, Japan. Married with one son and one daughter.

Grand Prix 1996 Record

Grand Prix	Grid	Qual Time	Fin	Laps	Race Time	Reason
Australian	15th	1:35.715	11th	55	1.32:51.827	*+3 laps down*
Brazilian	16th	1.20.427	9th	69	1.51:00.929	*+2 laps down*
Argentinian	13th	1:32.407	–	28		Clutch
European	16th	1:21.812	dq†	65	1.33:31.599	*+2 laps down*
San Marino	16th	1:29.892	–	45		Lost drive
Monaco	15th	1.22.460	–	2		Throttle/accident
Spanish	16th	1:24.401	–	8		Electrics
Canadian	17th	1:23.599	–	6		Accident
French	14th	1:18.242	–	33		Engine
British	12th	1:29.913	–	12		Engine
German	16th	1:48.381	–	19		Accident
Hungarian	14th	1:20.499	7th	74	1.46.49.846	*+3 laps down*
Belgian	17th	1:55.371	8th	44	1.29.55.352	
Italian	16th	1:28.234	10th	51	1.19.12.208	*+2 laps down*
Portuguese	14th	1:23.013	12th	68	1.41.50.550	*+2 laps down*
Japanese	14th	1:42.711	–	37		Engine

† Finished 12th but disqualified.

1996 Position Summary

Contested:	16	Finished:	6
		(7 but disqualified at European)	
Pole Positions:	0	Fastest Laps:	0
Points:	0		
1st-6th:	0		

Grand Prix Record

Contested:	78	(1992-1996)
Pole Positions:	0	
Fastest Laps:	0	
Points:	5	1994 (5)
1st:	0	
2nd:	0	
3rd:	0	
4th:	0	
5th:	2	1994 (Bra, San)
6th:	1	1994 (GB)

Year	Team	No.	Grand Prix
1992	Larousse Venturi Lamborghini		
		14	SA, Mex, Bra, San, Can, Fra, GB, Ger, Hun, Bel, Ita, Por, Jap, Aus
1993	Tyrrell Yamaha	16	SA, Bra, Eur, San, Esp, Mon, Can, Fra, GB, Ger, Hun, Bel, Ita, Por, Jap, Aus
1994	Tyrrell Yamaha	16	Bra (2), Pac, San (2), Mon, Esp, Can, Fra, GB (1), Ger, Hun, Bel, Ita, Por, Eur, Jap, Aus
1995	Tyrrell Yamaha	16	Bra, Arg, San, Esp, Mon, Can, Fra, GB, Ger, Hun, Bel, Ita, Por, Pac, Jap, Aus
1996	Tyrrell Yamaha	16	Aus, Bra, Arg, Eur, San, Mon, Esp, Can, Fra, GB, Ger, Hun, Bel, Ita, Por, Jap

LAMY, Pedro   Portugal

1996: Minardi Ford   *1997: –*

Portugal's only Grand Prix driver had a steady season as the number one Minardi driver. Even so it was not without its farcical moments, not least in Monaco and Spain where he and team driver Giancarlo Fisichella managed to take each other out of both races on opening laps. Fisichella proved to be a thorn in his side, often out-qualifying and out-performing him.

Australia proved to be Lamy's best performance in qualifying, but clutch problems proved to be his undoing, forcing him into the spare car while on the grid. Having been hit by Rosset at the second race start, his seat belt was not adjusted properly and, despite three stops to try and rectify the problem, he had to stop for safety reasons.

In South America Lamy looked to be capable of excelling in Brazil. Having started in 20th position he amazingly made his way through the field up to 11th position on the very first lap. An incident with Ukyo Katayama's Tyrrell saw him spin back down the procession but he soldiered on to finish in 11th position ahead of Martin Brundle's Jordan. In Argentina a drive flange failure ended his race when he looked set to complete his second finish of the season.

Two successive finishes did come as the show moved into Europe. Twelfth at the European GP was bettered by what was to be a season's best in San Marino – 9th – which was achieved even after incurring a pit lane speeding penalty. After the disasters in Monaco and Spain another accident forced Lamy to retire from the Canadian GP after being rammed by Brundle's Jordan. Twelfth position was achieved at both Magny-Cours and Hockenheim but gear selection problems meant a non-finish at Silverstone, perhaps not surprising as Lamy had not been able to do any testing at the circuit due to team funding problems. After suspension problems in Hungary an encouraging race at Spa saw Lamy finish 10th, despite having to use the spare car once again. More engine problems meant an early retirement at Monza but another two successive finishes (for only the second time all season) at Estoril and Suzuka at least brought some joy to the season. He might have hoped for a higher finish at his home Portuguese GP, but an overheating clutch on the formation lap caused the car to stall on the grid and he had to start the race from the pit lane two laps down.

Born: 20/3/72, Aldeia Garcia, Portugal. Single.

Grand Prix 1996 Record

Grand Prix	Grid	Qual Time	Fin	Laps	Race Time	Reason
Australian	17th	1:36.109	–	43		Seat belt defect
Brazilian	20th	1.21.491	10th	68	1.50:02.877	+3 laps down
Argentinian	19th	1:33.727	–	39		CV joint
European	19th	1:23.139	12th	65	1.34:03.416	+2 laps down
San Marino	18th	1:30.471	9th	61	1.36:59.418	+2 laps down
Monaco	19th	1:23.350	–	0		Accident
Spanish	18th	1:25.274	–	0		Accident
Canadian	19th	1:24.262	–	44		Accident
French	18th	1:19.210	12th	69	1.37:47.135	+3 laps down
British	19th	1:31.454	–	21		Gear selection
German	18th	1:49.461	12th	43	1.22.08.733	+2 laps down
Hungarian	19th	1:21.713	–	24		Suspension
Belgian	19th	1:56.830	10th	43	1.28.39.042	+1 lap down
Italian	18th	1:28.933	–	12		Engine
Portuguese	19th	1:24.510	16th	65	1.41.05.173	+5 laps down
Japanese	18th	1:44.874	12th	50	1.32.59.965	+2 laps down

1996 Position Summary

Contested:	16	Finished:	8
Pole Positions:	0	Fastest Laps:	0
Points:	0		
1st-6th:	0		

Grand Prix Record

Contested:	28	(1993-1996)
Pole Positions:	0	
Fastest Laps:	0	
Points:	1	1995 (1)
1st:	0	
2nd:	0	
3rd:	0	
4th:	0	
5th:	0	
6th:	1	1995 (Aus)

Year	Team	No.	Grand Prix
1993	Lotus Ford	4	Ita, Por, Jap, Aus
1994	Lotus Mugen Honda	4	Bra, Pac, San, Mon
1995	Minardi Ford	8	Hun, Bel, Ita, Por, Eur, Pac, Jap, Aus (1)
1996	Minardi Ford	16	Aus, Bra, Arg, Eur, San, Mon, Esp, Can, Fra, GB, Ger, Hun, Bel, Ita, Por, Jap

LARINI, Nicola   Italy

1996: (Test Driver: Ferrari)   *1997: Sauber Petronas*

Nicola Larini has only one full season to his credit, but as he proved in his last outing for Ferrari in San Marino in 1994, he is a more than adequate deputy, and has served Ferrari well as their test driver for the past three seasons. His second place behind Michael Schumacher in the ill-fated San Marino Grand Prix in May 1994 ended the worst run of failing to score a point in Formula One – 43 races. He made his debut back in 1987 for the Coloni team, and also drove for Osella and Ligier before his move to the biggest name in Italian motor sport.

Last season he also took part in the International Touring Car Championship with Alfa Romeo before taking up the number two driving spot with Sauber-Petronas in the close season.

Born: 19/3/64, Camaiore, Italy. Married with two daughters.

Grand Prix Record

Contested:	44	(1987-1994)
Fastest laps:	0	
Pole Positions:	0	
Points:	6	
1st:	0	
2nd:	1	1994 (San)
3rd:	0	
4th:	0	
5th:	0	
6th:	0	

Year	Team	No.	Grand Prix
1987	Coloni	5	Por, Esp, Mex, Jap, Aus
1988	Osella Alpha Romeo Turbo	10	Mon, USAE, Fra, GB, Ger, Bel, Ita, Por, Esp, Jap
1989	Osella Turbo	9	Bra, San, Can, GB, Hun, Ita, Esp, Jap, Aus

1990	Ligier-Ford	16	USA, Bra, San, Mon, Can, Mex, Fra, GB, Ger, Hun, Bel, Ita, Por, Esp, Jap, Aus
1992	Ferrari	2	Jap, Aus
1994	Ferrari	2	Pac, San (6)

LAVAGGI, Giovanni   *Italy*

1996: Minardi Ford   *1997: –*

Giovanni Lavaggi's source of funding was his passport into a cash-starved Minardi for the final six races of the 1996 season, at the expense of Giancarlo Fisichella. As it was, the 107% qualifying rule proved to be the Italian's biggest problem as he fell foul of it no less than three times. Having failed to qualify in his first race at Hockenheim, it was no surprise that the Minardi team appealed over Damon Hill's pole time in an effort to get their money-bringer a race. The attempt was unsuccessful and Lavaggi had to wait until the next race at the Hungaroring to make his Minardi debut (he had four races with the now defunct Pacific Ford team in 1995). As it was he was over five seconds off the pace. One of the slowest drivers on the circuit he actually received a speeding penalty, albeit in the pit lanes, on lap 27. Classified in 10th position he didn't actually finish the race when he spun out on lap 74, by which time he was already eight laps down on the race leader!

The 107% rule excluded Lavaggi from the Belgian Grand Prix in Spa even though it was a much narrower margin than normal – 0.2 seconds. Italy and Portugal provided two qualification drives by Lavaggi but both put him in the final place on the grid. In Monza his qualification was ironically by 0.2 seconds but engine problems forced him to retire on lap five. At Estoril he finished with a steady drive and despite being hampered throughout the race by oil-pressure warning lights, he finished five laps down. Qualification at Suzuka proved to be an even greater problem with Lavaggi nearly a second outside the 107% time.

Despite these trials and tribulations Lavaggi is under no illusions about his ability and he seems to take it all in his stride. His money will ensure that he is likely to pop up somewhere during the season.

Born: 18/2/58, Augusta, Italy. Single.

Grand Prix 1996 Record

Grand Prix	Grid	Qual Time	Fin	Laps	Race Time	Reason
German	107%	1:51.357	dnq			
Hungarian	20th	1:22.468	10th †	69	1:41.39.024	*+8 laps down*
Belgian	107%	1:58.579	dnq			
Italian	20th	1:29.833	–	5		Engine
Portuguese	20th	1:25.612	15th	65	1:40.33.410	*+5 laps down*
Japanese	107%	1:46.795	dnq			

Did not race at: Australian, Brazilian, Argentinian, European, San Marino, Monaco, Spanish, Canadian, French, British.

† *Classified 10th but actually spun out on lap 74 – eight laps down.*

1996 Position Summary

Contested:	6	Finished:	2
Pole Positions:	0	Fastest Laps:	0
Points:	0		
1st-6th:	0		

Grand Prix Record

Contested:	10	(1995-96)
Pole Positions:	0	
Fastest Laps:	0	
1st-6th:	0	
Best Position: 10th		1995 Hun (actually spun off at Hun but classified 10th)

Year	Team	No.	Grand Prix
1995	Pacific Ford	4	Ger, Hun, Bel, Ita
1996	Minardi Ford	6	Ger, Hun, Bel, Ita, Por, Jap

MAGNUSSEN, Jan   Denmark

1996: (Test Driver: McLaren Mercedes)   *1997: Stewart Ford*

Jan Magnussen has a chance to make his mark on the Grand Prix circuit with the new Stewart Ford team he joined in October 1996. Magnussen's race experience in F1 is about as bare as it can get, having made just one start for McLaren as a substitute for Mika Hakkinen in the Pacific Grand Prix. Nevertheless it was a sound performance, putting the car 12th on the grid and finishing in a final 10th place, two laps down on race winner Michael Schumacher.

In 1996 he continued in his role as test driver for McLaren, combining as a Touring Car driver for the Mercedes AGM team in the ITC. In addition he had four drives in Indycar for the American Penske team.

A new talent in a new car may mean that Magnussen has a relatively quiet full debut season in F1 as the second driver to the Brazilian, Rubens Barrichello.

Born: 4/7/73, Roskilde, Denmark. Single. One son.

Grand Prix Record

Contested:	1	(1995)
Pole Positions:	0	
Fastest Laps:	0	
1st-6th:	0	
Best Position: 10th		1995 (Aus)

Year	Team	No.	Grand Prix
1995	McLaren Mercedes	1	Pac

MARQUES, Tarso   Brazil

1996: (Test Driver : Arrows Yamaha)   1997: (Test Driver : Minardi Ford)
Tarso Marques and his sponsorship were brought into the Minardi team for Giancarlo Fisichella for the two South American Grands Prix. In his first qualifying session the 20-year-old Brazilian installed himself 19th on the grid, only to find himself relegated to last spot when he missed a signal calling him in for weighing during the session. His first race was short-lived when he spun out and stalled his engine at the start.

In Argentina he showed great improvement, qualifying an impressive 14th on the grid, five places ahead of senior team-mate Pedro Lamy. Problems occurred on lap 32 though when he clashed with Martin Brundle's Jordan as the in-use safety car left the circuit. The incident caused too much damage for him to continue.

Marques had been expected to join up with the Minardi team for the European GP, but he failed to raise enough money to allow him to continue in the drive.

Born: 19/1/76, Curitiba, Brazil. Single.

Grand Prix 1996 Record

Grand Prix	Grid	Qual Time	Fin	Laps	Race Time	Reason
Brazilian	19th †	1.21.421	–	0		Spin
Argentinian	14th	1:32.502	–	33		Spin

† *relegated to 21st on grid for failing to stop for weighing. Started 20th after Pedro Diniz had to start from back of grid.*

Grand Prix Record

Contested:	2	Finished:	0
Pole Positions:	0	Fastest Laps:	0
Points:	0		
1st-6th:	0		
Best Finish:	–		

Year	Team	No.	Grand Prix
1995	Minardi Ford	2	Bra, Arg

MONTERMINI, Andrea   Italy

1996: Forti Ford   1997: –
Andrea Montermini might seem to have a hex on teams that employ his services. In 1995 he drove for Pacific who collapsed after the season had

finished. Last year he drove for the Forti team who didn't even see the season out, the British Grand Prix at Silverstone being their last track excursion.

Of the ten races he took part in 1996 he only managed to finish one – that in Argentina when he finished 10th, three laps down. In three others he started but failed to finish and in five others he fell foul of the 107% rule.

Qualification for the Australian Grand Prix was blighted, not least by the fact that his car caught fire in the team garage on the Friday night. His qualifying time on the Saturday was almost 10 seconds off that of pole. In Brazil things fared a little better. He qualified in last place but was upgraded to 20th position after the Minardi drivers were demoted into the last two places. The wet proved to be too difficult a test and after three spins he retired. There was joy in Argentina where Montermini achieved what was to be his only finish of the season, even though he came in three laps down.

The 107% rule proved too much in the first two Grands Prix in Europe and after managing to get onto the starting grid in Monaco he crashed out during the wet acclimatisation lap and failed to start. The 107% rule was again the deciding factor in Barcelona but there were starts, if not finishes, in both Canada and France. The retirement in Montreal due to loose ballast sloshing around the cockpit rather sums up the sort of season that Forti had in all.

Silverstone and the British GP proved to be the last time Montermini and Forti were seen on the circuit – neither went out in a blaze of glory though as the 107% rule proved too much of a barrier.

Born: 30/5/64, Sassuolo, Modena, Italy. Single.

Grand Prix 1996 Record

Grand Prix	Grid	Qual Time	Fin	Laps	Race Time	Reason
Australian	107%	1:42.087	dnq			
Brazilian	22nd	1.23.454	–	26		Spin
Argentinian	22nd	1.35.651	10th	69	1.55:36.450	*+3 laps down*
European	107%	1:25.053	dnq			
San Marino	107%	1:33.689	dnq			
Monaco	22nd	1:25.393	dns	0		Crash
Spanish	107%	1:27.358	dnq			
Canadian	22nd	1:26.109	–	22		Loose ballast
French	21st	1:20.647	–	2		Engine
British	107%	1:35.206	dnq			

Did not race at: German, Hungarian, Belgian, Italian, Portuguese, Japanese.

1996 Position Summary

Contested:	10	Finished:	1
Pole Positions:	0	Fastest Laps:	0
Points:	0		
1st-6th:	0		

Grand Prix Record

Contested:	27	
Pole Positions:	0	
Fastest Laps:	0	
Points:	0	
1st-6th:	0	
Best Finish:	8th	1995 (Ger)

Year	Team	No.	Grand Prix
1995	Pacific Ford	17	Bra, Arg, San, Esp, Mon, Can, Fra, GB, Ger, Hun, Bel, Ita, Por, Eur, Pac, Jap, Aus
1996	Forti Ford	10	Aus, Bra, Arg, Eur, San, Mon, Esp, Can, Fra, GB

MORBIDELLI, Gianni   Italy

1996: –   *1997: (Test Driver : Ferrari)*

Gianni Morbidelli finds himself back in F1 as test driver for Ferrari for the 1997 season due to the departure of Sauber-bound Nicola Larini. His last race was in 1995 at Adelaide where he came in third for Arrows behind Damon Hill's Williams and the Ligier of Olivier Panis. He joined Arrows from Minardi where he had spent two years. He made his debut in the Brazilian Grand Prix in 1990 for Dallara, and drove one race at the end of the following season for Ferrari, where he picked up his first points finish.

Born: 13/1/68, Italy. Single.

Grand Prix Record

Contested:	60	(1990-1995)
Pole Positions:	0	
Fastest Laps:	0	
1st:	0	
2nd:	0	
3rd:	1	1995 (Aus)
4th:	0	
5th:	1	1994 (Ger)
6th:	3	1991 (Aus), 1994 (Bel), 1995 (Can)

Year	Team	No.	Grand Prix
1990	Dallara Ford	1	Bra
	Minardi Ford	2	Jap, Aus
1991	Minardi Ferrari	15	USA, Bra, San, Mon, Can, Mex, Fra, GB, Ger, Hun, Bel, Ita, Por, Esp, Jap
	Ferrari	1	Aus (0.5)

111

1992	Minardi Lamborghini	15	SA, Mex, Bra, Esp, San, Mon, Can, Fra, GB, Ger, Bel, Ita, Por, Jap, Aus
1994	Footwork Ford	16	Bra, Pac,San, Mon, Esp, Can, Fra, GB, Ger (2), Hun, Bel (1), Ita, Por, Eur, Jap, Aus
1995	Arrows Hart	10	Bra, Arg, San, Esp, Mon, Can (1), Fra, Pac, Jap, Aus (4)

MULLER, Jorg   Germany

1996: –   *1997: (Test Driver : Arrows Yamaha)*

Muller competed for many years in the German Formula 3 Championship, winning the title in 1994 with 11 wins. In the same year he had his first test in a Formula One car with Ligier. In 1996 he became European Formula 3000 Champion and also won the Spa 24-hour race in a BMW. Following testing with Arrows during 1996 he was appointed as test driver for the 1997 season.
Born: 3/9/69, Kerkrade, Holland. Single.

Grand Prix Record

Contested:	0
Pole Positions:	0
Fastest Laps:	0
Points:	0
1st-6th:	0

NAKANO, Shinji   Japan

1996: –   *1997: Prost Mugen Honda*

Nakano is the fifth Japanese driver to secure a full-time drive in Formula One Grand Prix racing. Following lengthy testing, the Ligier team signed him to a one year contract during which the 25-year-old from Osaka will need to prove himself in the job.

He had a successful career in karting which led on to a season in Japanese F3 and then two seasons in Europe in Opel Lotus. In 1992 he returned to Japan and has been a regular in the F3 and F3000 season, before being a championship contender in Formula Nippon during 1996.
Born: 1/4/71, Osaka, Japan. Single.

Grand Prix Record

Contested:	0
Pole Positions:	0
Fastest Laps:	0
Points:	0
1st-6th:	0

PANIS, Olivier   France

1996: Ligier Mugen Honda   *1997: Prost Mugen Honda*

It's hard to believe that Olivier Panis will ever again be in a position to emulate his first Grand Prix win that came in 1996. The victory in Monaco must be his career highlight and may well remain so unless he can establish himself with a more dominant team or take his driving and his Ligier car to a new level. Both are possible. This should take nothing away from his win in the Principality which was just reward for a magnificent drive in tricky conditions. Much will be made of the retirements around him, but Panis lasted the pace and did what even the likes of World Champion Damon Hill has never achieved – won at Monaco.

Apart from the win his other three points came in Brazil and Hungary but beyond that he was destined to finish on the edge of the points. Changing those 7th and 8th positions into point finishes could transform the racing career of Olivier Panis. It should be remembered that Panis performed in amongst the upheavals experienced by the team as manager Tom Walkinshaw announced his withdrawal from the team to take over the Arrows set-up.

The much improved Ligier-Mugen V10 engine failed to push Panis up the grid and indeed his starting positions were very similar to those he achieved in 1995. Once again his nine finishes were always in positions which were distinct improvements over his starting position on the grid. A steady race in Melbourne saw him finish just outside the points – the re-start costing him perhaps a place in the points after he had made a good start in the original race. In Brazil he did even better when a lowly 15th (due to a spin during the qualifying session) on the grid was metamorphosed into a final 6th and a well earned point. Race traffic held up the progress of Panis in Brazil after a poor start and a poor grid position left him in an unfavourable position. Consistent driving and retirements in front of him gradually saw him move up through the field towards an 8th placing.

The first five races of the European season saw four non-finishes but sandwiched in amongst these was the great win in Monaco. Gearbox and engine problems took their toll at Imola and Montreal while a clash with Eddie Irvine at the Nurburgring caused him to retire early on. In Spain Panis qualified in a career-best 8th position only to find himself shunted off at the start of the race.

The win in Monaco was aided by some excellent race strategy by the Ligier team with Panis starting with a full tank of fuel in wet conditions and stopping just once. In his home race, Panis qualified 9th but found the Magny-Cours race blighted by fuel rig problems that forced him to make three stops. The light load did help him in setting the second-fastest lap time though on the way to a final 7th placing. Handling problems resulted in a disappointing weekend at Silverstone. Panis then found himself out-qualified by team-mate Pedro Diniz at Hockenheim but, despite tyre wear problems, he again produced a steady drive to finish 7th. Things improved for the

Hungarian GP, perhaps aided by Panis' signing a new four-year contract prior to the race. Despite a bad start, his one-stop strategy allowed him to obtain two points, despite finishing a couple of laps down.

The Belgian and Italian Grands Prix were the undoubted low lights for Panis' season. He crashed out at the first corner at Spa. At Monza he stalled on the formation lap and was then hit by Katayama on lap three, which forced him out of the race. Understeer problems prevailed throughout his weekend in Estoril but a 10th place finish at least restored some confidence after the previous two races. In the final race of the season Panis found himself behind Frentzen for much of the race and ultimately had to settle for 7th place.

For 1997 the Ligier team has undergone further French revolution with the team's acquisition and renaming by Alain Prost and with an engine deal with Peugeot on line for 1998 Olivier Panis has a real chance to assert himself in the world of Formula One.

Born: 2/9/66, Lyon, France. Married with one son.

Grand Prix 1996 Record

Grand Prix	Grid	Qual Time	Fin	Laps	Race Time	Reason
Australian	11th	1:35.330	7th	57	1.33:14.468	+1 lap down
Brazilian	15th	1.20.426	6th	70	1.50:34.031	+1 lap down
Argentinian	12th	1:32.177	8th	72	1.56:09.617	
European	15th	1:21.509	–	6		Accident damage
San Marino	13th	1:29.472	–	54		Gearbox
Monaco	14th	1:22.358	1st	75	2.00:45.629	
Spanish	8th	1:22.685	–	1		Accident damage
Canadian	11th	1:22.481	–	39		Engine
French	9th	1:17.390	7th	71	1.36:48.120	+1 lap down
British	16th	1:30.167	–	40		Handling
German	12th	1:46.746	7th	45	1.23:27.329	
Hungarian	11th	1:19.538	5th	76	1:47.40.381	+1 lap down
Belgian	14th	1:54.220	–	0		Accident
Italian	11th	1:26.206	–	2		Accident
Portuguese	15th	1:23.055	10th	69	1.41.34.267	+1 lap down
Japanese	12th	1:42.206	7th	52	1:33.56.301	

1996 Position Summary

Contested:	16	Finished:	9
Pole Positions:	0	Fastest Laps:	0
Points:	13		
1st:	1	2nd:	0
3rd:	0	4th:	0
5th:	1	6th:	1

Grand Prix Record

Contested:	49	(1994-1996)
Pole Positions:	0	

Fastest Laps:	0	
Points:	38	1994 (9), 1995 (16), 1993 (13)
1st:	1	1996 (Mon)
2nd:	2	1994 (Ger), 1995 (Aus)
3rd:	0	
4th:	2	1995 (Can, GB)
5th:	3	1994 (Aus), 1995 (Jap), 1996 (Hun)
6th:	4	1994 (Hun), 1995 (Esp, Hun), 1996 (Bra)

Year	Team	No.	Grand Prix
1994	Ligier Renault	16	Bra, Pac, San, Mon, Esp, Can, Fra, GB, Ger (6), Hun (1), Bel, Ita, Por, Eur, Jap, Aus (2)
1995	Ligier Mugen Honda	17	Bra, Arg, San, Esp (1), Mon, Can (3), Fra, GB (3), Ger, Hun (1), Bel, Ita, Por, Eur, Pac, Jap (2), Aus (6)
1996	Ligier Mugen Honda	16	Aus, Bra (1), Arg, Eur, San, Mon (10), Esp, Can, Fra, GB, Ger, Hun (2), Bel, Ita, Por, Jap

ROSSET, Ricardo   Brazil

1996: Arrows Hart   *1997: Lola Ford*

Ricardo Rosset has made a rapid rise through the racing ranks in the past three years. Starting in F3 and finishing as runner-up in the FIA F3000 International Championship in 1995, he graduated to the Arrows team in 1996 as the number two driver to Jos Verstappen and had an 8-8 season.

Financial troubles haunted the team in pre-season, but after the opening race in Melbourne the announcement that Tom Walkinshaw was to take over started to have a good effect as the cash situation improved and Walkinshaw brought in sponsors.

Eight finishes from his first 16 Grand Prix starts was a fair season for the debutant, especially given that only half of these failures were due to accidents. Qualifying was always a problem for the Brazilian and he never got off the last few rows of the grid. His 9th placing in Melbourne was an excellent start to his F1 career and, despite suffering a spin at the hands of Pedro Lamy, he ultimately finished two laps down. In his home town race, Rosset found himself suffering the other side of F1 when he slipped into a wall at high speed. In Argentina the gremlins got into his car's fuel pump and ended his race early on.

Having finished 11th at the European GP with a solid performance, a broken refuelling rig following a pit refuelling accident involving team-mate Verstappen meant that he was unable to take on more fuel and had to retire. It was a bad omen for the Brazilian who then only managed to complete nine laps in the next three races. Only the blame for the third could be placed elsewhere as he was 'Katayamed' on lap seven.

Things improved in France where Rosset at least finished, even if it was three laps down. At Silverstone he qualified in 17th position only to be relegated to the back of the grid after failing to stop for a scrutineering check. An electric failure on lap 14 completed a dismal weekend. Another 11th position at Hockenheim was followed by a career-best race and 8th position at the Hungaroring, ahead of Michael Schumacher.

A broken steering arm forced Rosset out at Monza but the Brazilian was able to complete the season with two finishes, 14th at Estoril despite all sorts of car problems, and 13th at Suzuka which included a 10 second stop-go penalty.

Born: *27/7/68, Sao Paulo, Brazil. Single.*

Grand Prix 1996 Record

Grand Prix	Grid	Qual Time	Fin	Laps	Race Time	Reason
Australian	18th	1:36.198	9th	56	1.33:21.629	+2 laps down
Brazilian	17th	1.20.440	–	24		Collision
Argentinian	20th	1:33.752	–	24		Fuel pump
European	20th	1:23.620	11th	65	1.33:33.929	+2 laps down
San Marino	20th	1:31.316	–	40		Broken refueling rig
Monaco	20th	1:24.976	–	3		Accident
Spanish	20th	1:25.621	–	0		Accident
Canadian	21st	1:25.193	–	6		Accident
French	19th	1:19.242	11th	69	1.37:00.175	+3 laps down
British	17th †	1:30.529	–	13		Electrics
German	19th	1:49.551	11th	44	1.23:23.171	+1 lap down
Hungarian	18th	1:21.590	8th	74	1:47.07.362	+3 laps down
Belgian	18th	1:56.286	9th	43	1:28.21.974	+1 lap down
Italian	19th	1:29.181	–	36		Steering arm
Portuguese	17th	1:24.230	14th	68	1:40.44.958	+5 laps down
Japanese	19th	1:45.412	13th	50	1:33.34.388	

† *Time disallowed/disqualified and forced to start from back of grid in 20th position.*

1996 Position Summary

Contested:	16	Finished:	8
Pole Positions:	0	Fastest Laps:	0
Points:	0		
1st-6th:	0		

Grand Prix Record

Contested:	16
Pole Positions:	0

Fastest Laps:	0	
1st-6th:	0	
Best Finish:	8th	1996 (Hun)

Year	Team	No.	Grand Prix
1996	Arrows Hart	16	Aus, Bra, Arg, Eur, San, Mon, Esp, Can, Fra, GB, Ger, Hun, Bel, Ita, Por, Jap

SALO, Mika   Finland

1996: Tyrrell Yamaha   *1997: Tyrrell Ford*

After the first two races of the season Mika Salo could be forgiven for feeling a good deal of optimism for what lay ahead. In Australia he earned a point and then equalled his best ever finish when the show arrived in South America. Given his two similar successes in the final two races of 1995, things looked bright. But from there on matters took a turn for the worse, despite another points finish (albeit by default) in Monaco, not least through a succession of engine reliability and handling problems that saw him finish only five of the remaining 14 races.

In Melbourne Mika will have been well satisfied with his 10th position on the grid that had to be achieved in the spare car. He was relieved that the race was restarted after he stalled on the start grid, thus allowing him to continue after the restart despite nagging clutch problems throughout the race. Having left the world's largest island happy, Salo swapped a grid position for a race position. One position down on the starting grid he finished 5th for only the third time in his career, having at one point been as high as 3rd.

In Argentina things started to fall apart having qualified a disappointing 16th driving a car with little or no grip. A sticking electronic throttle was the downfall in the race despite three stops in an endeavour to fix it. In Europe things looked brighter and, having qualified 14th at the Nurburgring, Salo finished 10th only to be disqualified for finishing the race underweight.

San Marino provided Salo's best grid position of the year – 8th – and he made an excellent start which saw him move up into 4th spot. An engine failure on lap 24 ruined the weekend. In Monaco his 11th grid position was achieved in the spare car that was set up for his team-mate Ukyo Katayama. During the race he managed to get as far up the field as 4th and was taken out of the race in the penultimate lap when he ran into the back of Eddie Irvine's stationary car. Nevertheless, with the field already devoid of cars, he was classified in 5th position for only the fourth time in his career.

In Spain Salo fell foul of FIA rules. Having qualified 12th, he had engine problems on the formation lap and, having tried to start from the pits and suffered the same problem, he illegally switched to the spare car, which is not allowed after the start of a race and was duly black flagged. In Canada, 14th position on the grid was a result considering he had been plagued with gearbox problems throughout the weekend to limit his test and set-up time to almost non-existent levels. Having started the race in the spare car the engine finally gave up the ghost on lap 40.

A trio of finishes helped restore some confidence. Tenth at Magny-Cours was achieved with failing oil pressure and was followed by a relatively trouble-free race at Silverstone which was reflected in the 7th placing. At Hockenheim 9th place was commendable despite an overall lack of power from the Yamaha V10 engine.

In Hungary, an accident seconds after the start involving Verstappen and Diniz left Salo looking ahead to Spa where a 7th place was achieved thanks to some excellent driving to avoid the first corner pile-up and to making a clever refuelling stop when the safety car appeared on the circuit.

Engines continued to plague Salo with failures at Monza and Suzuka but there were no such problems at Estoril where Salo drove a good race to finish 11th.

Most observers regard him as a fine driver and the fact that he still managed to carry his reputation through what can only be considered a traumatic season for him speaks volumes for his talent. 1997 sees Salo in the final year of his current contract at Tyrrell and it would be a major surprise if he isn't whisked away by one of the bigger teams for 1998. Teaming up with Jos Verstappen and a Ford-backed engine in his 1997 Tyrrell could help provide a much better season.

Born: 30/11/66, Helsinki, Finland. Single.

Grand Prix 1996 Record

Grand Prix	Grid	Qual Time	Fin	Laps	Race Time	Reason
Australian	10th	1:34.832	6th	57	1.33:03.181	+1 lap down
Brazilian	11th	1.20.000	5th	70	1.50:26.315	+1 lap down
Argentinian	16th	1:32.903	–	36		Stuck throttle
European	14th	1:21.458	dq †	66	1.33:36.379	+1 lap down
San Marino	8th	1:28.423	–	23		Engine
Monaco	11th	1.22.235	5th	70		dnf – Accident
Spanish	12th	1:23.224	–	16		Black flag
Canadian	14th	1:23.118	–	39		Engine
French	13th	1:18.021	10th	70	1.36:52.589	+2 laps down
British	14th	1:29.949	7th	60	1.33.38.262	+1 lap down
German	15th	1:48.139	9th	44	1.22:22.768	+1 lap down
Hungarian	16th	1:20.678	–	0		Accident
Belgian	13th	1:54.095	7th	44	1.29.15.879	
Italian	17th	1:28.472	–	9		Engine
Portuguese	13th	1:22.765	11th	69	1.41.37.838	+1 lap down
Japanese	15th	1:42.840	–	20		Engine

† Finished 10th but disqualified for being underweight.

1996 Position Summary

Contested:	16	Finished:	7
Pole Positions:	0	Fastest Laps:	0
Points:	5		
1st:	0	2nd:	0
3rd:	0	4th:	0
5th:	2	6th:	1

Grand Prix Record

Contested:	35	(1994-1996)
Pole Positions:	0	
Fastest Laps:	0	
Points:	10	1995 (5), 1996 (5)
1st:	0	
2nd:	0	
3rd:	0	
4th:	0	
5th:	4	1995 (Ita, Por), 1996 (Bra, Mon)
6th:	2	1995 (Jap), 1996 (Aus)

Year	Team	No.	Grand Prix
1994	Lotus Mugen Honda	2	Jap, Aus
1995	Tyrrell Yamaha	17	Bra, Arg, San, Esp, Mon, Can, Fra, GB, Ger, Hun, Bel, Ita (2), Por, Eur, Pac, Jap (1), Aus (2)
1996	Tyrrell Yamaha	16	Aus (2), Bra (1), Arg, Eur, San, Mon, Esp, Can, Fra, GB, Ger, Hun, Bel, Ita, Por, Jap

SCHUMACHER, Michael   Germany

1996: Ferrari   *1997: Ferrari*

Ferrari paid Michael Schumacher $25 million to entice him away from Benetton where he had won two Drivers' World Championships and he was probably worth every penny of it. Schumacher was outstanding, taking a car that was essentially no better than the one that Alesi and Berger did a reasonable job with, and moving it up to another level. There were a few disasters on the way and days when the world looked like it was going to fall apart. However, Schumacher always made it clear that 1996 and possibly even 1997 was going to be about getting the car and team in the right frame of mind for a real World Championship assault, possibly in 1998.

Schumacher seemed to literally throw the car around the circuits at times during 1996, especially when it came to qualifying where he was never off the first two rows. He managed four pole positions during the course of the season and only one of his finishes came outside of the points.

In Australia a brake failure curtailed his race where he had qualified 4th behind team-mate Eddie Irvine – only the third time in 70 races he had been outshone by a team-mate. In Brazil he recorded the first of eight podium finishes of the year and was clearly delighted as Argentina approached. In Buenos Aires he started on the front row for the first time in a Ferrari having held pole for much of the qualifying period. Having maintained his position for much of the race it was debris from a previous coming together between Badoer and Diniz that took its toll on the Ferrari – forcing him to retire with rear wing damage.

The first four races of the European season provided no less than 22 championship points and included a non-finish at Monaco where, having qualified in pole position, he made a rare mistake that he later acknowledged as he simply slid into a barrier at Lowes on the very first lap! That aberration came on the back of two successive second places. At the Nurburgring he used a new helmet to improve airflow into his engine through his airbox. It seemed to work and after some exciting scraps with Hill and Villeneuve, he finally had to settle for second place behind the Canadian.

At San Marino Schumacher achieved his first pole position of the year using a special qualifying engine. Reverting to the standard engine for the race, his start was not as good as David Coulthard who then seemed to hold him up. Looking to secure 2nd spot, it nearly didn't happen as a brake disc fell apart on the final lap. The huge disappointment of Monaco was in stark contrast to the sheer delight experienced in Schumacher's first Ferrari win in Spain, which was achieved with a stunning drive which saw the German finish over 45 seconds ahead of Jean Alesi despite suffering with a misfire problem that effectively limited the power of his car for much of the race. Just when things looked to have taken a big upswing the team started to suffer problems. In Canada the car couldn't be fired up for the formation lap and so Michael had to start from the back of the grid before retiring with drive shaft problems. Things got worse when the show returned to Europe. At Magny-Cours, having secured pole position, the car failed to make even the start when a piston failed on the formation lap.

At Silverstone the race at least started for Schumacher. Having qualified third he found that was the total number of laps he could muster before the Ferrari's gearbox hydraulics failed and Schumacher retired with the car locked in sixth gear. He achieved another 3rd place on the grid in his home German Grand Prix and after some testing tussles with Coulthard and Alesi he stayed in touch to finish 4th. Having secured pole position from Damon Hill for the Hungarian GP, a faulty throttle finally took its toll, along with gearbox problems that left Schumacher forced to take slow corners by killing the engine and then switching it back on! With this in mind his 9th position classification was a good result after finishing the race seven laps down.

Spa and an ecstatic Monza were probably the highlights of the season. Both started from 3rd positions on the grid and both ended in victory. At Spa a new seven-speed gearbox was clearly beneficial especially at the start when he stormed into the lead and then had a terrific battle with Villeneuve to keep his victory intact. All that really needs to be said about the Italian GP was that it brought Schumacher a Ferrari victory at Monza for the first time since 1988 to send the tifosi home having seen an excellent drive.

Schumacher remained at his best in Estoril but the Portuguese GP battle was between Hill and Villeneuve for the championship. Nevertheless 3rd place continued the encouraging turn in fortunes which was bettered in Japan at Suzuka where second place secured Schumacher third place in the Drivers' Championship.

A new Ferrari for 1997 and a year's worth of development with the involvement of Schumacher should see the German gain more poles and more victories. Provided that the car and engine remain reliable throughout the season and not just in parts, Schumacher will undoubtedly be there or thereabouts when the final point count is made.

Born: 3/1/69, Kerpen, Germany. Married, one child.

Grand Prix 1996 Record

Grand Prix	Grid	Qual Time	Fin	Laps	Race Time	Reason
Australian	4th	1:33.125	–	33		Brakes failure
Brazilian	4th	1.19.474	3rd	70	1.50:00.569	
Argentinian	2nd	1:30.598	–	46		Rear wing
European	3rd	1:20.149	2nd	67	1.33:27.235	
San Marino	1st	1:26.890	2nd	63	1.35:42.616	
Monaco	1st	1:20.356	–	0		Accident
Spanish	3rd	1:21.587	1st	65	1.59:49.307	
Canadian	3rd	1:21.198	–	41		Driveshaft
French	1st	1:15.989	dns	0		Engine
British	3rd	1:27.707	–	3		Gearbox hydraulics
German	3rd	1:44.477	4th	45	1.22:24.934	
Hungarian	1st	1:17.129	9th	70	1:37.31.955	+7 laps down†
Belgian	3rd	1:51.778	1st	44	1.28.15.125	
Italian	3rd	1:24.781	1st	53	1:17.43.632	
Portuguese	4th	1:21.236	3rd	70	1:41.16.860	
Japanese	3rd	1:40.071	2nd	52	1:32.35.674	

† did not finish – engine

1996 Position Summary

Contested:	16	Finished:	10
Pole Positions:	4	Fastest Laps:	2
Points:	59		
1st:	3	2nd:	3
3rd:	2	4th:	1
5th:	0	6th:	0

Grand Prix Record

Contested:	85	
Pole Positions:	14	1994 (Mon, Esp, Can, Hun, Eur, Jap), 1995 (San, Esp, Can, Jap), 1996 (San, Mon, Fra, Hun)
Fastest Laps:	26	1992 (Bel, Aus), 1993 (Bra, Esp, Can, Fra, Ger), 1994 (Bra, Pac, Mon, Esp, Can, Hun, Eur, Aus), 1995 (Bra, Arg, Mon, Fra, Ger, Bel, Eur, Pac, Jap) 1996 (Esp, Ita)
Points:	362	1991 (4), 1992 (53), 1993 (52), 1994 (92), 1995 (102), 1996 (59)
1st:	22	1992 (Bel), 1993 (Por), 1994 (Bra, Pac, San, Can, Mon, Ger, Hun, Eur), 1995 (Bra, Esp, Mon, Fra, Ger, Bel, Eur, Pac, Jap), 1996 (Esp, Bel, Ita)
2nd:	14	1992 (Esp, Can, Aus), 1993 (San, Can, GB, Ger, Bel), 1994 (Esp, Jap), 1995 (Por), 1996 (Eur, San, Jap)
3rd:	10	1992 (Mex, Bra, Ger, Ita), 1993 (Bra, Esp, Fra), 1995 (Arg), 1996 (Bra, Por)
4th:	4	1992 (SA, Mon, GB), 1996 (Ger)
5th:	2	1991 (Ita), 1995 (Can)
6th:	2	1991 (Por, Esp)

Year	Team	No.	Grand Prix
1991	Jordan Ford	1	Bel
	Benetton Ford	5	Ita (2), Por (1), Esp (1), Jap, Aus
1992	Benetton Ford	16	SA (3), Mex (4), Bra (4), Esp (6), San, Mon (3), Can (6), Fra, GB (3), Ger (4), Hun, Bel (10), Ita (4), Por, Jap, Aus (6)
1993	Benetton Ford	16	SA, Bra (4), Eur, San (6), Esp (4), Mon, Can (6), Fra (4), GB (6), Ger (6), Hun, Bel (6), Ita, Por (10), Jap, Aus
1994	Benetton Ford	14	Bra (10), Pac (10), San (10), Mon (10), Esp (6), Can (10), Fra (10), GB, Ger, Hun (10), Bel, Eur (10), Jap (6), Aus
1995	Benetton Renault	17	Bra (10), Arg (4), San, Esp (10), Mon (10), Can (2), Fra (10), GB, Ger (10), Hun, Bel (10), Ita, Por (6), Eur (10), Pac (10), Jap (10), Aus
1996	Ferrari	16	Aus, Bra (4), Arg, Eur (6), San (6), Mon, Esp (10), Can, Fra, GB, Ger (3), Hun, Bel (10), Ita (10), Por (4), Jap (6)

SCHUMACHER, Ralf   **Germany**

1996: –   *1997: Jordan Peugeot*

There will be more eyes than normal on the 1997 Jordan debutant. As the younger brother of two time World Champion Michael, much will be expected from the 22-year-old.

His driving pedigree gave a rapid rise to fame, when he established himself in the competitive German Formula 3 Championship and then led the action in the Nippon F3000 championship. By 1995 he was really starting to carve out his own niche in the motorsport world with a series of impressive performances in international competition. Ralf won the prestigious F3 World Final in Macau, was runner-up at the Monaco F3 Grand Prix and also finished 2nd in the European F3 Championship race at Zandvoort. Back home in Germany there were impressive results too, with 2nd place overall in the national F3 Championships.

These results brought the offer of a test with the Le Mans F3000 Team in Suzuka. Ralf was offered the drive for 1996 and took up the challenge, moving to the Far East to take part in the All Nippon F3000 Championship. Nobody expected him to be quite so dominant in his first year in Japan, in such a highly competitive series. It went right down to the wire, but Ralf emerged triumphant to claim the Championship crown in the very last race of the season.

Alongside his F3000 drives, Ralf was also competing in the Japanese GT Series where he finished second. It was impressive results such as these which led to a test for the McLaren F1 team mid-way through 1996 but it was Eddie Jordan who snapped him up for his own team.

Born: 30/6/75, Huerth, Germany. Single.

Grand Prix Record

Contested:	0
Pole Positions:	0
Fastest Laps:	0
1st-6th:	0

SOSPIRI, Vincenzo   **Italy**

1996: (Test Driver :Benetton Renault)   *1997: Lola Ford*

Sospiri is making his F1 debut with Lola but has a winning pedigree at all levels of motor sport. It is perhaps surprising that he has had to wait so long for his chance at the top having been test driver with Benetton last season.

He started in karting and was four times Italian champion, twice European champion and in 1987, his final year, World champion. He moved up through F3 and F3000 to become International F3000 Champion in 1995.

Born: 7/10/66, Forli, Italy. Single.

Grand Prix Record

Contested:	0
Pole Positions:	0
Fastest Laps:	0
1st-6th:	0

TAKAGI, Toranosuke   Japan

1996: –   *1997: (Test Driver: Tyrrell Ford)*

Toro ensures that the Japanese connection remains with Tyrrell, joining them as the team's official test driver for 1997 with a view to making the step up into the drive hot-seat in 1998 (assuming that Mika Salo is snapped up at the end of the 1997 season by another team).

The 24-year-old will combine the role with continuing to drive in the All Japan Formula Nippon series – a contest in which he came 4th in 1996 as a driver for the Nakajima Planning team (a sponsor of Tyrrell in 1997) with whom he gained two wins, four poles and one fastest lap.

Born: 12/2/74, Shizuoka, Japan. Single.

Grand Prix Record

Contested:	0
Pole Positions:	0
Fastest Laps:	0
1st-6th:	0

TRULLI, Jarno   Italy

1996: (Test Driver : Benetton Renault)   *1997: Minardi Ford*

Another newcomer to Formula One, Trulli impressed throughout 1996 when he became the German F3 Champion as a member of the Benetton Junior Team. Gained some experience behind the F1 wheel during 1996 as a test driver with the Benetton team. Has a long history in karting, starting at the age of nine, and winning a succession of championships around the world.

Born: 13/7/74, Pescara, Italy. Single.

Grand Prix Record

Contested:	0
Pole Positions:	0
Fastest Laps:	0
1st-6th:	0

VERSTAPPEN, Jos   Holland

1996: Arrows Hart   *1997: Tyrrell Ford*

In his third season of Formula 1 Grand Prix racing Jos Verstappen had his first full quota of starts. Unfortunately his record of just four finishes did little to improve his otherwise good reputation on the circuit. Although generally regarded as a quick driver he had an accident-prone 1996 and suffered his fair share of car and engine problems. The season was started with the underfunded Arrows team but the arrival of Tom Walkinshaw should have brought improvement.

Verstappen had to retire due to engine problems in both Australia and Brazil, having worked his way as high as 6th during the latter race. Argentina was the high point of the season after which Verstappen suffered a disastrous run of non-finishes. Having recorded his best grid position for two seasons – 7th – he had an excellent race to record what was to be his only point of the season, bringing his all-time tally to 11.

From there on it was largely downhill without a finish for the next six races and starting from the sixth or seventh rows of the grid. Problems ranging from gearbox trouble, steering arm failure and even a broken refuelling rig at Imola which he damaged during a pit-stop, all took their toll.

There was a brief respite at Silverstone where the introduction of a completely revised Hart V8 engine offered more reliability and allowed what was only his second finish of the season. Then a trio of accidents meant a hat-trick of non-finishes. At Hockenheim he ran into the back of Katayama on the first lap; at Hungaroring he tangled with Salo and Diniz and at Spa he spun off at Stavelot – just 21 laps completed in three Grands Prix.

Any sort of finish was vital at Monza and it came despite Verstappen still suffering with a sore neck – a constant reminder of his Spa spin. Driving what could be called a careful race he finished in a comfortable 8th place. In Portugal engine problems resurfaced and its eventual failure meant he was only one of four drivers not to complete the race.

At Suzuka Verstappen found himself racing very much for his future in the sport as it was clear that he was not to be retained by Arrows for 1997. Racing in much the same vein as at Monza he finished in 11th position, just one lap down. With the arrival of Hill and Diniz at Arrows, Verstappen secured a potentially better drive at Tyrrell where, partnering Mika Salo, he could have his best season to date. Certainly with the backing of a Ford engine and what should be greater reliability, 1997 could tell if Verstappen is capable of realising his potential.

Born: 4/3/72, Montford, Holland. Married.

Grand Prix 1996 Record

Grand Prix	Grid	Qual Time	Fin	Laps	Race Time	Reason
Grand Prix	*Grid*	*Qual Time*	*Fin*	*Laps*	*Race Time*	*Reason*
Australian	12th	1:35.338	–	16		Engine
Brazilian	13th	1.20.157	–	19		Engine

Argentinian	7th	1:31.615	6th	72	1.56:04.235	
European	13th	1:21.367	–	38		Gearbox
San Marino	14th	1:29.539	–	38		Broken refueling rig
Monaco	12th	1:22.327	–	0		Accident
Spanish	13th	1:23.371	–	47		Spin
Canadian	13th	1:23.067	–	10		Engine
French	15th	1:18.324	–	10		Steering arm
British	15th	1:30.102	10th	60	1.34:05.550	*+1 lap down*
German	17th	1:48.512	–	0		Accident
Hungarian	17th	1:20.781	–	10		Accident
Belgian	16th	1:55.150	–	11		Accident
Italian	15th	1:27.270	8th	52	1:18.40.215	*+1 lap down*
Portuguese	16th	1:23.531	–	47		Engine
Japanese	17th	1:43.383	11th	51	1:33.22.955	*+1 lap down*

1996 Position Summary

Contested:	16	Finished:	4
Pole Positions:	0	Fastest Laps:	0
Points:	1		
1st:	0	2nd:	0
3rd:	0	4th:	0
5th:	0	6th:	1

Grand Prix Record

Contested:	31	(1994-1996)
Pole Positions:	0	
Fastest Laps:	0	
Points:	11	1994 (10), 1996 (1)
1st:	0	
2nd:	0	
3rd:	2	1994 (Hun, Bel)
4th:	0	
5th:	1	1994 (Por)
6th:	1	1996 (Arg)

Year	Team	No.	Grand Prix
1994	Benetton Ford	10	Bra, Pac, Fra, GB, Ger, Hun (4), Bel (4), Ita, Por (2), Eur
1995	Simtek Ford	5	Bra, Arg, San, Esp, Mon
1996	Arrows Hart	16	Aus, Bra, Arg (1), Eur, San, Mon, Esp, Can, Fra, GB, Ger, Hun, Bel, Ita, Por, Jap

VILLENEUVE, Jacques   Canada

1996: Williams Renault   *1997: Williams Renault*

Jacques Villeneuve was like a breath of fresh air in 1996. How exciting Formula 1 would be if each season could unearth just one true racer like the French-Canadian. Coming to F1 as the reigning Indycar champion, and son of Gilles, he had a big reputation to live up to. That it might put pressure or add stress to his season could be understood. If it did, it didn't show as he had arguably the best rookie season of all time. Certainly his stats told that story. His 13 finishes from 16 racing starts (81.25%) was the best of the season and secured him 78 points, not to mention six fastest laps.

Pre-season testing had gone well for Villeneuve but the proof of the pudding came in his debut race. What pudding it was as he stormed to a pole position at Melbourne and came within a whisker of winning. He led the race from team-mate Hill for much of the time but suddenly his engine started losing oil and he had to lay off the pace and allow Hill to pass him. Such was his lead he was able to hang on for second spot to finish nearly half a minute ahead of third placed Irvine. It set the scene for the championship battle that was to come. The doubters remained as to Villeneuve's potential and, having secured 3rd place on the starting grid, he spun off in Brazil having been placed under constant pressure by Jean Alesi. Another second place in Argentina was obtained through applying some racing nous. After a poor start that saw his 3rd position diminish to 9th, he made excellent use of the safety car when it came out to climb the position ladder and get within 12 seconds of triple-winning Damon Hill.

It looked to be just a matter of time until Villeneuve secured his first Grand Prix and it came at the Nurburgring. He started 2nd on the grid but raced into a lead which he effectively maintained despite great pressure from Schumacher, who was less than a second behind in the final stages. At Imola a puncture following a tangle with Alesi lost Villeneuve valuable time and he eventually had to retire with a broken rear suspension. There was little more joy at Monaco where he found it hard to come to terms with the street circuit, qualifying 10th – his worst of the season – and he was eventually bundled out of the race by Badoer. In Spain Villeneuve experienced racing in the rain for only the second time in his career. He coped well enough to finish 3rd.

On to Montreal and for his home town Grand Prix Villeneuve wished for a win. Having qualified second he had to be content with a similar finish – it might have been a different story had the yellow flags not come out just as he caught up to Herbert's Sauber. Another 2nd place came at Magny-Cours before Villeneuve was able to record his second victory at Silverstone, having led the race throughout. In Germany Villeneuve had to settle for 3rd place where his qualifying was hampered by a seized shock absorber reflected by his 6th position on the grid. A better performance at the Hungaroring followed and a bad start by Damon Hill allowed Villeneuve to better his grid position at the start and when the first round of pit-stops gave him the lead on lap 25 he never looked like losing it.

Spa seemed to be Villeneuve's favourite circuit. Qualifying first by more than half a second, he looked to be comfortably in the lead until the yellow flags came out around the track and with confusion on the radio, he lost time in the pits, ultimately relinquishing his lead to Schumacher who never surrendered it despite constant pressure from the Canadian.

As the Italian GP approached, Villeneuve found himself just 13 points behind Damon Hill and with a possible psychological advantage when his Williams team announced they would not be retaining the championship leader for 1997. But it was another type of barrier that hindered Villeneuve and Hill at Monza. Having qualified second, they hit one of the several tyre-barriers that had been installed at the last minute to prevent cars cutting corners. Unlike Hill, Villeneuve managed to keep his car on the course but finished outside the points.

The 13 point gap meant that Villeneuve had to win at Estoril to have any realistic chance of nicking the Drivers' Championship from under the nose of his team-mate. Win he did and it was done in emphatic style with what can only be described as an electrifying drive. Second on the grid and with a poor start, Villeneuve had to make up some 15 seconds on his team-mate. He did it and the race will be long remembered for the overtaking manoeuvre he performed on Schumacher in a ballsy Indycar style move at the Parabolica which saw him move into second place. He finally took the lead through pit stops to set up an amazing finale for Suzuka.

Villeneuve went to Japan knowing that his team-mate needed just a point for the championship. He had to win and hope for the best. He made the task easier by out-qualifying Hill for pole position, but a poor start by Villeneuve made a difficult task an almost impossible one by dropping him back to 7th. The season ended spectacularly when Villeneuve's rear wheel came away while on his 37th lap to bounce dangerously into the crowd, thankfully with no injury to anyone.

Villeneuve had to settle for second place in the Drivers' Championship and a team title to his name. Not bad for a rookie, especially when it is remembered that Villeneuve was new to many of the Grand Prix circuits. To combat this he spent many hours playing computer games which realistically modelled many of the tracks. With a year's experience and knowledge in hand, he has a realistic chance of securing the Drivers' World Championship.

Born: 9/4/71, St Jean-sur-Richelieu, Quebec, Canada. Single.

Grand Prix 1996 Record

Grand Prix	Grid	Qual Time	Fin	Laps	Race Time	Reason
Australian	1st	1:32.371	2nd	58	1.32:28.511	
Brazilian	3rd	1.19.254	–	26		Spin
Argentinian	3rd	1:30.907	2nd	72	1.55:07.489	
European	2nd	1:19.721	1st	67	1.33:26.473	

San Marino	3rd	1:27.220	11th †	57	1.27:49.134	Suspension
Monaco	10th	1.21.963	–	66		Accident
Spanish	2nd	1:21.084	3rd	65	2.00:37.695	
Canadian	2nd	1:21.079	2nd	69	1.36:07.648	
French	6th	1:16.905	2nd	72	1.36:36.922	
British	2nd	1:27.070	1st	61	1.33:00.874	
German	6th	1:44.842	3rd	45	1.22:17.343	
Hungarian	3rd	1:17.259	1st	77	1.46.21.134	
Belgian	1st	1:50.574	2nd	44	1:28.20.727	
Italian	2nd	1:24.521	7th	52	1:18.14.701	
Portuguese	2nd	1:20.339	1st	70	1:40.22.915	
Japanese	1st	1:38.909	–	36		Lost wheel

† *Retired due to suspension problems but classified 11th.*

1996 Position Summary

Contested:	16	Finished:	13
Pole Positions:	3	Fastest Laps:	6
Points:	78		
1st:	4	2nd:	5
3rd:	2	4th:	0
5th:	0	6th:	0

Grand Prix Record

Contested:	16	(1996)
Pole Positions:	3	1996 (Aus, Bel, Jap)
Fastest Laps:	6	1996 (Aus, Can, Fra, GB, Por, Jap)
Points:	78	1996 (78)
1st:	4	1996 (Eur, GB, Hun, Por)
2nd:	5	1996 (Aus, Arg, Can, Fra, Bel)
3rd:	2	1996 (Esp, Ger)
4th:	0	
5th:	0	
6th:	0	

Year	Team	No.	Grand Prix
1996	Williams Renault	16	Aus (6), Bra, Arg (6), Eur (10), San, Mon, Esp (4), Can (6), Fra (6), GB (10), Ger (4), Hun (10), Bel (6), Ita, Por (10), Jap

WURZ, Alexander   Austria

1996: –   *1997: (Test Driver: Benetton Renault)*
Alexander Wurz came through the normal karting ranks as a youngster before
progressing to Formula Ford 1600 (1991-92) and Formula 3 (1993-95). In

June 1996 he became the youngest driver ever to win at Le Mans and thus put himself in the world spotlight. In autumn 1996 he was given the chance to test for Benetton and the team was so impressed wlth his technical feedback and lap times that he was subsequently asked to join as official test driver for the 1997 season.

Born: 15/2/74, Waithofen, Austria. Engaged.

Grand Prix Record

Contested:	0
Pole Positions:	0
Fastest Laps:	0
1st-6th:	0

Team
Directory

Arrows

Danka Arrows Yamaha
Arrows Grand Prix International

TWR Group Ltd, Leafield Technical Centre, Leafield, Witney,
Oxon, OX8 5PF

Tel: +44 (0)1993 871000   Fax : +44 (0)1993 871100

Chairman/CEO: Tom Walkinshaw
Designer: Frank Dernie
Team Manager: John Walton
Chief Mechanic: Les Jones
Drivers/Engineer: Damon Hill (1)   /   Vincent Gaillardot
                    Pedro Diniz (2)   /   Steve Clarke
Test Driver: Jorg Muller
Sponsors: Danka, Zepter International, Parmalat, Power House,
                  Yamaha Motor Co., Bridgestone Corporation, Brastemp,
                  Remus, Quest International, Cadcentre, Kibon, Arisco,
                  Reporter Parfum, Amik, Packplast.

Brief History

1977: Arrows Grand Prix founded. 1978: Riccardo Patrese scores Arrows'
first point with sixth at Long Beach. Patrese takes second in Sweden – the
team's best finish to date. Patrese banned for involvement in the accident that
killed Ronnie Peterson. 1981: Patrese takes only pole position to date at Long
Beach. 1984: Arrows switch to BMW Turbo engines. 1987: Megatron supply
engines to Arrows after BMW pulls out. 1989: Arrows open new $10 million
technical centre in Milton Keynes. 1989: Arrows are bought by Wataru
Ohashi's Footwork Corporation. 1995: Jackie Oliver takes control after
Footwork pull out. 1996: Tom Walkinshaw buys controlling interest in team
and relocates works. Reigning World Champion Damon Hill signs for team.

Grand Prix Record

Contested:	288	
Victories:	0	(Best Finish: 2nd – 4 times)
Pole Positions:	1	
Fastest Laps:	0	
Constructors' World Titles:	0	(Best: 4th 1988)
Drivers' World Championships:	0	(Best: =7th 1988)

Most Points in a Season: 23   (1988)
Total World Championship Points: 141

Review

The 1997 season is the 20th consecutive year that the Arrows team has contested the FIA Formula One World Championship. They start it with a completely new owner and management team in place and the reigning World Champion, Damon Hill, driving for them. But whether that will be enough for them to chalk up their first victory remains to be seen. Their 141 points at the start of the season places them eighth in the list of 48 teams that have contested races on the Grand Prix circuit.

Last season can be viewed as one in which the team was rebuilt. They had arrived at the Australian Grand Prix in financial difficulty with just four of the Hart V8 engines being taken to Melbourne – and by the end of that first month the team had been sold to Tom Walkinshaw and incorporated into the TWR Group. From there on it was a process of rebuilding with the 1997 season in mind, the team being relocated to Witney in Oxfordshire and personnel being changed.

The 1997 car is the first since Tom Walkinshaw took over and in the acquisition of Damon Hill he has produced another great coup. Gone is the traditional Hart engine and in its place is a partnership with Yamaha and a new V10 engine.

Last season the team managed only 12 finishes from the 32 car starts with number one driver Jos Verstappen managing just three of those. Verstappen's ability to drive fast was often in evidence but his sixth place in Brazil, after qualifying seventh, was the team's only point of the season. Many of his retirements were down to accidents – not all of which were his own fault. Reliability was a problem. Ricardo Rosset managed more finishes with his eighth at Hungaroring being his best place of the season.

An Arrows car will have a number one on it for the first time during 1997 and while a victory may be out of the question for Damon Hill, a regular finish amongst the low end of the points would be considered a good season. Pedro Diniz took a lot of criticism during 1996, especially from other drivers, but what he has taken to Arrows is an estimated $10 million in sponsorship, while Harvey Postlethwaite, Tyrrell Technical Director, voted him as being the most improved driver of the year. He could continue to surprise more people in 1997.

Drivers and Results 1996

Driver	Races	Com	Ret	Dnq	HP	Pts	Psn	Comp%
Ricardo Rosset	16	8	8	0	8	0	–	50.00
Jos Verstappen	16	4	12	0	6	1	16/16	25.00

Grand Prix	Ricardo Rossett	Jos Verstappen
Australian	9th	Retired
Brazilian	Retired	Retired
Argentinian	Retired	6th
European	11th	Retired
San Marino	Retired	Retired
Monaco	Retired	Retired
Spanish	Retired	Retired
Canadian	Retired	Retired
French	11th	Retired
British	Retired	10th
German	11th	Retired
Hungarian	8th	Retired
Belgian	9th	Retired
Italian	Retired	8th
Portuguese	14th	Retired
Japanese	13th	11th

Arrows Yamaha A18 Specifications

Engine:	**Yamaha OXIIA**
Type:	V10 (72 degree)
Capacity:	2996cc
Valve mechanism:	DOHC, direct lifter type, cam gear drive
Fuel injection:	Zytek
Ignition:	Magneti Marelli
Dry weight:	Less than 105kg
Dimensions:	575 mm (length), 499mm (width), 373mm (height)

Car	
Chassis:	Arrows manufactured Carbon Monocoque
Suspension:	Pushrod operated six damper system with dynamic dampers
Steering:	Arrows
Cooling system:	Secan oil and water radiators
Transmission:	Arrows 6-speed semi-automatic, in-line configuration
Clutch:	AP Racing (Carbon)
Brakes:	Brembo Al-Be composite callipers, Carbone Industrie discs and pads
Wheels:	BBS one piece 13x12 front, 13x13.7 rear
Tyres:	Bridgestone
Instruments:	Arrow data display
Seat belts:	Sabelt
Steering wheel:	Personal
Extinguisher:	SPA extinguishant/Arrows integral shaped container

Dimensions

Overall Length:	4700mm	Wheelbase:	3000mm
Front Track:	1650mm	Rear Track:	1600mm

Engines 1978-97

1978-83: Ford. 1984-86: BMW Turbo. 1987-88: Megatron Turbo. 1989-90: Ford Turbo. 1991: Porsche. 1992-94: Mugen-Honda. 1995-96: Hart. 1997: Yamaha.

Drivers 1978-97

1978: R.Patrese. 1979: R.Patrese & J.Mass. 1980: R.Patrese & J.Mass. 1981: R.Patrese, S.Stohr & G.Villeneuve. 1982: M.Surer, M.Baldi & B.Henton. 1983: M.Surer, C.Serra, T.Boutsen. 1984: T.Boutsen, M.Surer. 1985: T.Boutsen & G.Berger. 1986: T.Boutsen, M.Sure & C.Danner. 1987: D.Warwick & E.Cheever. 1988: D.Warwick & E.Cheever. 1989: D.Warwick, E.Cheever & M.Donnelly. 1990: M.Alboreto & I.Capelli. 1991: M.Alboreto, A.Caffi & S.Johansson. 1992: M.Alboreto & A.Suzuki. 1993: D.Warwick & A.Suzuki. 1994: C.Fittipaldi & G.Morbidelli 1995: G.Morbidelli, T.Inoue & M.Papis. 1996: J.Verstappen & R.Rosset. 1997: D.Hill & P.Diniz.

Grand Prix Best Performance

2nd position four times: 1978 Sweden (Patrese), 1980 USA (Patrese), 1981 San Marino (Patrese), 1985 San Marino (Boutsen).

Benetton

Mild Seven Benetton Renault

Benetton Formula Ltd
Whiteways Technical Centre, Enstone, Chipping Norton, Oxon, OX7 4EE
Tel: +44 (0)1608 678000   Fax: +44 (0)1608 678800

Chairman:	Luciano Benetton
MD:	Flavio Briatore
Tech. Director:	Pat Symonds
Team Manager:	Joan Villadelprat
Chief Mechanic:	Mick Ainsley-Cowlishaw
Chief Designer:	Nick Wirth
Drivers/Engineer:	Jean Alesi (7) / Alan Permane
	Gerhard Berger (8) / Rod Nelson
Test Driver:	Alexander Wurz
Sponsors:	Mild Seven, Benetton Sportsystem, Renault, Bitburger.

Brief History

1986: Benetton Formula One established after taking over the old Toleman team. 1987: Gerhard Berger wins in Mexico to give Benetton their first victory. 1990: Nelson Piquet leads home fellow Brazilian Roberto Moreno for first one-two. 1992: Michael Schumacher wins his first Grand Prix in Belgium. 1994: Michael Schumacher wins the Drivers' World Championship. 1995: Michael Schumacher wins second Drivers' World Championship and Benetton win first Constructors' World Championship.

Grand Prix Record

Contested:	234	(161 excluding Toleman)
Victories:	26	
Pole Positions:	13	
Fastest Laps:	33	
Constructors' World Titles:	1	(1995)
Drivers' World Championships:	2	(1994, 1995)
Most Points in a Season:	137	(1995)
Total World Championship Points:	705.5	

Having had two seasons of dominance, 1996 was a season of change for the Benetton team. Two new but very experienced drivers found themselves suffering a number of niggling problems with their cars and in particular with the rear suspension, balance – especially with low fuel loads – and airbox pressure. The latter was a particular problem for the tall Gerhard Berger, who also suffered throughout the first half of the season with the after effects of pneumonia. It all led to a disappointing start to the season for the team and seemed to create not a small amount of unrest within the camp itself not helped by rumours and speculation throughout the season.

After the first two races, Alesi and Berger had only managed one finish each and, as reigning Constructors' Cup holders, Benetton found themselves already 17 points behind arch-rivals Williams even though both drivers had managed point finishes.

Hard work helped overcome some of the air pressure problems for Berger in Argentina allowing him to dominate second position only to suffer a broken rear suspension although this undoubtedly came about from the bumpy nature of the track. Alesi maintained his momentum though, taking an excellent third position.

Suspension development continued towards the European Grand Prix but understeer was now a major problem as Alesi crashed out on lap two after hitting Salo's Tyrrell. Berger at least finished but only ninth after stalling in the pits.

An unhappy Flavio Briatore had a much-published pep talk with both drivers and his team prior to Imola in an effort to get things moving. With the cars still lacking balance, both drivers got in the points with Berger finishing third to provide a first podium finish of the year.

Berger's retirement at Monaco was to be the first of three successive non-finishes and while it was the undoubted low point of the season for him, it also marked the start of a recovery, and driving to a 4th position at Magny-Cours, he at last looked to have thrown off the effects of his illness. Two weeks later he recorded his best finish of the season by coming in second at Silverstone.

In the meantime Alesi was entering his most consistent spell on the way to his best season's points tally ever, despite the twitchy nature of the car. Four second places and four thirds, two fourths and never out of the points whenever he finished prove what a consistent season he had.

Alesi and Berger are teamed again for the 1997 season but it seems unlikely that they will be capable of returning the World Championship to Benetton. Fast approaching 38, Berger is in the twilight of his F1 career but it should certainly be possible for him and Alesi to record at least a victory for their team during the season.

A new Renault engine, the RS9, should help. Designed by the Renault Sport team, the RS9 is a completely different type of engine from the RS8 used in 1996. It is based on a study initiated in 1995 and features leading-edge technology. The most significant change is the degree at which the cylinders are angled. The cylinder rows form an angle of 71 degrees instead of 67 on the RS8 and the other engines since the RS1. The overall design of the RS9 has also taken account of recent developments in chassis design in terms of weight and positioning of the engine's centre of gravity. Its maximum engine speed is 500 to 600 rpm higher than that of the RS8, which makes the RS9 an even higher performance engine than its predecessors.

The B197 is the last car designed by Rory Byrne for Benetton. He has left the team and has been replaced by ex-Simtek boss Nick Wirth who will be in charge of development throughout the season and into 1998. How that affects the team remains to be seen. 1997 is the last year Renault will be powering Benetton and everyone will want to at least try to go out in a blaze of glory.

Drivers and Results 1996

Driver	Races	Com	Ret	Dnq	HP	Pts	Psn	Comp%
Jean Alesi	16	11	5	0	2	47	4/16	68.75
Gerhard Berger	16	9	7	0	2	21	6/16	56.25

Grand Prix	Jean Alesi	Gerhard Berger
Australian	Retired	4th
Brazilian	2nd	Retired
Argentinian	3rd	Retired
European	Retired	9th
San Marino	6th	3rd
Monaco	Retired	Retired
Spanish	2nd	Retired
Canadian	3rd	Retired
French	3rd	4th
British	Retired	2nd
German	2nd	13th
Hungarian	3rd	Retired
Belgian	4th	6th
Italian	2nd	Retired
Portuguese	4th	6th
Japanese	Retired	4th

Benetton B197 Specifications

Engine:	**Renault RS9**
Cylinders:	10 cylinders (71 degree angle)
Valves:	40

Dimensions:	623 mm (length), 542 mm (width), 395 mm (height)
Management:	Magneti Marelli electronic engine management and static ignition.

Car

Chassis:	Carbon fibre composite monocoque manufactured by Benetton Formula
Suspension:	Double wishbone and pushrod with Benetton designed and manufactured. Front suspension system located on top of the monocoque
Transmission:	Benetton semi-automatic six-speed gearbox. Triple-plate clutch
Fuel system:	ATL rubber fuel cell mounted within monocoque structure behind cockpit
Oil system:	Oil tank within bell-housing providing two gallon/nine litres capacity
Cooling system:	Separate water and oil cooling; water radiators in each sidepod
Electrical:	Hardware and software developed jointly by Benetton and Magneti Marelli
Braking systems:	Carbon fibre discs and pads

Dimensions

Overall Length:	4500mm	Wheelbase:	2800mm
Front Track:	1690mm	Rear Track:	1618mm
Height:	950mm		

Jean Alesi in the rain

Engines 1981-97

(1981-85: Toleman). 1981-85: Hart Turbo. 1986: BMW Turbo. 1987: Ford Turbo. 1988-94: Ford. 1995-97: Renault.

Drivers 1981-97

1981: B.Henton & D.Warwick. 1982: D.Warwick & T.Fabi. 1983: D.Warwick & B.Giacomelli. 1984: A.Senna, J.Cecotto, S.Johansson & P.Martini. 1985: T.Fabi & P.Ghinzani. 1986: T.Fabi & G.Berger. 1987: T.Boutsen & T.Fabi. 1988: A.Nannini & T.Boutsen. 1989: A.Nannini, J.Herbert & E.Pirro. 1990: A.Nannini, N.Piquet & R.Moreno. 1991: N.Piquet, R.Moreno & M.Schumacher. 1992: M.Schumacher & M.Brundle. 1993: M.Schumacher & R.Patrese. 1994: M.Schumacher, J.Verstappen, J.J. Lehto & J.Herbert. 1995: M.Schumacher & J.Herbert. 1996-97: J.Alesi & G.Berger. *NB: Team name Toleman 81-85.*

Grand Prix Wins

1986 Mexico (Berger); 1989 Japan (Nannini); 1990 Japan (Piquet), Australia (Piquet); 1991 Canada (Piquet); 1992 Belgium (M.Schumacher); 1993 Portugal (M.Schumacher); 1994 Brazil (M.Schumacher), Pacific (M.Schumacher), San Marino (M.Schumacher), Monaco (M.Schumacher), Canada (M.Schumacher), France (M.Schumacher), Hungary (M.Schumacher), Europe (M.Schumacher); 1995 Brazil (M.Schumacher), Spain (M.Schumacher), Monaco (M.Schumacher), France (M.Schumacher), Britian (Herbert), Germany (M.Schumacher), Belgium (M.Schumacher), Italy (Herbert), Europe (M.Schumacher), Pacific (M.Schumacher), Japan (M.Schumacher).

Ferrari

Scuderia Ferrari Marlboro

Ferrari SpR
Via Ascari 55-57, 41053 Maranello, Modena, Italy
Tel: +39 536 949 111   Fax: +39 536 949 436

Chairman:	Luca Di Montezemolo
Tech. Director:	Ross Brawn
Designers:	Paolo Martinelli (engine), Roberto Dalla (electronics) and Mario Almondo (production)
Team Manager:	Jean Todt
Chief Mechanic:	Nigel Stepney
Drivers/Engineer:	Michael Schumacher (5) / Ignazio Lunetta
	Eddie Irvine (6) / Luca Baldisserri
Test Driver:	Gianni Morbidelli
Sponsors:	Marlboro, Fiat, Shell, Asprey, Magneti Marelli, Telecom Italia, Goodyear, Pioneer, Arexons, BBS, Brembo, SKF, Cerruti 1881, Momo, NGK, TRW Sabelt, USAG, Veca.

Brief History

1898: Enzo Ferrari born in Modena, Italy. 1929: Enzo Ferrari forms his company. 1947: Franco Cortese wins the Grand Prix of Rome to record Ferrari's first race win. 1951: Jose Gonzalez records Ferrari's first Formula One victory. 1952: Alberto Ascari wins the Drivers' World Championship in a Ferrari. 1953: Ascari wins back-to-back titles driving for the Modena-based team. 1956: Juan-Manuel Fangio wins World Championship with Ferrari. 1958: Mike Hawthorn becomes the third Ferrari driver to win the title. 1961: Phil Hill leads Ferrari to the 'double' of both Drivers' and Constructors' titles. 1964: John Surtees takes the World Championship in a Ferrari. 1969: Lowest ever Ferrari score of 7 points achieved in Constructors' World Championship. 1975: Niki Lauda takes title in a Ferrari ahead of Emerson Fittipaldi. 1977: Lauda repeats his success of two years earlier. 1979: Jody Scheckter wins his only World Championship driving a Ferrari. 1983: Ferrari win the last of their eight World Constructors' Championships. 1996: Ferrari give double World Champion Michael Schumacher a record $25 million two-year contract.

Grand Prix Record

Contested:	570
Victories:	108

Pole Positions:	118	
Fastest Laps:	124	
Constructors' World Titles:	8	(61, 64, 75, 76, 77, 79, 82, 83)
Drivers' World Championships:	9	(52, 53, 56, 58, 61, 64, 75, 77, 79)
Most Points in a Season:	113	(1979)
Total World Championship Points:	1991.5	

Review

Australia saw the debut race for both Michael Schumacher and Eddie Irvine in the newly designed John Bernard F310 powered by the first Ferrari V10 engine. Gone was the familiar roar of the V8. Late delivery of the car meant there had been little time for testing and what time there was, was dominated by the German as it was for much of 1996.

Modifications continued throughout the season but the general aerodynamic set-up of the car was never really perfected with understeer into corners and oversteer out of them plaguing both drivers. Changes were made throughout the season but neither driver ever seemed completely happy with what was achieved. Gearbox reliability was another big factor, especially for Eddie Irvine who seemed to suffer from it race after race, and it was a major factor in many of his retirements. A switch back to the 1995 gearbox seemed to improve performance in the early part of the European season but it was only when the new seven-speed system was introduced later in the season at Spa that a real Ferrari revival started to take place. This came on the back of a series of dreadful failures that seemed to place Ferrari Sporting Director Jean Todt's position in some doubt.

Schumacher had said that it was going to be a difficult season for Ferrari and that efforts were building to a championship further down the line. On reflection there was development but the highs and lows of the season must have been more dynamic than even he could have imagined.

Eddie Irvine came to the team as the number two driver and clearly was. Despite his lack of testing time he became only the third team-mate to out-qualify the world champion in 70 races when the two came together for the first race of the season in Australia, a race in which he secured the team's first points and first podium finish of the season – ahead of Schumacher!

A steady start in Australia and South America saw the car developed further and when they returned to Europe Schumacher took his first podium at the Nurburgring. The San Marino GP saw the introduction of a special qualifying engine and set-up and it worked a treat with Schumacher securing his first pole position of the season. It wasn't all rosy though as the German's rear suspension collapsed the moment he secured his pole. Problems were also beginning to surface with the clutch and this would make starting difficult for both drivers for much of the rest of the season.

Having uncharacteristically crashed into Loews on the first lap at Monaco from his second successive pole position, a first Ferrari win came in

Barcelona as Schumacher produced one of the drives of the season. The win took the team to Canada and the scene of their only 1995 triumph with some confidence, which ultimately proved to be misplaced as both drivers failed to finish. A new high nose cone had been introduced for the race in an effort to help stability. But it was engine problems that manifested themselves to leave Schumacher on the starting grid as the formation lap took place when the engine wouldn't fire up due to low fuel pressure and so he had to start from the back of the grid. Irvine's race didn't last longer than the second lap when a front suspension push-rod broke.

If Spain was bad for the team then France was a disaster – the only highlight being Schumacher's third pole position of the year. A new clutch system was in use but handling was still a problem for both drivers. Having pipped Hill for pole a piston collapsed during the formation lap and ended Michael's race before it started. Irvine lasted a little longer – lap six – before his gearbox caved to leave Ferrari plenty of time to pack up before the race was completed.

The setbacks continued at Silverstone and just when things looked like they couldn't get any worse, they did. Schumacher lost hydraulic pressure on lap two, leaving him in sixth gear and forcing retirement. Irvine suffered a differential bearing failure signalled by a plume of smoke that completed another disastrous weekend for the Maranello team and a second successive non-finish.

The team at least managed a finish in the form of Schumacher at Hockenheim following major modifications in several areas, not least in the hydraulic system, gearbox and suspension. The Hungarian GP relieved the pressure even more with both drivers securing Ferrari's best overall grid position of the year. Schumacher achieved his fourth pole position and Irvine was on the second row behind him in fourth place. Neither driver finished when a sticking throttle valve terminated Schumacher's race late on and Irvine suffered another gearbox failure.

The Belgian GP was probably the race where the car itself was the most impressive for Schumacher, undoubtedly helped by the introduction of a new seven-speed gearbox which changed its way onto a win. Irvine of course suffered when his gearbox again gave up for the umpteenth time. The next Ferrari win was a home base triumph at Monza courtesy of Schumacher. In the penultimate race of the season at Estoril Ferrari recorded only its third double finish of the season with Eddie Irvine collecting his first points since Imola.

Ferrari's goal in the final race at Suzuka was to ensure they finished second in the Constructors' Cup. With a solid performance in Portugal behind them there was no reason to make any changes to the cars. The outgoing World Champion's second position ensured that happened. Irvine produced a good drive and rose to fourth position at times in the race only to finish the season on a sour note when he was hit by Berger on lap 39 and taken out of the race. Schumacher's points ensured that Ferrari finished ahead of Benetton but a massive 105 points behind Williams in the Constructors' Cup. In the Drivers' Championship Schumacher surrendered his crown for third place with Irvine finishing 10th.

In 1997 Ferrari will surely get even better. Unless there is a disaster of monumental proportions then Schumacher will continue to add to his tally of Grand Prix wins and it may be enough to secure him a third Drivers' Championship. He has also promised to give Eddie Irvine a helping hand during 1997 with more practice time and the benefit of his considerable experience. This will certainly need to happen if Ferrari have ambitions towards winning a Constructors' Cup in the next two years as Eddie will need to get amongst the points on a regular basis.

Drivers and Results 1996

Driver	Races	Com	Ret	Dnq	HP	Pts	Psn	Comp%
Eddie Irvine	16	5	11	0	3	11	10/16	31.25
M. Schumacher	16	10	6	0	1	59	3/16	62.50

Grand Prix	Eddie Irvine	Michael Schumacher
Australian	3rd	Retired
Brazilian	7th	3rd
Argentinian	5th	Retired
European	Retired	2nd
San Marino	4th	2nd
Monaco	Retired	Retired
Spanish	Retired	1st
Canadian	Retired	Retired
French	Retired	Dns
British	Retired	Retired
German	Retired	4th
Hungarian	Retired	9th
Belgian	Retired	1st
Italian	Retired	1st
Portuguese	5th	3rd
Japanese	Retired	2nd

Ferrari F310B Specifications

Engine:	**3000 Ferrari (046/2)**
Cylinders:	V10 (75 degrees)
Capacity:	2998.1cc
Valves:	40
Injection:	Magneti Marelli
Spark Plugs:	Champion
Electronics:	Magneti Marelli

Car

Gearbox:	Transverse sequential 6 speed & reverse		
Clutch:	Manual command on steering wheel		
Front Suspension:	Push-Rod	Rear Suspension:	Push-Rod
Dampers:	Ferrari	Tyres:	Goodyear
Brake Pads:	Brembo	Brake Callipers:	Brembo
Steering:	Momo	Instruments:	Magneti Marelli
Wheel Diameter (Front/Rear): 13" & 13"			
Wheel Rim Widths (Front/Rear): 11.7" & 13.75"			

Dimensions

Overall Length:	4358mm	Wheelbase:	2935mm
Front Track:	1690mm	Rear Track:	1605mm
Overall Width:	1995mm	Height:	968mm

Engines 1950-97

1950-80: Ferrari. 1981-88: Ferrari Turbo. 1989-97: Ferrari.

Drivers 1950-97

1950: A.Ascari, L.Villoresi, R.Sommer, D.Serafini, P.Whitehead. 1951:
A.Ascari, L.Villoresi, J.Gonzalez, P.Taruffi. 1952: A.Ascari, G.Farina,
L.Villoresi, P.Taruffi, P.Whitehead. 1953: A.Ascari, G.Farina, L.Villoresi,
M.Hawthorn. 1954: G.Farina, J.Gonzalez, M.Hawthorn, U.Maglioli,
M.Trintignant, R.Manzon. 1955: M.Hawthorn, M.Trintignant, G.Farina,
U.Maglioli & J.Gonzalez. 1956: J.Fangio, P.Collins, E.Castelotti, L.Musso,
O.Gendibien, A.de Portigo & M.Trintignant. 1957: P.Collins, M.Hawthorn,
L.Musso, M.Trintignant, C.Perdisa, E.Castellotti, A.de Portigo & W.Von
Trips. 1958: M.Hawthorn, P.Collins, L.Musso, W.Von Trips, P.Hill &
O.Gendibien. 1959: T.Brooks, P.Hill, J.Behra, D.Gurney, C.Allison &
O.Gendibien. 1960: P.Hill, W.Von Trips, R.Ginther, C.Allison &
W.Mairesse. 1961: P.Hill, W.Von Trips, R.Ginther, G.Baghetti &
W.Mairesse. 1962: P.Hill, W.Mairesse, G.Baghetti, L.Bandini &
R.Rodriguez. 1963: W.Mairesse, J.Surtees, L.Bandini & L.Scarfiotti. 1964:
J.Surtees & L.Bandini. 1965: J.Surtees & L.Bandini. 1966: J.Surtees,
L.Bandini, M.Parkes & L.Scarfiotti. 1967: L.Bandini, C.Amon, M.Parkes &
L.Scarfiotti. 1968: J.Ickx, C.Amon & A.de Adamich. 1969: C.Amon &
P.Rodriguez. 1970: J.Ickx, L.Giunti & C.Regazzoni. 1971: J.Ickx,
C.Regazzoni & M.Andretti. 1972: J.Ickx, C.Regazzoni & M.Andretti. 1973:
J.Ickx & A. Merzario. 1974: C.Regazzoni & N.Lauda. 1975: C.Regazzoni &
N.Lauda. 1976: N.Lauda, C.Regazzoni & C.Reutemann. 1977: N.Lauda,
C.Reutemann & G.Villeneuve. 1978: C.Reutemann & G.Villeneuve. 1979:
J.Scheckter & G.Villeneuve. 1980: J.Scheckter & G.Villeneuve. 1981:
G.Villeneuve & D.Pironi. 1982: G.Villeneuve, D.Pironi, P.Tambay &

M.Andretti. 1983: P.Tambay & R.Arnoux. 1984: M.Alboreto & R.Arnoux. 1985: M.Alboreto, R.Arnoux & S.Johansson. 1986: M.Alboreto & S.Johansson. 1987: M. Alboreto & G.Berger. 1988: M.Alboreto & G.Berger. 1989: N.Mansell & G.Berger. 1990: A.Prost & N.Mansell. 1991: A.Prost, J.Alesi & G.Morbidelli. 1992: J.Alesi, I.Capelli & N.Larini. 1993: J.Alesi & G.Berger. 1994: J.Alesi, G.Berger & N.Larini. 1995: J.Alesi & G.Berger. 1996-97: M. Schumacher & E. Irvine.

Grand Prix Wins

1951 Britain (Gonzalez), Germany (Ascari), Italy (Ascari); 1952 Switzerland (Taruffi), Belgium (Ascari), Britain (Ascari), German (Ascari), Netherlands (Ascari), Italy (Ascari); 1953 Argentina (Ascari), Netherlands (Ascari), Belgium (Ascari), France (Hawthorn), Britain (Ascari), Germany (Farina), Swiss (Ascari); 1954 Britain (Gonzalez), Spanish (Hawthorn); 1955 Monaco (Trintignant); 1956 Argentina (Musso/Fangio), Belgium (Collins), France (Collins), Britain (Fangio), Germany (Fangio); 1958 France (Hawthorn), Britain (Collins); 1959 France (Brooks), Germany (Brooks); 1960 Italy (Hill); 1961 Netherlands (von Trips), Belgium (Hill), France (Baghetti), Britain (von Trips), Italy (Hill); 1963 Germany (Surtees); 1964 Germany (Surtees), Austria (Bandini), Italy (Surtees); 1966 Belgium (Surtees), Italy (Scarfiotti); 1968 France (Ickx); 1970 Austria (Ickx), Italy (Regazzoni), Canada (Ickx), Mexico (Ickx); 1971 South Africa (Andretti), Netherlands (Ickx); 1972 Germany (Ickx); 1974 Spain (Lauda), Netherlands (Lauda), Germany (Regazzoni); 1975 Monaco (Lauda), Belgium (Lauda), Sweden (Lauda), France (Lauda), Italy (Regazzoni), United States (Lauda); 1976 Brazil (Lauda), South Africa (Lauda), Long Beach (Regazzoni), Belgium (Lauda), Monaco (Lauda), Britain (Lauda); 1977 Brazil (Reutemann), South Africa (Lauda), Germany (Lauda), Netherlands (Lauda); 1978 Brazil (Reutemann), Long Beach (Reutemann), Britain TP (Reutemann), United States (Reutemann), Canada (G.Villeneuve); 1979 South Africa (G.Villeneuve), Long Beach (G.Villeneuve), Belgium (Scheckter), Monaco (Scheckter), Italy (Scheckter), United States (G.Villeneuve); 1981 Monaco (Villenueve), Spain (G.Villeneuve); 1982 San Marino (Pironi), Netherlands (Pironi), Germany (Tambay); 1983 San Marino (Tambay), Canada (Arnoux), Germany (Arnoux); 1984 Belgium (Alboreto); 1985 Canada (Alboreto), Germany (Alboreto); 1987 Japan (Berger), Australia (Berger); 1988 Italy (Berger); 1989 Brazil (Mansell), Hungary (Mansell), Portugal (Berger); 1990 Brazil (Prost), France (Prost), Britain (Prost), Portugal (Mansell), Spain (Prost); 1994 Germany (Berger); 1995 Canada (Alesi); 1996 Spain, Belgium, Italy (M.Schumacher).

Jordan

Benson & Hedges Total Jordan Peugeot
Jordan Grand Prix Ltd

Buckingham Road, Silverstone, Towcester, Northants, NN12 8JT

Tel: +44 (0)1327 857153   Fax: +44 (0)1327 858120

MD:	Eddie Jordan
Tech. Director:	Gary Anderson
Chief Mechanic:	Tim Edwards
Drivers/Engineer:	Ralf Schumacher (11) / Andrew Green
	Giancarlo Fisichella (12) / Andy Tilley
Test Driver:	None
Sponsors:	Benson & Hedges, Total, AMK, APE, Beta, Cadtek, Carrs Paints, Control Techniques, Diavia, Goodyear, Fanghi d'alga Guam, Hewlett Packard, Kremlyovskaya Vodka, Motorscan, Osama, OZ Wheels, Pepsi, Rockport, Ruffles, Sally Freight, Scania, Sparco, Uliveto, Unipart.

Brief History

1980: Eddie Jordan forms Jordan Motor Racing Team. 1987: Johnny Herbert wins British Formula 3 Championship driving a Jordan. 1988: Jean Alesi takes the International F3000 title for Jordan. 1990: Jordan F1 formed. 1991: Jordan score their first F1 points with Andrea de Cesaris fourth in Canada. 1993: Jordan signs a deal to use Hart engines until the end of the 1994 season. 1995: Exclusive deal with Peugeot engines.

Grand Prix Record

Contested:	97	
Victories:	0	(Best Finish: 2nd)
Pole Positions:	1	
Fastest Laps:	1	
Constructors' World Titles:	0	(Best: 5th 1994)
Drivers' World Championships:	0	(Best: 6th 1994)
Most Points in a Season:	28	(1994)
Total World Championship Points:	88	

The preamble to the 1996 season was full of great optimism for the Jordan team and although Rubens Barrichello managed to get in the points on a fairly consistent basis, the lack of even a single podium finish must rank as a great disappointment. The newly acquired Benson and Hedges sponsorship and Peugeot engine looked set to provide Eddie Jordan with a combination capable of getting into the top four. As it was, 22 Constructors' Cup points placed them fifth overall – the same as in 1995 where at least there had been podium finishes.

Fourth was the best that either driver managed, Barrichello at Buenos Aires and Silverstone and Brundle at Monza. Yet despite a double retirement at Melbourne things looked better in Barrichello's homeland of Brazil. At Interlagos Rubens, whose home is almost on the starting grid, qualified second and looked capable of moving towards the cult status enjoyed by Senna. He fought a hard race in heavy rain and ultimately spun off leaving team-mate Brundle to provide the team's first finish of the year. That was a blessing to Brundle in a season which most will remember as the one in which he wrote off his new Jordan 196 in spectacular fashion at Melbourne. An accident triggered by Panis and Coulthard saw him flying upside down into the gravel, breaking the chassis in two. Luckily he was unhurt and made the restart but the omens were bad and his whole season would prove to be worse than he would have liked.

Three finishes and seven points were followed by three retirements as the first half of the Brazilian's season came and went. Brundle managed two sixth places and four retirements over the same period.

By now the brilliant yellow of the Jordan had been replaced by the more palatable gold one associated with Benson & Hedges and in the remaining eight races Barrichello and Brundle both managed six finishes with the Brazilian outscoring his team-mate by a single point during that time.

Perhaps not surprisingly both drivers have now been replaced at Jordan. Barrichello has signed a four-year deal with the new Stewart team and Brundle a TV contract to co-present ITV's coverage of the Grand Prix season. Incoming are Ralf Schumacher, who as brother of Michael will ensure plenty of media coverage for Eddie Jordan's team, and Giancarlo Fisichella who now has a chance to show if he is as good as most commentators, this one included, believe him to be. Whether Jordan can break out of fifth gear remains to be seen – they should be capable of more points than they achieved in 1996.

Drivers and Results 1996

Driver	Races	Com	Ret	Dnq	HP	Pts	Psn	Comp%
Rubens Barrichello	16	9	7	0	4	14	8/16	56.25
Martin Brundle	16	9	7	0	4	8	11/16	56.25

Grand Prix	Rubens Barrichello	Martin Brundle
Australian	Retired	Retired
Brazilian	Retired	12th
Argentinian	4th	Retired
European	5th	6th
San Marino	5th	Retired
Monaco	Retired	Retired
Spanish	Retired	Retired
Canadian	Retired	6th
French	9th	8th
British	4th	6th
German	6th	10th
Hungarian	6th	Retired
Belgian	Retired	Retired
Italian	5th	4th
Portuguese	Retired	9th
Japanese	9th	5th

Martin Brundle's 1996 Jordan

Jordan 197 Specifications

Engine: **Peugeot A14EV4 3 litre**

Cylinders:	V10 (72 degrees)
Valves:	40 – 4 per cylinder, with pneumatic return
Injection:	Peugeot
Capacity:	2998 cc
Electronics:	TAG Electronic control
Dimensions:	620mm (length), 512mm (width), 393mm (height)

Car

Chassis:	Full carbon fibre composite monocoque
Suspension:	Composite pushrods activating twin Penske dampers, unequal length aerodynamic wishbones, composite top wishbone, steel lower wishbone, steel fabricated uprights and front/rear roll-bar
Transmission:	In-house design. Seven speed (plus reverse) longitudinal gearbox with electo-hydraulic sequential gear change
Clutch:	Triple plate Jordan Peugeot racing clutch
Brakes:	Brembo braking systems. SEP carbon discs and pads.
Wheel rims:	OZ Racing forged according to Jordan's specifications.
Tyres:	Goodyear
Fuel tank:	Capacity 145 litres

Dimensions

Overall Length:	4450mm	Wheelbase:	2950mm
Front Track:	1700mm	Rear Track:	1618mm
Overall Width:	2000mm	Height:	950mm

Engines 1991-97

1991: Ford. 1992: Yamaha. 1993-94: Hart. 1995-97: Peugeot.

Drivers 1991-97

1991: A.de Cesaris, B.Gachot, R.Moreno, M.Schumacher & A.Zanardi. 1992: S.Modena & M.Gugelmin. 1993: R.Barrichello, I.Capelli, T.Boutsen, M.Apicella, E.Nespatti & E.Irvine. 1994: R.Barrichello, E.Irvine, A.Suzuki & A.de Cesaris. 1995: R.Barrichello & E.Irvine. 1996: R.Barrichello & M.Brundle. 1997: R.Schumacher & G.Fisichella.

Grand Prix Best Performance

2nd Position once: 1995 Canada (Barrichello)

Lola

Mastercard Lola Formula One Team

Lola Cars
Cleb Road, St Peters Hill, Huntingdon, Cambridgeshire, PE18 7DS
Tel: +44 (0)1480 451301   Fax: +44 (0)1480 456722

Chairman/MD:	Eric Broadley MBE
Chief Designer:	Eric Broadley MBE
Team Manager:	Ray Boulter
Operations Mgr:	Alan Harrison
Chief Mechanic:	Dave Luckett
Drivers/Engineer:	Ricardo Rosset (24) / Alex Zoechling
	Vincenzo Sospiri (25) / Dave Wynne
Test Driver:	Andrea Montermini
Sponsors:	Mastercard, Pennzoil, Koni Shock Absorbers, Sparco Raceware, MBK Scooters, Harbones Renault Truck Distributors, Mechanix Workwear, Honda Industrial Power equipment, SIKA Flooring, Toshiba, Sally Ferries.

Brief History

1958: Lola Cars Limited formed. 1962: Commissioned for Fl design for John Surtees and Roy Salvadori. 1964: John Surtees wins inaugural North American Can-Am Championship. Graham Hill wins Indy 500 in T90. GT40 wins Le Mans. 1967: Bobby Brown wins Formula A/5000 Championship in T140. 1969: GT4O wins Le Mans 24-hour. 1974: T370 Formula 1 commissioned by Graham Hill. Driven by Hill to establish Embassy-Hill in Grand Prix racing. 1975: Lola's 1000th car manufactured. 1977: T333 wins US F5000 title. 1978: Al Unser wins Indy 500 and becomes first driver to win all three 500-mile races in one season. 1979: T530 wins Can-Am title. 1984: Mario Andretti wins IndyCar World Championship in Lola-Cosworth. 1987: Bobby Rahal wins IndyCar World Championship in Lola-Cosworth. 1990: Outright winner European and Japanese F3000 Championships. Al Unser wins IndyCar World Championship in Lola-Chevrolet. 1991: Michael Andretti wins IndyCar World Championship in Lola-Chevrolet. 1992: Bobby Rahal wins IndyCar World Championship in Lola-Chevrolet. Outright winner Japanese F3000 Championship. 1993: Nigel Mansell wins IndyCar World Championship in Lola-Chevrolet. Outright winner Japanese F3000 Championship. 1995: Lola wins in all four formulas entered, IndyCar, IndyLights, F3000 and F3000 Japan. Win FIA contract to design/build new F3000 formula chassis exclusively from 1996. Appointed by ARS to become exclusive supplier for IndyLights for 1997. 1997: Lola return to F1 in their own right.

Grand Prix Record

Contested:	0	(158)
Victories:	0	(0)
Pole Positions:	0	(1)
Fastest Laps:	0	(0)
Constructors' World Titles:	0	(Best: 4th 1962)
Drivers' World Championships:	0	
Most Points in a Season:	0	
Total World Championship Points:	0	(46)

(Figures in brackets are those achieved by teams using Lola chassis.)

Review

New to Formula One in their own right, Lola are not new to racing and have been chassis suppliers to other F1 teams during the period 1962 to 1993. For the 1997 season the Lola name will not only be for their car chassis but also the V10 engine that they hope will ultimately challenge the supremacy of the French, Italian and German power-plants that presently head the Formula One results.

The Lola project is backed by a consortium of international high-tech companies with operations in the UK. The five-year project will cost somewhere between £5 million and £10 million.

The engine, which will be capable of 18,000 rpm and 750 hp, is being designed by Al Melling's MCD international consultancy in Lancashire and the major components, cylinder blocks, heads and castings, are produced by the Hertfordshire-based Urbanhurst. MBE Systems in Gloucestershire provide the advanced electronic engine management systems and the engines are to be built at Lola's Cambridgeshire base. The car will start the season using a Ford V8 Zetec R power unit until the in-house engine is built and fully tested.

Lola Cars Limited was originally launched in 1958, and is now the longest established member of the successful British motorsports industry. Graham Hill achieved success with them in 1966, gaining the first of the company's three victories in the Indianapolis 500. Nigel Mansell is another winning name and his IndyCar championship in 1993 was one of five the company have won. Over the past four decades Lola Cars have also achieved major successes world-wide in Formula 3000 (Japan and Europe), Sports Cars and Indy Lights, as well as having scored F1 World Championship points as a constructor.

Mastercard have been secured as the team's major sponsor and their driver team will consist of the Brazilian driver Ricardo Rosset and Italian F1 newcomer Vincenzo Sospiri.

The last time a Lola chassis took to the circuit prior to 1997 was in 1993 when Luca Badoer and Michele Alboreto raced at Estoril in the Portuguese Grand Prix for the BMS Scuderia Italia team.

Lola T97/30 Specifications

Engine:	**Ford V8 Zetec R**
Car	
Chassis:	Carbon aluminium honeycomb monocoque designed in-house by Lola
Transmission:	Semi-automatic transverse gearbox, six-speed unit, operated by paddles on steering wheel
Clutch:	AP Racing carbon clutch
Electronics:	PI data acquisition systems
Suspension:	Wishbones all round using pushrod system
Brakes:	Metal Matrix Construction AP callipers with Carbone Industrie/AP carbon discs all round
Wheels:	One-piece forged OZ single hexagonal nut fixing wheels to Lola design
Tyres:	Bridgestone

Engines 1997

1997: Ford.

Drivers 1997

1997: R.Rosset & V.Sospiri.

McLaren

West McLaren Mercedes

McLaren International Ltd
Unit 22, Woking Business Park, Albert Drive, Woking, Surrey, GU21 5JY
Tel: +44 (0)1483 728211   Fax: +44 (0)1483 720157
MD: Ron Dennis
Chief Designers: Neil Oatley
                   Mario Illien (engine)
                   Henri Durand (aerodynamics), Dieter Gundel (systems),
                   Patric Lowe (R&D), Steve Nichols (vehicle engineering),
                   Jim Coates (electronic systems)
Drivers/Engineer: Mika Hakkinen (9)   /   Roger Higgins
                   David Coulthard (10) /   Tim White
Test Driver: Jan Magnussen
Sponsors: West, Mercedes-Benz, Mobil, Tag Heuer, Loctite, Boss,
                   Camozzi, Goodyear, British Aerospace, SAP, Sun
                   Microsystems, Cadence, Targetti, Kenwood, Eibach
                   Springs, Enkei, Computervision.

Brief History

1959: Bruce McLaren makes his F1 debut driving for the Cooper works team.
1963: Bruce McLaren Motor Racing Ltd founded. 1966: McLaren make their
Grand Prix debut at Monaco. 1968: Bruce McLaren wins in Belgium for his
own team's first F1 victory. McLaren finish second behind Lotus in
Constructors' World Championship. 1970: Bruce McLaren killed at
Goodwood whilst testing a CanAm sportscar. 1973: Emerson Fittipaldi leads
McLaren to the Drivers' & Constructors' Championship double. 1976: James
Hunt takes the Drivers' World Championship by a point from Niki Lauda.
1984: Niki Lauda beats team-mate Alain Prost by just half a point to take the
Drivers' title. 1985: Alain Prost takes the title ahead of Michele Alboreto.
1986: Prost retains his title after Nigel Mansell goes out in the final race at
Adelaide. 1988: Senna takes the title by three points from Prost. McLaren
post a record Constructors' Championship score of 199 points. 1989: Prost
takes the title from Senna by 16 points for another McLaren 'double'. 1990:
Senna regains the title from Prost by seven points. 1991: Senna wins his third
World Drivers' Championship.

Grand Prix Record

Contested:	443	
Victories:	104	
Pole Positions:	79	
Fastest Laps:	69	
Constructors' World Titles:	7	(74, 84, 85, 88, 89, 90, 91)
Drivers' World Championships:	9	(74, 76, 84, 85, 86, 88, 89, 90, 91)
Most Points in a Season:	199	(1988)
Total World Championship Points:	1984.5	

Review

The 1996 season was another winless season for the Woking team who had promised much more in the lead-up to the season. Australia 1993 was the last McLaren win but there is no doubting that they have the talent and the car to get back onto the podium's top spot. Luck may be all that is lacking now – if they had had some at Monaco and also at Spa when a double top looked likely until the pace car spoiled things, they may have already turned that particular corner.

The Mercedes engine, now proven during 1996, should be one of the best in F1, rivalling the Renault and Peugeot for top-end power. Certainly improvements during last season left it looking as though it was the most potent powerplant on the track. The key now is the chassis and improvements have been made here, especially on the front wing mounting points which, it was discovered, had been flexing, which was causing downforce to fluctuate.

What McLaren do have is a talented drive duo of Mika Hakkinen and David Coulthard. Few can have anything but admiration for the way Mika Hakkinen recovered from the huge practice accident he had at Adelaide at the end of 1995. Many observers had written off his chances of racing competitively again. He proved them wrong and only failed to finish in four of his 16 races, and in 10 of those 12 races he finished in the points, amassing 31 in all – his best season ever!

After a season at the front with Williams, David Coulthard moved to McLaren with great hopes for 1996. In general when the car ran well so did Coulthard and his blinding starts, especially at Imola where he grabbed the lead from fourth on the grid, were an eye-catcher.

The MP4-12 is the designation of the 1997 car which incorporates numerous design innovations. In line with the updated FIA technical regulations the MP4-12 features a rear impact zone, collapsible steering column, reduced winglets areas and suspension designed within the limited aspect ratios designated by the technical regulations. The design is similar to that introduced at the Belgian Grand Prix in 1996.

There have also been a range of aerodynamic changes and further use of composites within the rear suspension. A newly packaged version of the longitudinal transmission introduced in 1996 will be in place for a second season and the cooling system philosophy has also been changed to capitalise on internal air flow.

For 1997 McLaren are without their almost symbolic red and white livery and Marlboro sponsor (whose name can now be found on the Ferrari). A bright (very bright) orange (shades of the early 1996 Jordan?) will distinguish the West McLaren Mercedes on the circuit. West are a tobacco brand of the Reemstma company. With a change of sponsor may come the change in fortunes that McLaren seeks.

Drivers and Results 1996

Driver	Races	Com	Ret	Dnq	HP	Pts	Psn	Comp%
David Coulthard	16	9	7	0	2	18	7/16	56.25
Mika Hakkinen	16	12	4	0	3	31	5/16	75.00

Grand Prix	David Coulthard	Mika Hakkinen
Australian	Retired	5th
Brazilian	Retired	4th
Argentinian	7th	Retired
European	3rd	8th
San Marino	Retired	8th
Monaco	2nd	Retired
Spanish	Retired	5th
Canadian	4th	5th
French	6th	5th
British	5th	3rd
German	5th	Retired
Hungarian	Retired	4th
Belgian	Retired	3rd
Italian	Retired	3rd
Portuguese	13th	Retired
Japanese	8th	3rd

McLaren MP4-12 Specifications

Engine:	**Mercedes-Benz**
Type:	V10 (75 degree)
Cylinders:	10 – 4 valves per cylinder
Injection:	TAG 2000 electronic system
Oil:	Mobil 1
Dimensions:	590mm (length), 546.4mm (width), 483mm (height)

Car

Chassis:	McLaren moulded carbon fibre/honeycombed composite
Transmission:	McLaren longitudinal six speed semi-automatic. Control by TAG electronic system. McLaren drive shafts and CV assemblies
Suspension:	Inboard spring/damper operated by pushrod and bellcrank with a double wishbone system
Springs:	Eibach
Dampers:	Penske
Brakes:	AP Racing callipers and master cylinders
Tyres:	Goodyear
Race wheels:	Enkei
Water Radiators:	McLaren/Calsonic
Oil Radiators:	McLaren/Calsonic

Engines 1966-95

1966-82: Ford. 1983-87: TAG-Porsche Turbo. 1988: Honda Turbo. 1989-92: Honda. 1993: Ford. 1994: Peugeot. 1995-97: Mercedes.

Mika Hakkinen

Drivers 1966-97

1966: B.McLaren. 1967: B.McLaren. 1968: D.Hulme & D.Gurney. 1969: B.McLaren, D.Hulme & V.Elford. 1970: B.McLaren, D.Hulme, D.Gurney & J.Surtees. 1971: D.Hulme, P.Gethin & J.Oliver. 1972: D.Hulme & P.Revson. 1973: D.Hulme, P.Revson, J.Scheckter. 1974: E.Fittipaldi & D.Hulme. 1975: E.Fittipaldi & E.Mass. 1976: J.Hunt & E.Mass. 1977: J.Hunt & E.Mass. 1978: J.Hunt & P.Tambay. 1979: J.Watson & P.Tambay. 1980: J.Watson & A.Prost. 1981: J.Watson & A.de Cesaris. 1982: N.Lauda & J.Watson. 1983: N.Lauda & J.Watson. 1984: N.Lauda & A.Prost. 1985: N.Lauda, A.Prost & J.Watson. 1986: A.Prost & K.Rosberg. 1987: A.Prost & S.Johansson. 1988: A.Prost & A.Senna. 1989: A.Prost & A.Senna. 1990: A.Senna & G.Berger. 1991: A.Senna & G.Berger. 1992: A.Senna & G.Berger. 1993: A.Senna, M.Andretti & M.Hakkinen. 1994: M.Hakkinen, M.Brundle & P.Alliot. 1995: M.Hakkinen, N.Mansell, M.Blundell & J.Magnussen. 1996-97: M. Hakkinen & D. Coulthard.

Grand Prix Wins

1968 Belgium (McLaren), Italy (Hulme), Canada (Hulme); 1969 Mexico (Hulme); 1972 South Africa (Hulme); 1973 Sweden (Hulme), Britain (Revson), Canada (Revson); 1974 Argentina (Hulme), Brazil (Fittipaldi), Belgium (Fittipaldi), Canada (Fittipaldi); 1975 Argentina (Fittipaldi), Spain (Mass), Britain (Fittipaldi); 1976 Spain (Hunt), France (Hunt), Germany (Hunt), Canada (Hunt), United States (Hunt); 1977 Britain (Hunt), United States (Hunt), Japan (Hunt); 1981 Britain (Watson); 1982 Long Beach (Lauda), Belgium (Watson), Detroit (Watson), Britain (Lauda); 1983 Long Beach (Watson); 1984 Brazil (Prost), South Africa (Lauda), San Marino (Prost), France (Lauda), Monaco (Prost), Britain (Lauda), Germany (Prost), Austria (Lauda), Netherlands (Prost), Italy (Lauda), Europe (Prost), Portugal (Prost); 1985 Brazil (Prost), Monaco (Prost), Britain (Prost), Austria (Prost), Netherlands (Lauda), Italy (Prost); 1986 San Marino (Prost), Monaco (Prost), Austria (Prost), Australia (Prost); 1987 Brazil (Prost), Belgium (Prost), Portugal (Prost); 1988 Brazil (Prost), San Marino (Senna), Monaco (Prost), Mexico (Prost), Canada (Senna), Detroit (Senna), France (Prost), Britain (Senna), Germany (Senna), Hungary (Senna), Belgium (Senna), Portugal (Prost), Spain (Prost), Japan (Senna), Australia (Prost); 1989 San Marino (Senna), Monaco (Senna), Mexico (Senna), United States (Senna), France (Prost), Britain (Prost), Germany (Senna), Belgium (Senna), Italy (Prost), Spain (Senna); 1990 United States (Senna), Monaco (Senna), Canada (Senna), Germany (Senna), Belgium (Senna), Italy (Senna); 1991 United States (Senna), Brazil (Senna), San Marino (Senna), Monaco (Senna), Hungary (Senna), Belgium (Senna), Japan (Berger), Australia (Senna); 1992 Monaco (Senna), Canada (Berger), Hungary (Senna), Italy (Senna), Australia (Berger); 1993 Brazil (Senna), Europe (Senna), Monaco (Senna), Japan (Senna), Australia (Senna).

Minardi

Minardi Team

Minardi Scuderia Italia
Minardi Team SpA, Via Spalenzani 21, 48018 Faunze, Ravenna, Italy
Tel: +39 546 620480   Fax: +39 546 620998

President:	Gian Carlo Minardi
Vice President:	Gabriele Rumi
Team Manager:	Frederic Dhainaut
Chief Designer:	Mauro Gennari
Tech. Coord:	Gabbriele Tredozi
Elecronics:	Alessandro Iacoponi
Driver/Engineer:	Ukyo Katayama (20) / Marco Calovolo
	Jarno Trulli (21) / Gabriele Dellicolli
Test Driver:	Tarso Marques
Sponsors:	Bossini, Brembo, Bridgestone, Carbone Industrie, Cimatron, Diemme, Doimo, Donatl, Fiamm, Fondmetal, Hartpower, Hewlett Packard, Ircis, Magneti Marelli, Microsystem, Mild Seven, Milpass, RBM, Setrans, Sparco, TRW Sabelt, Valleverde.

Brief History

1979: Minardi formed by Gian Carlo Minardi. 1985: Minardi make their Formula One debut in Brazil. 1988: Pierluigi Martini picks up Minardi's first points with sixth in Canada. 1990: Minardi record their only front row start with Martini behind Gerhard Berger in America. 1993: Christian Fittipaldi takes Minardi's highest placing of fourth in South Africa. Minardi's best finish of eighth with seven points in the Constructors' World Championship.

Grand Prix Results

Contested:	188	
Victories:	0	(Best Finish: 4th – three times)
Pole Positions:	0	
Fastest Laps:	0	
Constructors' World Titles:	0	(Best: 7th 1991)
Drivers' World Championships:	0	(Best: 10th 1994)
Most Points in a Season:	7	(1993)
Total World Championship Points:	27	

Review

The lead-up to the 1997 season saw a number of significant changes at Minardi. At the end of 1996 the company reorganised and installed a new board of directors, still led by Gian Carlo Minardi (President and Managing Director), with a view to initiate a long term plan to create a more competitive team in the FIA Formula One World Championship. As part of this goal the team also acquired new suppliers and a new engine. With Yamaha now installed at Arrows, the Hart V8 engine is now exclusively that of Minardi – this is the first time in 10 years that Minardi have had an exclusive engine deal. The Minardi-Hart will receive the important technical support of Magneti Marelli who will provide the latest version of their software for engine and gearbox management and data acquisition.

Minardi also signed a two-year collaboration agreement with Bridgestone. After six years' excellent co-operation with Goodyear, Minardi has chosen this new technical direction with the intention of making available its own results to the Japanese company, as a contribution to the development of their racing tyres.

The Minardi M197 may well be a more reliable car for 1997 but they will also need more reliability from their drivers. Minardi were the only F1 team last season to use more than two drivers – juggling with four overall for financial reasons – and in Giancarlo Fisichella they may have unearthed a real star for the future – but he has departed for Jordan. Pedro Lamy was the only Minardi driver to compete in all their Grands Prix, finishing in half of them but never above ninth place, achieved at Imola.

The most frustrating aspect of the Minardi drivers last season was their ability to run into each other, thus proving to be their own worst enemies.

For 1997 Ukyo Katayama and his sponsorship monies have been obtained and he will hope for a better season than his last for Tyrrell. He is joined by Italian F1 newcomer Jarno Trulli.

Drivers and Results 1996

Driver	Races	Com	Ret	Dnq	HP	Pts	Psn	Comp%
G. Fisichella	8	2	6	0	11	0	–	25.00
P. Lamy	16	8	8	0	9	0	–	50.00
G.Lavaggi	6	2	1	3	10	0	–	33.33
T.Marques	2	0	2	0	–	0	–	0.00

Grand Prix	G.Fisichella	P.Lamy	G.Lavaggi	T.Marques
Australian	Retired	Retired	–	–
Brazilian	–	10th	–	Retired
Argentinian	–	Retired	–	Retired
European	13th	12th	–	–
San Marino	Retired	9th	–	–

Monaco	Retired	Retired	–	–
Spanish	Retired	Retired	–	–
Canadian	Retired	Retired	–	–
French	Retired	12th	–	–
British	11th	Retired	–	–
German	–	12th	Dnq	–
Hungarian	–	Retired	10th	–
Belgian	–	10th	Dnq	–
Italian	–	Retired	Retired	–
Portuguese	–	16th	15th	–
Japanese	–	12th	Dnq	–

Minardi M197 Specifications

Engine:	**Hart 830 AV7**
Injection:	Magneti Marelli electronic
Electronics:	Magneti Marelli
Fuel tank:	ALT
Fuel:	Minardi

Minardi '97 Line-up

Car

Chassis:	Carbon fibre monocoque
Suspension:	Inboard spring via rocker and pushrod to wishbone
Brake Pads:	Carbon Industrie
Brake Discs:	Brembo
Cooling system:	Water radiators (x2), oil radiator (x1)
Gearbox:	6 speed plus reverse. Longitudinal Minardi Xrtac gearbox with Minardi electrohydraulic system
Wheels:	Fondmetal: 11"x13" (front), 13.7"x13" (rear)
Tyres:	Bridgestone
Seatbelts:	TRW Sabelt

Dimensions

Overall Length:	44405mm	Wheelbase:	2900mm
Front Track:	1680mm	Rear Track:	1620mm
Overall Width:	2000mm	Height:	950mm

Engines 1985-97

1985-87: Motori Moderni Turbo. 1988-90: Ford Cosworth. 1991: Ferrari. 1992: Lamborghini. 1993-96: Ford Cosworth. 1997: Hart.

Drivers 1985-97

1985: P.Martini. 1986: A.de Cesaris & A.Nannini. 1987: A.Nannini & A.Campos. 1988: L.Perez Sala, A.Campos & P.Martini. 1989: P.Martini, L.Perez Sala & P.Barilla. 1990: P.Martini, P.Barilla & G.Morbidelli. 1991: P.Martini, G.Morbidelli & R.Moreno. 1992: G.Morbidelli, C.Fittipaldi & A.Zanardi. 1993: C.Fittipaldi, F.Barbazza, P.Martini & J-M.Gounon. 1994: P.Martini & M.Alboreto. 1995: P.Lamy, L.Badoer & P.Martini. 1996: P. Lamy & T.Inoue. 1997: U.Katayama & J.Trulli.

Grand Prix Best Performance

4th position three times: 1991 San Marino (Martini), Portugal (Martini); 1993 South Africa (Martini).

Prost

Equipe Prost Gauloises Blondes

Technopole de la Nievre, 58470 Magny-Cours, France
Tel: +33 3 86 60 62 00   Fax: +33 3 86 21 22 96

Owner:	Alain Prost
MD:	Bruno Michel
Sporting Manager:	Cesare Fiorio
Chief Mechanic:	Robert Dassaud
Chief Designer:	Loic Bigois
Drivers/Engineer:	Olivier Panis (14) / Renato Muscati
	Shinji Nakano (15) / Humphrey Corbett
Test Driver:	–

Brief History

1976: Ligier enter F1 at the end of the 1976 season. Jacques Laffite takes pole and sets the fastest lap in Italy. 1979: Laffite wins the opening two Grands Prix in Argentina and Brazil. 1980: Ligier finish second in the Constructors' World Championship behind Williams. 1983: Ligier fail to score a point in the season for the first time in their history. 1996: Tom Walkinshaw leaves for Arrows. 1997: Alain Prost takes control of Ligier and renames team to Prost Grand Prix.

Grand Prix Record

Contested:	326	
Victories:	9	
Pole Positions:	9	
Fastest Laps:	11	
Constructors' World Titles:	0	(Best: 2nd 1980)
Drivers' World Championships:	0	(Best: 4th 1979, 1980, 1981)
Most Points in a Season:	66	(1980)
Total World Championship Points:	389	

Review

What a year for Ligier! First they lost the backing and expertise of Tom Walkinshaw, then Olivier Panis stayed the course for a memorable win at Monaco – their first victory since 1981 – and then just weeks away from the start of the 1997 season, Alain Prost took control of the French team and announced that French manufacturer Peugeot will supply engines to the team from 1998. With the agreement of the other teams the Ligier team is also allowed to change its name to Prost Grand Prix.

On the circuit in 1996 there were more retirements than finishes and the euphoria of that win in Monaco perhaps overshadowed a season on the outskirts of consistent scoring. Ligier were expected to fall apart when Walkinshaw left but instead Panis drove the race of his life and read the conditions better than the majority of the drivers around him. True, Damon Hill looked to have the race sewn up, but Grand Prix racing is about finishing and Panis did it first and nothing else should detract from that particular fact.

Panis, you feel, is on the verge of turning from a good driver into a very good driver and the arrival of Prost may help facilitate this. He finished more races than he retired from and although he managed a sixth in Brazil and a fifth in Hungary he was only just outside the points on numerous other occasions. The line is fine and even a slight improvement could help him turn the corner and prove that what he did once, he can do again.

Team-mate Pedro Diniz was the subject of criticism from various parties but his financial backing was probably as important to Ligier last year as anything, especially after Walkinshaw departed. Two points were managed from six finishes but there were signs of improvement throughout the season after a poor start and an horrific-looking fire in Argentina.

For 1997 Panis is joined by newcomer Shinji Nakano who has a year to prove himself. Don't be surprised if 1998 sees another new driver to partner Panis – French of course.

Drivers and Results 1996

Driver	Races	Com	Ret	Dnq	HP	Pts	Psn	Comp%
Pedro Diniz	16	6	10	0	6	2	15/16	37.50
Olivier Panis	16	9	7	0	1	13	9/16	56.25

Grand Prix	Pedro Diniz	Olivier Panis
Australian	10th	7th
Brazilian	8th	6th
Argentinian	Retired	8th
European	10th	Retired
San Marino	7th	Retired
Monaco	Retired	1st
Spanish	6th	Retired
Canadian	Retired	Retired
French	Retired	7th
British	Retired	Retired
German	Retired	7th
Hungarian	Retired	5th
Belgian	Retired	Retired

Italian	6th	Retired
Portuguese	Retired	10th
Japanese	Retired	7th

Prost JS45 Specifications

Engine: **Mugen Honda**

Type:	V10 MF-310H B
Cylinders:	10
Valves:	40 – 4 valves per cylinder
Capacity:	3000 cc
Power:	More than 670 bhp
Injection:	Honda PGM-F1
Timing:	Pneumatic valve return system (PVRS)
Dimensions:	625mm (length), 525mm (width), 470mm (height)

Car

Chassis:	Carbon fibre composite monocoque manufactured by Prost Grand Prix
Suspension:	Double wishbone and push-rod (rear) with suspension units located on top of monocoque (front)
Brakes:	Brembo and/or AP one-piece callipers and master cylinders with Carbone Industries carbon fibre discs

Olivier Panis – Monaco 1996

Transmission:	Transverse semi-automatic six-speed gearbox. Multi-plate clutch			
Fuel system:	ATL rubber fuel cell mounted within the monocoque structure behind the cockpit			
Oil system:	Eight litre capacity oil tank			
Cooling system:	Separate water radiators in each side pod plus oil radiator on right-hand side of engine			

Dimensions

Overall Length:	4335mm	Wheelbase:	2995mm
Front Track:	1693mm	Rear Track:	1608mm
Overall Width:	1995mm	Height:	950mm

Engines 1976-97

1978-78: Matra. 1979-80: Ford. 1981-84: Matra. 1984-86: Renault Turbo. 1987: Megatron Turbo. 1988: Judd. 1989-90: Ford. 1991: Lamborghini. 1992-94: Renault. 1995-97: Mugen-Honda.

Drivers 1976–97

1976: J.Laffite. 1977: J.Laffite. 1978: J.Laffite. 1979: J.Laffite, P.Delailler & J.Ickx. 1980: J.Laffite & D.Pironi. 1981: J.Laffite, J-P Jarier, J-P Jabouille & P.Tambay. 1982: J.Laffite & E.Cheever. 1983: J-P Jarier & R.Boesel. 1984: A.de Cesaris & F.Hesnault. 1985: J.Laffite, A.de Cesaris & P.Streiff. 1986: R.Arnoux, J.Laffite & P.Alliot. 1987: R.Arnoux & P.Ghinzani. 1988: R.Arnoux & S.Johansson. 1989: R.Arnoux & O.Grouillard. 1990: P.Alliot & N.Larini. 1991: T.Boutsen & E.Comas. 1992: T.Boutsen & E.Comas. 1993: M.Brundle & M.Blundell. 1994: E.Bernard, O.Panis, J.Herbert & F.Lagorce. 1995: M.Brundle, A.Suzuki & O.Panis. 1996: P.Diniz & O.Panis. 1997: O.Panis & S.Nakano.

Grand Prix Wins

1977 Sweden (Laffite); 1979 Argentina (Laffite), Brazil (Laffite), Spain (Depailler); 1980 Belgium (Pironi), Germany (Laffite); 1981 Austria (Laffite), Canada (Laffite); 1996 Monaco (Panis).

Sauber

Red Bull Sauber Petronas

Team Sauber Formel 1
Wildbachstrasse 9, 8340 Hinwil, Switzerland
Tel: +41 1 938 1400   Fax: +41 1 938 1670

Team Principal:	Peter Sauber
Team Director:	Max Welti
Chief Designer:	Leo Ress
Team Manager:	Beat Zehnder
Chief Mechanic:	Ernst Keller
Drivers/Engineer:	Johnny Herbert (16) / Gilles Alegoet
	Nicola Larini (17) / Willy Rampf
Test Driver:	Norberto Fontana
Sponsors:	Red Bull, Baumier, Brembo, Emil Frey, Giroflex, Goodyear, Helbling Informatik, IBM, Lista, MacNeal-Schwendler, Magneti Marelli, Man Nutzfahrzeuge, Modellbau Bubeckk, OMP, Sachs, Silicon Graphics, Speedline.

Brief History

1993: Sauber record a scoring finish in their first Grand Prix with J.J. Lehto taking fifth in South Africa. The team end the season sixth in the Constructors' World Championship with 12 points.

Grand Prix Record

Contested:	65	
Victories:	0	(Best Finish: 3rd – once)
Pole Positions:	0	
Fastest Laps:	0	
Constructors' World Titles:	0	(Best: 6th 1993)
Drivers' World Championships:	0	(Best: 8th 1994)
Most Points in a Season:	18	(1995)
Total World Championship Points:	53	

Review

Now in its fifth year as a Grand Prix team, Sauber had perhaps their best result even after the 1996 Grand Prix season had finished. In November 1996 the company signed an agreement outlining technical co-operation with Ferrari that effectively secures the Sauber-Petronas team a two-year contract with the traditional Italian race outfit and access to highly modern engine technology based on Ferrari's experience. Team Principal Peter Sauber commented, 'For us this agreement signifies the most important step ever since we decided to enter Formula One, not only have we got an absolutely competitive engine for the 1997 season that bears comparison, but we now also acquire engine competence thus finally allowing us to plan strategically in this area.'

For the 1997 season the Sauber-Petronas V10 engines will be built and revised by a group of about 20 specialists in Maranello, Italy who operate independently from the Ferrari race engine department. All engineers and mechanics in the group have previously worked on other motor racing projects such as Formula One, the IMSA programme or the ITC programme. A small group of engineers at Sauber Petronas Engineering will be working closely with the specialists in Maranello from the beginning.

This selling of technology by one team to another is ground-breaking and may well be a way ahead for many smaller teams who could conceivably be used on a nursery basis. However, it has also presented the team with some blinding headaches, not least with a dramatic race against time in order to complete the new car in time for the season's opening!

The C16 chassis is significantly narrower in the front area and, following the latest trend, the front nose box with the integrated crash structure has been made even higher and narrower. Some visible changes have been made in the cockpit area which is also narrower around the side crash structure. And the lower cockpit side design is a result of the aerodynamic findings of last season. It aims to improve the air flow in the airbox area from where the engine receives the air it needs.

The rear of the C16 has not been spared from the general slimming diet. It is also narrower. Further significant changes are the so-called ear wings – for improving downforce – which have been placed between the side pods and rear tyres, a place designated by the new FIA Technical Regulations.

The news is sure to be a boost to the team's number one driver Johnny Herbert who had an indifferent time last year. Much of this could be put down to the lack of testing which was dominated by the German Heinz-Harald Frentzen who has now left for Williams. When Herbert did get the practice time he required later in the season his results improved. Indeed he finished one more race than Frentzen and at Monaco he achieved Sauber's best finish of the year when coming home 3rd for their only podium placement.

Frentzen made the news in 1996 mainly because it was announced that he would replace Damon Hill at Williams. After an 8th place at Melbourne he failed to finish in the next five races and only got amongst the points twice in a disappointing season.

For 1997 Nicola Larini joins Johnny Herbert in the cockpit. Getting the C16 chassis to match the Ferrari engine technology might make for another slow start to the season, but the potential for more consistent points finishes is there.

Drivers and Results 1996

Driver	Races	Com	Ret	Dnq	HP	Pts	Psn	Comp%
H-H. Frentzen	16	6	10	0	4	7	12/16	37.50
Johnny Herbert	16	7	8	0	3	4	14/16	43.75

Grand Prix	H-H Frentzen	Johnny Herbert
Australian	8th	Dns
Brazilian	Retired	Retired
Argentinian	Retired	9th
European	Retired	7th
San Marino	Retired	Retired
Monaco	Dnf	3rd
Spanish	4th	Retired
Canadian	Retired	Retired
French	Retired	Dq
British	8th	9th
German	8th	Retired
Hungarian	Retired	Retired
Belgian	Retired	Retired
Italian	Retired	9th
Portuguese	7th	8th
Japanese	6th	10th

Johnny Herbert

Sauber Ford C15 Specifications

Engine: **Sauber-Petronas**
Type: V10 (75 degrees)
Valves: 40
Capacity: 2998.1 cc
Valve Mechanism: Pneumatic
Management: Magneti Marelli
Ignition System: Magneti Marelli, static
Dimensions: 598mm (length), 540mm (width), 432mm (height)

Car
Chassis: Carbon fibre monocoque
Suspension: Upper and lower wishbones, combined spring/damper
                  units (Sachs), mounted inboard with pushrod actuation
Brakes: Eight-piston callipers (Brembo) front and six-piston
                  callipers rear; carbon pads and discs (Carbone Industrie)
Transmission: Semi-automatic, longitudinally mounted, six-speed
                  transmission (Sauber), carbon clutch (Sachs)

Dimensions

Overall Length:	4410mm	Wheelbase:	2940mm
Front Track:	1660mm	Rear Track:	1610mm
Overall Width:	2000mm	Height:	1000mm

Engines 1993-97

1993: Sauber. 1994: Mercedes. 1995-96: Ford. 1997: Sauber-Petronas.

Drivers 1993-97

1993: K. Wendlinger & JJ.Lehto. 1994: K.Wendlinger, H-H.Frentzen, J.J.Lehto & A.de Cesaris. 1995: H-H.Frentzen, J-C.Boullion & K.Wendlinger. 1996: J. Herbert & H-H.Frentzen. 1997: J.Herbert & N.Larini.

Grand Prix Best Performance

3rd position once: 1995 Italy (Frentzen).

Stewart

Stewart Ford

Stewart Grand Prix Ltd

16 Tanners Drive, Blakelands, Milton Keynes, Bucks, MK14 5BW
Tel: +44 (0)1908 216122   Fax: +44 (0)1908 216892

Chairman:	Jackie Stewart
MD:	Paul Stewart
TD:	Alan Jenkins
Team Managers:	David Stubbs (Race)
	Andy Miller (Technical)
Drivers/Engineer:	Rubens Barrichello (22) / Jean-François Sinteff
	Jan Magnussen (23) / Malcolm Tierney
Test Driver:	–
Sponsors:	Visit Malaysia, HSBC Group, Hewlett-Packard, MSC, OMP, EDS Unigraphics, Hertz, Sanyo, Texaco.

Brief History

1996: Stewart Grand Prix formed. 1997: First season F1 racing.

Grand Prix Record

Contested:	0
Victories:	0
Pole Positions:	0
Fastest Laps:	0
Constructors' World Titles:	0
Drivers' World Championships:	0
Most Points in a Season:	0
Total World Championship Points:	0

Review

In London on 10 December 1996 the first Formula One car from Stewart Grand Prix was launched, the SF-1. In under nine months the car had been created from scratch and a brand new team built around it. The whole car design process had been undertaken by computer from the outset.

The story goes that three times World Champion Jackie Stewart was approached by Ford in the summer of 1995 to see if he would consider adding his name to a new F1 team. Having already had great success with Paul Stewart Racing (Jackie's son) the plunge was taken at the end of the same year and their base at Milton Keynes expanded to take on the additional staff required. By March 1996 design on the SF-1 had started in earnest using state-of-the-art computer-aided design systems. The search was also on for major backers and partners to help finance the growth and general research and development. The team signed a deal with HSBC Holdings in September worth £25 million over five years and this was followed by others including one with the Malaysian tourist board. The cars will carry the Malaysian flag alongside the Racing Stewart tartan.

The team had hoped that they would have been able to capture Damon Hill's signature but by the end of October both Jan Magnussen and Rubens Barrichello had signed three- and four-year deals respectively.

Barrichello offers driving experience to the Stewart team while Magnussen comes with just one outing for McLaren to his name. Consistently finishing in the mid-ranks will be considered a success for the first year.

Stewart Ford SF1 Specifications

Engine:	**Ford Zetec-R V10**
Cylinders:	10 (72 degree) – 40 valves
Capacity:	2998cc
Management:	Ford electronics
Ignition:	Cosworth
Spark plugs:	Champion
Dimensions:	605mm (length), 520mm (width), 460mm (height)
Car	
Chassis:	Carbon fibre monocoque
Transmission:	Semi-automatic six-speed, longitudinally mounted
Clutch:	High-pressure hydraulic system, AP Racing triple-plate clutch
Suspension:	Upper and lower wishbones, combined spring/damper units mounted with pushrod actuation. Choice of twin or triple Stewart/Penske damper layout
Brakes:	Twin AP Racing four-piston callipers (front). Twin AP Racing six-piston callipers (rear)
Brake pads:	Carbone Industrie carbon fibre discs and pads
Wheels:	BBS forged magnesium, 12"x13" front, 13.4"x13" rear

Engines 1997

1997: Ford.

Drivers 1997

1997: R.Barrichello & J.Magnussen.

Tyrrell

Tyrrell Ford

Tyrrell Racing Organisation Ltd
Long Reach, Ockham, Woking, Surrey, GU23 6PE
Tel: +44 (0)1483 284955   Fax: +44 (0)1483 284892

Chairman:	Ken Tyrrell
MD Commercial:	Bob Tyrrell
MD Engineering:	Dr Harvey Postlethwaite
Sporting Director:	Satoru Nakajima
Dep.Tech.Dir:	Mike Gascoyne
Team Manager:	Steve Nielsen
Chief Mechanic:	Nigel Steer
Electronics Eng:	Chris White
Software Eng:	Chris Hills
Drivers/Engineer:	Jos Verstappen (18) / Tim Densham
	Mika Salo (19) / David Brown
Test Driver:	Toranosuke Takagi
Sponsors:	PIAA Corporation, Ford, Goodyear, Koni, Parametric Technology, Motion Systems, Mitech, Morse, Tamiya

Brief History

1970: Jackie Stewart takes pole position for Tyrrell in Montreal in their first race in Formula One. 1971: Stewart wins the second race of the season in Spain to record Tyrrell's first win in only their fifth race; they go on to win the Constructors' World Championship with more than double the points of second-placed BRM. 1972: Tyrrell win four races but finish second to Lotus in the Championship. 1973: Five races won but runners-up to Lotus for the second year running. 1978: Patrick Depailler wins in Monaco for his only Grand Prix win for Tyrrell. 1982: Michele Alboreto wins in Las Vegas for Tyrrell's first win for four years. 1983: Alboreto wins in Detroit for Tyrrell's last victory to date. 1984: Tyrrell fail to score a point in the Constructors' Championship for the first time. 1989: After six years without success, Jonathan Palmer records the fastest lap in the Canadian Grand Prix.

Grand Prix Record

Contested:	385
Victories:	23
Pole Positions:	14

Fastest Laps:	20	
Constructors' World Titles:	1	(1971)
Drivers' World Championships:	2	(1971, 1973)
Most Points in a Season:	82	(1973)
Total World Championship Points:	615	

Review

After two seasons where hopes were high but returns low it has been all-change for the Surrey-based team. A new engine and a new driver line-up have helped to renew hopes for 1997 which in many respects cannot fail to be better that 1996.

Hopes were high when the new 024 chassis was released. It looked sleek and the new Yamaha was the lightest engine as well as the smallest allowing the team more freedom in the way the chassis worked. As it turned out, the engine was far from reliable and Katayama and Salo finished less than half of the races they started and just three points were scored.

Having promised much in 1994 Ukyo Katayama had a worse season last year than he did in 1995 and failed to secure a point-scoring position, seventh being his best at the Hungarian Grand Prix. In many respects it was no surprise when he wasn't listed as a Tyrrell driver for 1997, Minardi providing him with his seat for the season.

Mika Salo is now in his third (and possibly final) season with Tyrrell and despite the season's shortcomings still did enough to impress. Indeed he started 1996 very positively taking sixth place in Australia and then going one better in Brazil to come home fifth. Indeed the Tyrrell team might have had good cause to be confident about what lay ahead at this point because Katayama had managed to finish both races, albeit lower down the field. But then the Japanese failed to record a finish in the next nine races (although he did finish at the Nurburgring only to be disqualified), while Salo suffered the same fate and disqualification in his next six outings. When Salo did get back on track, seventh was the best he could manage which was also matched by Katayama once. Overall, apart from engine reliability, handling and balance seem to have been problematical throughout the season.

For 1997 the Tyrrell 025 is to be powered by a new-generation Ford V8 engine, which is being developed by Cosworth Racing, Ford's technology partner in Formula One. It was showing a distinct improvement in horsepower during pre-season testing and hopefully it will prove to be more reliable that the 1996 Yamaha engine.

Salo has been retained for a third year and he is joined by Jos Verstappen. The Dutchman had a disappointing season at Arrows during 1996 and will need to start turning his much-vaunted potential into point finishes on a regular basis for Tyrrell in 1997.

Drivers and Results 1996

Driver	Races	Com	Ret	Dnq	HP	Pts	Psn	Comp%
Ukyo Katayama	16	6	10	0	7	0	–	37.50
Mika Salo	16	7	9	0	5	5	13/16	43.75

Grand Prix	Ukyo Katayama	Mika Salo
Australian	11th	6th
Brazilian	9th	5th
Argentinian	Retired	Retired
European	Dq	Dq
San Marino	Retired	Retired
Monaco	Retired	Retired
Spanish	Retired	Retired
Canadian	Retired	Retired
French	Retired	10th
British	Retired	7th
German	Retired	9th
Hungarian	7th	Retired
Belgian	8th	7th
Italian	10th	Retired
Portuguese	12th	11th
Japanese	Retired	Retired

Tyrrell 025 Specifications

Engine: **Ford ED3 V8**

Injection:	Cosworth
Ignition:	Cosworth
Spark Plugs:	Champion

Car

Chassis:	Moulded carbon fibre and honeycomb structure
Suspension:	Combined spring and damper units operated by push rods and rockers, third spring, mechanical anti-roll bar
Dampers:	Koni
Wheels:	Forged magnesium: Front – 4-spoke, 12" wide. Rear – 5-spoke, 13.7" wide
Brakes:	AP Racing. Front – 2x6 piston callipers. Rear – 2x4 piston callipers
Brake Discs:	Hitco carbon
Fuel tank:	ATL Kevlar bladder
Instruments:	Pi Research System, integrated digital display
Gearbox:	Tyrrell longitudinal three-shaft 6-speed unit
Gear Selection:	Pneumatic, sequential, semi-automatic

Drive Shafts:	Tyrrell Trilobe
Clutch:	AP Racing carbon plate
Differential:	Tyrrell Viscous Coupling

Dimensions

Overall Length.	4430mm	Wheelbase:	2990mm
Front Track:	1700mm	Rear Track:	1610mm
Overall Width:	2000mm	Height:	950mm

Engines 1970-97

1970-85: Ford. 1985-86: Renault Turbo. 1987-90: Ford. 1991: Honda. 1992 Ilmor. 1993-96: Yamaha. 1997: Ford.

Drivers 1970-97

1970: J.Stewart & F.Cevert. 1971: J.Stewart & F.Cevert. 1972: J.Stewart & F.Cevert. 1973: J.Stewart & F.Cevert. 1974: J.Scheckter & P.Depailler. 1975 J.Scheckter & P.Depailler. 1976: J.Scheckter & P.Depailler. 1977: R.Peterson & P.Depailler. 1978: P.Depailler & D.Pironi. 1979: J-P.Jarier & D.Pironi 1980: J-P.Jarrier, D.Daly & M.Thackwell. 1981: E.Cheever, R.Zunino & M.Alboreto. 1982: M.Alboreto, B.Henton & S.Borgudd. 1983: M.Alboreto & D.Sullivan. 1984: S.Bellof, M.Brundle, S.Johansson & M.Thackwell. 1985 M.Brundle, S.Johansson, S.Bellof, I.Capelli & P.Streiff. 1986: M.Brundle & P.Streiff. 1987: J.Palmer & P.Streiff. 1988: J.Palmer & J.Bailey. 1989 J.Palmer, M.Alboreto, J.Alesi & J.Herbert. 1990: S.Nakajima & J.Alesi 1991: S.Nakajima & S.Modena. 1992: A.de Cesaris & O.Grouillard. 1993 A.de Cesaris & U.Katayama. 1994: U.Katayama & M.Blundell. 1995 U.Katayama, M.Salo & G.Tarquini. 1996: U.Katayama & M.Salo. 1997 J.Verstappen & M.Salo.

Grand Prix Wins

1971 Spain (Stewart), Monaco (Stewart), France (Stewart), Britain (Stewart) Canada (Stewart), United States (Cevert); 1972 Argentina (Stewart), France (Stewart), Canada (Stewart), United States (Stewart); 1973 South Africa (Stewart), Belgium (Stewart), Monaco (Stewart), Netherlands (Stewart) Germany (Stewart); 1974 Sweden (Scheckter), Britain (Scheckter); 1975 South Africa (Scheckter); 1976 Sweden (Scheckter); 1978 Monaco (Depailler); 1982 Las Vegas (Alboreto); 1983 Detroit (Alboreto).

Williams

Rothmans Williams Renault
Williams Grand Prix Engineering Ltd
Grove, Wantage, Oxfordshire, OX12 0QD
Tel: +44 (0)1235 777700   Fax: +44 (0)1235 777739

Chairman/MD:	Frank Williams
Tech. Director:	Patrick Head
Designers:	Geoff Willis/Gavin Fisher
General Manager:	David Williams
Team Manager:	Dickie Stanford
Chief Mechanic:	Carl Gaden
Systems Manager:	Allan Challis
Drivers/Engineer:	Jacques Villeneuve (3) / Jock Clear
	Heinz-Harald Frentzen (4) / Tim Preston
Test Driver:	Jean-Christophe Boullion
Sponsors:	Rothmans, Renault, Castrol, Goodyear, Komatsu, Automotive Products, Magneti Marelli, Champion, Sparco, Andersen Consulting, Cermica, Mirage SpA, Sonox, Henderson Investors, Auto Motor und Sport, Falke.

Brief History

1969: After building his business up, Frank Williams starts running cars. 1970: Piers Courage killed during the Dutch Grand Prix driving a private session. 1973: Entered Formula One under the name of ISO. 1976: Disappointing partnership with oil man Walter Wolf. 1978: Williams Grand Prix Engineering founded. Australian Alan Jones signed to drive. 1979: Clay Regazzoni wins in Britain for Williams' first Grand Prix victory. 1980: Alan Jones wins the Drivers' World Championship with Williams taking the Constructors' title for the first time. 1986: Frank Williams seriously injured in a car crash and confined to a wheelchair. 1992: Nigel Mansell becomes the first driver to win the opening five rounds of a season and achieves a record of nine victories in total as Williams take the Drivers' and Constructors' World Championships. 1993: Alain Prost wins his fourth World title and announces his retirement from the sport. 1994: Williams record their seventh Constructors' Championship victory to bring them level with Lotus in the all-time record. 1996: Williams win eighth Constructors' Championship, Damon Hill wins first Drivers' World Championship, Jacques Villeneuve runner-up in first season.

Grand Prix Record

Contested:	299	
Victories:	95	
Pole Positions:	97	
Fastest Laps:	100	
Constructors' World Titles:	8	(80, 81, 86, 87, 92, 93, 94, 96)
Drivers' World Championships:	6	(80, 82, 87, 92, 93, 96)
Most Points in a Season:	175	(1996)
Total World Championship Points:	1787.5	

Review

As many had predicted Williams regained their Constructors' Cup title, equalling the record number of wins held by Ferrari. Damon Hill at last won his World Drivers' Championship and, as now seems the norm with Williams Champions, didn't have his contract renewed as the German, Heinz-Harald Frentzen, was preferred as partner to the rookie Jacques Villeneuve, who stormed onto the Grand Prix scene in 1996.

That Williams had the best car in 1996 is undisputed and their driver combination proved to be equally impressive as their drivers notched up an impressive 13 wins, 12 poles and 11 fastest laps. There was never any doubt that they would win the Championship long before the final race.

The stage was set at Melbourne in the first race of the season where Villeneuve, who pipped Hill for pole position, led him for so long and looked set to become only the third driver in history to win on his F1 debut. An oil problem put paid to that as Hill swept past him to take the first of three successive wins. In fact Hill only failed to finish four races, two of those down to driver error. When Hill did finish it was always in the points. In qualifying he dominated, never off the front row of the grid and nine times on pole. Villeneuve was equally impressive and with just three retirements he had the greatest race completion rate of any driver. Of his 13 finishes only two came outside the points.

With Hill dominating in South America the return to Europe and the Nurburgring saw Villeneuve secure his first Grand Prix win in what was only his fourth race in Formula One. The Williams team at this point had already amassed more points than all the opposition put together! At Imola Hill dominated and won again while Villeneuve finished outside the points for the first time.

At Monaco things went wrong. Hill was leading comfortably when he retired in plumes of smoke with engine failure while Villeneuve fared no better, colliding with a back marker. In the rains of Spain Schumacher excelled and Villeneuve did well to come home third while Hill spun off, leaving him with two successive non-finishes.

In Canada Jacques desperately wanted to win on the circuit named after his father, but he had to settle for second spot as Hill won again. It was the same story at Magny-Cours two weeks later but Villeneuve got back to winning ways at Silverstone while Hill spun out with wheel-bearing failure.

It was at the German Grand Prix that rumours first surfaced about Hill being replaced by Heinz-Harald Frentzen for the 1997 season. Hill answered his critics by taking victory in the race with Villeneuve trailing in third. The championship race was now just between the two Williams drivers.

At the tight Hungaroring Villeneuve again took victory from Hill and with Hill having to settle for fifth in Spa, Villeneuve's second place allowed him to close the points gap between the two of them. At the Italian Grand Prix it was announced that Hill's contract would not be renewed for 1997. Whether this affected the championship leader is debatable as he had a brush with tyres at a chicane and spun out early on. Villeneuve failed to take advantage of the situation though and finished outside the points for only the second time.

At Estoril Villeneuve led Hill home in a thrilling race most memorable for a stunning passing manoeuvre by the Canadian to get by Michael Schumacher. The win set up a thrilling championship conclusion. Hill had only to score a point to ensure his place in the history books while Villeneuve had to win the race with Hill scoring no points at all. Hill drove the perfect race leading the field home quite comfortably, by which time he was already World Champion with Villeneuve having shed a wheel early in the race.

The Constructors' Cup had long before been won. Williams scored twice as many points as second-placed Ferrari, thereby equalling their record of championship wins.

Williams will be amongst the teams to beat during 1997. Frentzen has always been viewed as a potential champion in the making and the expectation will be for him to succeed especially under pressure from the brilliant Villeneuve. A potential problem might be the Williams split with ace designer Adrian Newey, who at the end of 1996 resigned from the team, leaving Geoff Willis and Gavin Fisher to carry on development in the interim. And on top of this is the manslaughter trial which Frank Williams and co. face in Italy over the death of Ayrton Senna. It will be another interesting season.

Drivers and Results 1996

Driver	Races	Com	Ret	Dnq	HP	Pts	Psn	Comp%
Hill	16	12	4	0	1	97	1/16	75.00
Villeneuve	16	13	3	0	1	78	2/16	81.25

Grand Prix	Damon Hill	Jacques Villeneuve
Australian	1st	2nd
Brazilian	1st	Retired
Argentinian	1st	2nd

European	4th	1st
San Marino	1st	11th
Monaco	Retired	Retired
Spanish	Retired	3rd
Canadian	1st	2nd
French	1st	2nd
British	Retired	1st
German	1st	3rd
Hungarian	2nd	1st
Belgian	5th	2nd
Italian	Retired	7th
Portuguese	2nd	1st
Japanese	1st	Retired

Williams FW19 Specifications

Engine: **Renault V10, RS9**
Cylinders: 10 in V configuration 67 degrees
Valves: Pneumatically controlled
Spark Plugs: Champion
Electronics: Magneti Marelli
Dimensions: 623mm (length), 542mm (width), 395mm (height)

Car
Chassis: Carbon Aramid epoxy composite, manufactured by Williams using Fiberite products
Transmission: Six-speed Williams transverse semi-automatic
Clutch: AP Racing
Cooling system: Two Secan water radiators either side of chassis; two IMI oil radiators
Brakes: Carbone Industrie discs and pads operated by AP callipers.
Lubricants: Castrol
Wheels: OZ, 13"x11.5" front, 13"x13.7" rear
Tyres: Goodyear Eagle radials
Cockpit Instru.: Williams digital data display

Dimensions

Overall Length:	4150mm	Wheelbase:	2890mm
Front Track:	1670mm	Rear Track:	1600mm

Engines 1973-97

1973-83: Ford. 1984-87: Honda Turbo. 1988: Judd. 1989-97: Renault.

Drivers 1973-97

1973: H.Ganley, H.Pescarolo & N.Galli. 1974: A.Merzario, J-P.Jabouille & T.Belso. 1975: A.Merzario, J.Laffite & J.Scheckter. 1976: J.Ickx, M.Leclerc & A.Merzario. 1977: P.Neve. 1978: A.Jones. 1979: A.Jones & C.Regazzoni. 1980: A.Jones & C.Reutemann. 1981: A.Jones & C.Reutemann. 1982: K.Rosberg, D.Daly, C.Reutemann & M.Andretti. 1983: K.Rosberg, J.Laffite & J.Palmer. 1984: K.Rosberg & J.Laffite. 1985: K.Rosberg & N.Mansell. 1986: N.Mansell & N.Piquet. 1987: N.Mansell, N.Piquet & R.Patrese. 1988: N.Mansell, R.Patrese, M.Brundle & J.Schlesser. 1989: T.Boutsen & R.Patrese. 1990: T.Boutsen & R.Patrese. 1991: N.Mansell & R.Patrese. 1992: N.Mansell & R.Patrese. 1993: A.Prost & D.Hill. 1994: A.Senna, D.Hill, D.Coulthard & N.Mansell. 1995: D.Hill & D.Coulthard. 1996: D.Hill & J. Villeneuve.

Grand Prix Wins

1979 Britain (Regazzoni), Germany (Jones), Austria (Jones), Netherlands (Jones), Canada (Jones); 1980 Argentina (Jones), Monaco (Reutemann), France (Jones), Britain (Jones), Canada (Jones), United States (Jones); 1981 Long Beach (Jones), Brazil (Reutemann), Belgium (Reutemann), Las Vegas (Jones); 1982 Switzerland (Rosberg); 1983 Monaco (Rosberg), 1984 Dallas (Rosberg), 1985 Detroit (Rosberg), Europe (Mansell), South Africa (Mansell), Australia (Rosberg); 1986 Brazil (Piquet), Belgium (Mansell), Canada (Mansell), France (Mansell), Britain (Mansell), Germany (Piquet), Hungary (Piquet), Italy (Piquet), Portugal (Mansell); 1987 San Marino (Mansell), France (Mansell), Britain (Mansell), Germany (Piquet), Hungary (Piquet), Austria (Mansell), Italy (Piquet), Spain (Mansell), Mexico (Mansell); 1989 Canada (Boutsen), Australia (Boutsen); 1990 San Marino (Patrese), Hungary (Boutsen); 1991 Mexico (Patrese), France (Mansell), Britain (Mansell), Germany (Mansell), Italy (Mansell), Portugal (Patrese), Spain (Mansell); 1992 South Africa (Mansell), Mexico (Mansell), Brazil (Mansell), Spain (Mansell), San Marino (Mansell), France (Mansell), Britain (Mansell), Germany (Mansell), Portugal (Mansell), Japan (Riccardo Patrese); 1993 South Africa (Prost), San Marino (Prost), Spain (Prost), Canada (Prost), France (Prost), Britain (Prost), Germany (Prost), Hungary (Hill), Belgium (D.Hill), Italy (D.Hill); 1994 Spain (D.Hill), Britain (D.Hill), Belgium (D.Hill), Italy (D.Hill), Portugal (D.Hill), Japan (D.Hill), Australia (Mansell); 1995 Argentina (D.Hill), San Marino (D.Hill), Hungary (D.Hill), Portugal (Coulthard), Australia (D.Hill); 1996: Australia (D.Hill), Brazil (D.Hill), Argentina (D.Hill), Europe (J.Villeneuve), San Marino (D.Hill), Canada (D.Hill), France (D.Hill), British (J.Villeneuve), Germany (D.Hill), Hungary (J.Villeneuve), Portugal (J.Villeneuve), Japan (D.Hill).

Retired Teams

Forti

Forti Grand Prix
Forti Course, SrL, Via Luigi Einaudi 33, Allessandria 15100, Italy
Tel: +39 131 246890   Fax: +39 131 246891

Grand Prix Record

Contested:	27	
Victories:	0	(Best Finish: 7th 1995)
Pole Positions:	0	
Fastest Laps:	0	
Constructors' World Titles:	0	
Drivers' World Championships:	0	
Most Points in a Season:	0	
Total World Championship Points:	0	

Review

Twenty-seven Grands Prix, no wins, no points and sadly by the time of the British Grand Prix at Silverstone no more money to continue in the show. The team brought in Sauber's Ford Zetec V8 for the start of the season which was mounted first in the 1995 chassis for the first few races and then in the 1996 development which was more of a retrograde step.

Despite the lack of funds and with the help of sponsorship deals that Pedro Diniz had been able to bring to the team for the 1995 season, the team had secured a good driving partnership in Badoer and Montermini. But the fact that they only recorded three finishes between them in a combined total of 20 starts hides another story. The big battle proved to be the 107% qualification rule and both drivers took their own places in history when they failed to get inside the marker for the first race of the season in Melbourne.

South America proved to be more fruitful with ex-Ferrari and Ligier team manager Cesare Fiorio joining to add his considerable experience. In Brazil both drivers were some five seconds off the pace but inside the 107% factor and had their grid positions upgraded to 19th and 20th following the demotion of Marques and Diniz. Montermini finally spun out for good but Badoer finished last and four laps down. Both drivers were on the starting grid in Argentina and had a reversal in roles with Montermini finishing.

At the Nurburgring both drivers were again thwarted by the 107% rule but at least managed to show off their new 1996 chassis on race day. The new FG03 looked a big improvement for Badoer who qualified well inside the 107% rule at Imola and finished 10th despite having his gearbox jammed in fifth for the last ten laps! Montermini wasn't so lucky though and once again missed the race courtesy of the 107% rule.

In Monaco both qualified and both failed to finish (but then most drivers did) and Badoer found himself with a two-race ban, suspended for three races, after taking out Villeneuve on lap 60. By the Spanish Grand Prix Cesare Fiorio had left to rejoin Ligier and the Shannon Racing Group had acquired a stake in Forti, a fact which was reflected in the cars' new green and black livery which wasn't shown on race day as both cars failed to make the required qualifying time.

South America had been fruitful and so was North America. At Montreal Luca Badoer out-qualified Ricardo Rosset – the first time a Forti driver had got the better of a driver from another team in 1996. The glory was short-lived as both drivers retired – Montermini due to loose ballast sloshing around his cockpit.

The French Grand Prix was the beginning of the end. Although both drivers qualified they both came out of the race relatively early, fuelling rumours that the engines were in desperate need of rebuilding but without the funds to facilitate this. By Silverstone two weeks later the team didn't have enough money to take part in the free practice sessions and could only drive some laps in qualifying which were too slow to come within the 107% boundary. The proposed contract with a new partner, Shannon Racing (Finfirst), was apparently cancelled. Hope lingered on as the season continued without them and the ownership of the team was challenged in and out of the courts before Guido Forti finally got his team back. Ever hopeful Forti were one of the signatories of the Concorde Agreement in October but it may be some time before we see them again, if ever.

Drivers and Results 1996

Driver	Races	Com	Ret	Dnq	HP	Pts	Psn	Comp%
Luca Badoer	10	2	4	4	10	0	–	20.00
Andrea Montermini	10	1	4	5	10	0	–	10.00

Grand Prix	Luca Badoer	Andrea Montermini
Australian	Dnq	Dnq
Brazilian	11th	Retired
Argentinian	Retired	10th
European	Dnq	Dnq
San Marino	10th	Dnq
Monaco	Retired	Dns
Spanish	Dnq	Dnq

Canadian	Retired	Retired
French	Retired	Retired
British	Dnq	Dnq

Engines 1995-96

1995-96: Ford.

Drivers 1995-96

1995: P.Diniz & R.Moreno. 1996: A.Montermini & L.Badoer.

Grand Prix Best Performance

7th position once: 1995 Australia (Diniz).

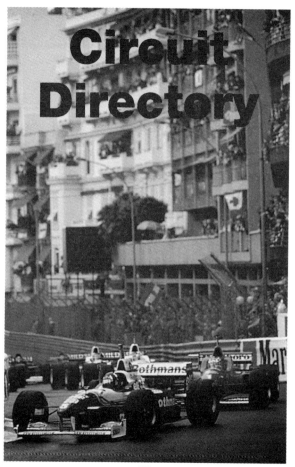

Circuit Directory

A1-Ring

Austrian Grand Prix – September 21 1997
Lap Distance: 2.67 miles/4.319 kms
Race Distance 189.57 miles/306.649 kms – 71 laps

The A1-Ring is an updated and re-designed version of the famous old Osterreichring. It lies in a green, hilly area of Austria known as Styria, roughly central in a triangle formed by the cities of Vienna, Salzburg and Graz.

Originally built in 1968, a total of 18 Grand Prix were held there between 1970 and 1987, with the final event needing three starts to get it underway! Since then over £17 million has been spent on turning the circuit into one of the most modern in the world, which includes brand new circuit and state-of-the-art facilities. The circuit combines a number of long straights with tight and sweeping corners that will test drivers and keep teams on their toes when it comes to car set-ups.

The Circuit

The starting line and grid are located in front of the medical centre and from here the cars power their way down past the garages at 180mph. Changing down from 6th gear and breaking hard the **Castrol Curve** is a sharp right-hand turn that leads into the fastest part of the circuit. At top speed the stands of the Naturtribune West flash past on the left as the track curves slightly out to the left.

At the end of the straight the **Remus Kurve** looms – very tight it takes the cars through 150 degrees and onto another top-speed straight past the Naturtribune Nord stands. The end of this straight marks the entry to the most curvaceous part of the circuit which swings inside and out. The **Gosset Kurve** is a double right hand turn, the entry being slower than the shallower exit. The **Nicki Lauda Kurve** is an open sweeping turn around to the right which leads into another similar turn called the **Power Horse Kurve**.

Out onto a fourth long straight the cars run parallel to the start-finish line as they approach the **A1 Kurve**. This is an open right-hand turn that leads into a short straight from where cars can re-enter the pit-lane. The **Mopikom Kurve** slows the cars down through 4th gear as they turn right before accelerating out across the finish line.

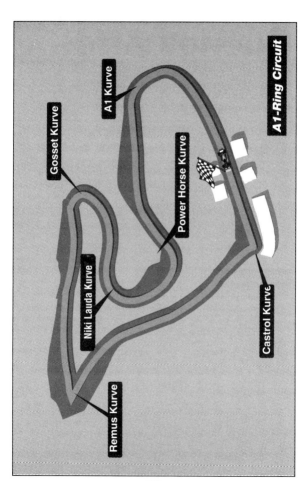

A1-Ring Circuit

A1 Kurve

Gosset Kurve

Power Horse Kurve

Niki Lauda Kurve

Remus Kurve

Castrol Kurve

Buenos Aires

Autodromo de la Ciudad de Buenos Aires
Argentine Grand Prix – April 13 1997
Lap Distance: 2.64 miles/4.259 kms
Race Distance   190.08 miles/306.654 kms – 72 laps

The Autodromo is located in the park Almirante Brown on the southern outskirts of the city of Buenos Aires. The track was originally built with the support of President Peron, in the era of the legendary Juan Manuel Fangio. First used in 1952 the Grand Prix returned to Buenos Aires last year after an absence of 14 years. It was the site of the first F1 race to incur fatalities when Farina's Ferrari killed nine spectators in the first race to be held there in 1953. This season will be the 19th Grand Prix held on the circuit.

A circuit that is well liked by most drivers. It is one of the smallest but is technically difficult because of its twisty nature and also the change in gradient – the track goes up and down and as such can be a little bumpy. Because of these factors, cars need to be set up for maximum grip. Passing is not impossible but very difficult and is often best attempted on the start/finish straight.

The Circuit

Off the starting straight and up to 6th gear and 180mph and drivers approach the **Curvon**. This is the first corner turning to the right at 80mph in 3rd gear. The **Curva de la Confiteria** is an inner left-hand loop that is entered at 155mph in 5th gear, quickly changing down to 2nd gear and 65mph at its apex. A change to 3rd gear and the loop is exited at about 110mph.

The **No8 Curvon** marks the end of the inner loop as the cars sweep tightly back round on themselves in 3rd gear at 95mph. Coming out of the turn the drivers find themselves on the second longest straight which is taken flat out at 180mph before they enter the **Curva de Ascari**. This is a sweeping right-hand turn which marks the beginning of the entry to the Esses at a speed of 175mph.

Entrada a los mixtos (Extrada a Esses) is a tight hairpin. Hard braking brings the cars down into 2nd gear and a sedate 55mph before entering the Esses at **Viborita** which is a double sweep left and then right, both in 3rd gear, but slowing from 95mph to about 75mph as the Esses are completed.

Curva del Ombú is another 3rd gear bend taken at about 100mph. This used to signal the end of the lap before the circuit was redesigned, now

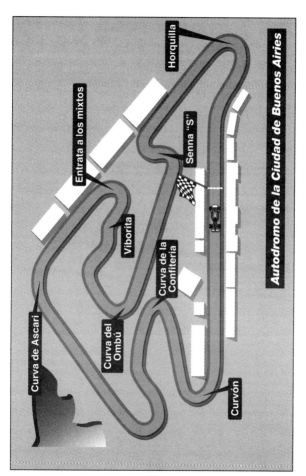

Autodromo de la Ciudad de Buenos Aries

Horquilla

Entrata a los mixtos

Senna "S"

Viborita

Curva de Ascari

Curva del Ombú

Curva de la Confiteria

Curvón

189

though the drivers continue down a shortened version of the old pit lane to the left right wiggle that marks the **Senna S**. What used to be called Tobogan is approached in 5th gear at 150mph, after which a rapid change down reduces speed to 55mph through the S bend. Hard on the accelerator out of Senna up to 155mph in 5th gear comes **Horquila**, braking hard back down to 2nd gear and 55mph. The final 90 degree bend brings the cars out onto **Tribunas** the longest straight and it's full speed ahead and across the finishing line in 6th gear at 180mph.

5-Year Record

Year	1st	2nd	3rd	4th	5th	6th
1992-94	No Grand Prix at this circuit					
1995	Hill (Williams)	Alesi (Ferrari)	Schumacher (Benetton)	Herbert (Benetton)	Frentzen (Sauber)	Berger (Arrows)
1996	Hill (Williams)	Villeneuve (Williams)	Alesi (Benetton)	Barrichello (Jordan)	Irvine (Ferrari)	Verstappen (Arrows)

Qualifying

1996	1995	1994
Hill (Williams)	Coulthard (Williams)	No race
1m 30.346	1m 53.241	–

Commentary

Damon Hill will be going for a hat-trick of wins in Argentina and is likely to be the only previous winner of the race on the starting grid. Last season he clinched his 13th pole position in Argentina and secured his fourth consecutive Grand Prix win and 16th in total. Williams-Renault will also be looking for a third consecutive win with Jacques Villeneuve hoping to go one better than last year's second place. Alesi loves the circuit and drove brilliantly last year, finishing third despite having stalled his car in the pits.

The changeable nature of the weather is often a big factor in both qualifying and the race itself. In dry conditions a lap time closest to 90 seconds should be enough to secure pole position.

At last year's race Brazilian Ricardo Rosset, driving for Arrows, was fined US$10,000 and warned about his future conduct by the FIA after he passed the chequered flag twice during practice on the Saturday. This year he will be in a Lola car.

Catalunya

Circuit de Catalunya
Spanish Grand Prix, Barcelona – May 25 1997
Lap Distance   2.937 miles/4.727 km
Race Distance   191.69 miles/307.255 km – 65 laps

Located 12 miles north-east of Barcelona, Catalunya is one of five circuits to play host to the Spanish Grand Prix. Held here since 1991, the circuit continues to be improved and upgraded on an annual basis making it one of the most advanced circuits in the world. Despite that it remains bumpy and the track surface has ripples on it, complete with demanding fast corners and long high straights. In many respects the circuit is like Estoril but has many more run-off areas which make it popular with the drivers from a safety point of view.

Technically the circuit is challenging with a good mixture of slow second gear and fast fourth gear corners. Setup is of paramount importance as teams try to trade the downforce they require for corners with reduction in drag for the fast straights.

The Circuit

From the starting line cars accelerate downhill at 180mph to **Elf**. The approach to Elf is downhill until almost the corner itself when it rises to the left. This corner is taken in 3rd gear at 85mph on the inside so that the car can drift out to the left for the next bend taken in 3rd at 100mph. **Curvone Renault** is a sweeping, long 180 degree right hander, entered in 4th gear and completed in 5th gear at 155mph.

Out of Renault accelerating to about 165mph before the circuit loops back on itself at **Revolt Repsol**. Entered in 3rd gear at 75mph and exited in 5th gear at 140mph along a short straight to **Revolt Seat**. This tight left-hand hairpin drops the cars downhill at around 60mph through two gentler left handers before entering **Revolt Wurth (5)**. Here the track takes a sharp left-hand which is almost 90 degrees. Here the track takes a sharp left-hand turn which is almost 90 degrees and is entered in 3rd gear at 80mph. On exit the circuit turns a gradual right as 5th gear and 145mph is hit before **Revolt Camposa**. This right hander is blind but can be navigated safely in 4th leading and then down the short straight on the run into 180 degree hairpin **Revolt La Caixa** which is taken in 3rd gear at 65mph as it climbs to the right into the final two 100 degree bends at **Banc Savadell**. Entered in 3rd at 80mph it is exited in 4th gear as the car accelerates towards the penultimate corner, another right hander that turns into a short straight leading to the final bend which is taken almost flat-out in fifth at about 140mph.

5-Year Record

Year	1st	2nd	3rd	4th	5th	6th
1992	Mansell (Williams)	Schumacher (Benetton)	Alesi (Ferrari)	Berger (McLaren)	Alboreto (Footwork)	Martini (Dallara)
1993	Prost (Williams)	Senna (McLaren)	Schumacher (Benetton)	Patrese (Benetton)	Andretti (McLaren)	Berger (Ferrari)
1994	Hill (Williams)	Schumacher (Benetton)	Blundell (Tyrrell)	Alesi (Ferrari)	Martini (Minardi)	Irvine (Jordan)
1995	Schumacher (Benetton)	Herbert (Benetton)	Berger (Ferrari)	Hill (Williams)	Irvine (Jordan)	Panis (Ligier)
1996	Schumacher (Ferrari)	Alesi (Benetton)	Villeneuve (Williams)	Frentzen (Sauber)	Hakkinen (Jordan)	Diniz (Ligier)

Qualifying

1996	1995	1994
D. Hill (Williams)	M.Schumacher (Benetton)	M.Schumacher (Benetton)
1m 20.650	1m 21.452	1m 21.908

Commentary

Michael Schumacher will be looking for his third successive win in Barcelona this year. His 1996 victory was his first for Ferrari in a race that will be remembered for his battle with Alesi's Benetton – the car in which Schumacher won in 1995. The weather took its toll last year with only six cars completing the course and it was a weekend in which Jacques Villeneuve was fined $5000 for speeding in the pit lane on the Saturday morning.

For qualifying, a time close to 80 seconds should secure pole position which was achieved by Damon Hill in 1996.

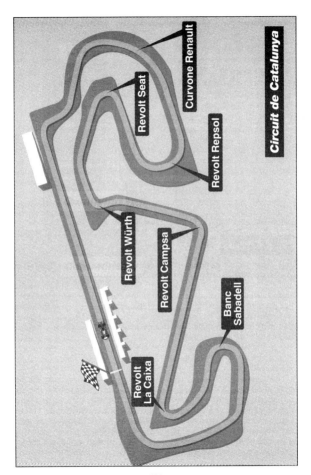

Circuit de Catalunya

Curvone Renault

Revolt Seat

Revolt Repsol

Revolt Würth

Revolt Campsa

Banc Sabadell

Revolt La Caixa

Estoril

Autodromo do Estoril
Portuguese Grand Prix – October 26 1997
Lap Distance: 2.701 miles/4.36 km
Race Distance: 192.339 miles/309.56 km – 71 laps

On the west coast of Portugal just 20 miles from Lisbon this circuit is a great favourite amongst the teams for testing. Constructed in 1972 it has staged the Portuguese Grand Prix since 1984 when the Grand Prix roadshow returned to this part of the Iberian Peninsula. A twisty, bumpy circuit but with one fast corner and a variety of slow ones it remains probably the most liked of all the circuits amongst the drivers. Drivers generally describe it as rough and tough and there are very few opportunities for overtaking.

For 1997 Estoril stages the finale to the world championship calendar so as to allow engine manufacturers Renault a European send-off to their current involvement in Formula 1 Grand Prix racing.

The Circuit

The circuit has a very long and fast pit straight that is followed by two 90 degree right-hand corners. The first of these is **Turn 1** by the Pirelli Bridge and this is approached at 180mph, is entered in 5th gear at 130mph and exited with the help of a low kerb. Next up at the Martini Bridge is **Turn 2** and the cars enter into the second right hander which is taken in 5th gear at 145mph. **Turn 3** is a very bumpy right hander entered in 5th gear but taken in 2nd with the cars breaking from 160mph to 60mph. **Turn 4** is an open 180-degree turn that is entered in 3rd gear at 115mph before changing down to 2nd and breaking to 40mph and accelerating out at full speed. More a kink than a corner, **Turn 5** can be taken almost flat out but slows the cars to around 160mph.

The **Parabolica Interior (Turn 6)** is another 180-degree turn taken in 2nd gear at 60mph. A fast entry and exit make for hard braking and fast accelerating. **Turn 7** is an off-camber, downhill right hander that is negotiated in 2nd gear at under 70mph. On exit cars speed-up to 115mph before the entry to **Curva do Tanque (Turn 8)** – modified so that cars arrive at the corner much earlier than previously. It is a 120-degree turn followed by a straight of just 200 metres; taken in 3rd at 110 mph as the cars climb a gradient (also known as the Corkscrew).

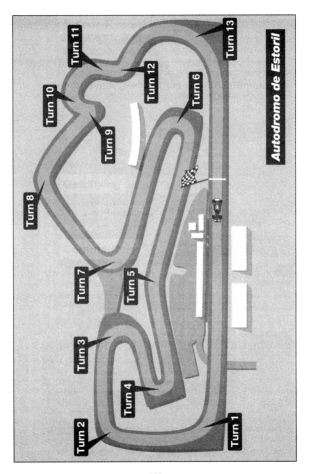

Autodromo de Estoril

Turn 9 and Turn 10 form a near hairpin taken in 1st gear at 30mph before looping on an arch-like right hander that takes the cars from 2nd to 3rd gear and 125mph. This is followed by the Turn 11 and Turn 12 which form the Esses which is a left-right sweep taken in 3rd but with speeds limited to 75mph for the most part. This then sets drivers up for Turn 13 – Parabolica – a magnificent sweeping, long right-hand turn taken in 5th gear with speeds in the order of 130mph, turning into the finishing straight where, on one of the longest straights in Grand Prix, drivers make the most of their cars' performance.

5-Year Record

Year	1st	2nd	3rd	4th	5th	6th
1992	Mansell (Williams)	Berger (McLaren)	Senna (McLaren)	Brundle (Benetton)	Hakkinen (Lotus)	Alboreto (Footwork)
1993	Schumacher (Benetton)	Prost (Williams)	Hill (Williams)	Alesi (Ferrari)	Wendlinger (Sauber)	Brundle (Ligier)
1994	Hill (Williams)	Coulthard (Williams)	Hakkinen (McLaren)	Barrichello (Jordan)	Verstappen (Benetton)	Brundle (McLaren)
1995	Coulthard (Williams)	Schumacher (Benetton)	Hill (Williams)	Berger (Ferrari)	Alesi (Ferrari)	Frentzen (Sauber)
1996	Villeneuve (Williams)	Hill (Williams)	Schumacher (Ferrari)	Alesi (Benetton)	Irvine (Ferrari)	Berger (Benetton)

Qualifying

1996	*1995*	*1994*
D. Hill (Williams)	D.Coulthard (Williams)	G.Berger (Ferrari)
1m 20.330	1m 20.537	1m 20.608

Commentary

Estoril is a very happy hunting ground for the Williams team as they have won five out of the last six Grands Prix held there. To that you can also add three runners-up spots as well in the same period. The 1997 event should be no different with Jacques Villeneuve going for a second sucessive win. His victory in 1996 was one of the drives of the season.

Last year's qualifying session was also one of the closest ever. Williams Renault drivers Damon Hill and Jacques Villeneuve were separated by just nine-thousandths of one second (that's 0.009) at Estoril. That would have been a gap of just 75cm if the two cars had started side by side!

Hockenheim

Hockenheimring
German Grand Prix – July 27 1997
Lap Distance   4.234 miles/6.815 km
Race Distance   189.90 miles/306.675 km – 45 laps

Located some 50 miles south of Frankfurt and 15 miles west of Heidelberg the circuit was originally built as a test circuit for Mercedes cars. The German Grand Prix has been staged here since 1986 and it is, for the majority, an open circuit that is very fast throughout. The exception to this is the Stadium complex near the starting grid where the track twists back and forth through 360 degrees in front of the grandstands.

This makes it a very difficult circuit to set-up for. Car settings are compromised for top speeds down the straights and downforce on the slow corners. At over four miles in length it is one of the longest Grand Prix circuits and is often more infamously remembered as the circuit that took the life of Jim Clarke in April 1968. Weather is often very changeable as the circuit plunders its way through dense pine tree forests which themselves can create dangerous patches of fog and mist.

The Circuit

From the start-finish line cars approach **Nork Kurve** a fast right hander that is taken in 4th gear at 125mph and exited in 5th ready to move up to 6th accelerating to over 190mph for the long run to the first chicane. The posthumously named **Jim Clark Kurve** slows cars to 2nd gear as they brake rapidly to 60mph before accelerating back up to 190mph deep into the forest.

Before the **Ostkurve** the drivers get busy coming into it. The previous straight turns into a sharp right-left turn taken in 2nd gear at 90mph before it becomes a long right-hand bend about 350 metres before Ostkurve is entered – a chicane which is a right-left taken in second gear leading into a long, fast right hander and on to the next straight. The **Ayrton Senna Kurve** which is also known as Bremskurve 3 is approached down the back straight at 190mph. The left-right turn slows the cars drastically to 60mph as it's taken in 2nd gear and then full-power as the cars accelerate back up to 190mph before the Stadium complex begins to come into view.

The Agip Kurve is a fast right-hander that is taken in 4th gear at 110mph and leads quickly into the **Sachs Kurve** as drivers shift down to a 60mph 2nd gear for the hairpin that has a well earned reputation for being slippery. The final section in the stadium that leads back to the start line, the **Sud** or **Opel Kurve** is a double apex hairpin taken in 3rd gear at an average of 90mph leading into the finishing straight where cars can accelerate to 175mph.

5-Year Record

Year	1st	2nd	3rd	4th	5th	6th
1992	Mansell (Williams)	Senna (McLaren)	Schumacher (Benetton)	Brundle (Benetton)	Alesi (Ferrari)	Comas (Ligier)
1993	Prost (Williams)	Schumacher (Benetton)	Brundell (Ligier)	Senna (McLaren)	Patrese (Benetton)	Berger (Ferrari)
1994	Berger (Ferrari)	Panis (Ligier)	Bernard (Ligier)	Fittipaldi (Arrows)	Morbidelli (Arrows)	Comas (Larrousse)
1995	Schumacher (Benetton)	Coulthard (Williams)	Berger (Ferrari)	Herbert (Benetton)	Boullion (Sauber)	Suzuki (Ligier)
1996	Hill (Williams)	Alesi (Benetton)	Villeneuve (Williams)	Schumacher (Ferrari)	Coulthard (McLaren)	Barrichello (Jordan)

Qualifying

1996	1995	1994
D. Hill (Williams)	D. Hill (Williams)	G. Berger (Ferrari)
1m 43.912	1m 44.385	1m 43.582

Commentary

Damon Hill secured his 18th pole position last year with only seconds of the qualifying session remaining. It was his second successive pole at the German Grand Prix. Hill went on to win his seventh race of the year, but it was Gerhard Berger in the Benetton who really caught the eye. He led for much of the race only to be let down when his engine blew.

It was here last year that speculation was rife in the pit paddock that Damon Hill would be replaced at Williams by Heinz-Harald Frentzen. The weekend will also be remembered for the no-show of the Forti F1 team who had run out of funding (see *Retired Teams* section).

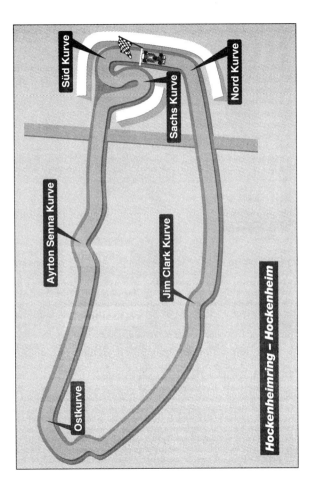

Süd Kurve

Nord Kurve

Sachs Kurve

Ayrton Senna Kurve

Jim Clark Kurve

Ostkurve

Hockenheimring – Hockenheim

Hungaroring

Hungaroring
Hungarian Grand Prix – August 10 1997
Lap Distance   2.465 miles/3.968 km
Race Distance   189.74 miles/305.536 km – 77 laps

Just 12 miles to the north-east of Budapest, Hungaroring is a modern Grand Prix complex that has been created with F1 in mind. It has hosted the Hungarian Grand Prix since 1986 but is not the best liked of tracks amongst the drivers. Bumpy and slippery, there is limited scope for overtaking with no fast corners which can make the race rather processional in nature. Grid position is therefore all important as is downforce and the circuit is second only to Monaco in this respect.

The Circuit

From the start-finish line it's full power to **Turn 1**. This is a long right-hand downhill bend taking the drivers through 180 degrees, entered in 3rd gear at 75mph, exited in 4th at 135mph. The camber on this corner can also catch drivers out or at the very least see them slipping out of the drive line and into the dirty sections of the track which does not benefit their tyres or subsequent grip. A short straight brings the cars into **Turn 2** and then **Turn 3** and here there is a choice of two lines but whether the car turns in early or late makes little difference to the amount of oversteer experienced as this long left hander begins to sweep right. 100mph in 2nd gear as the cars turn through another near 180 degrees decending first before climbing out of it.

Cars approach **Turn 4** leaving the straight at around 165mph, changing down from 6th to 4th gear while braking to 110 mph before climbing uphill on the approach to **Turn 5** – another long right hander negotiated in 3rd gear at 80mph and accelerated out of in 4th gear to 140mph.

Tune 6 leads to the highest part of the curcuit and is a right-left chicane that is entered in 2nd gear at 55mph and exited in 3rd at 115mph. **Turn 7** comes quickly and the approach to this left hander is bumpy. 3rd gear maintained throughout, 75mph being the slowest point at the apex of the curve. **Turn 8** is a right hander and is exited in 5th with the left hander taken flat out. A curving straight forms **Turn 9** and leads into **Turn 10** which is not as fast as it looks as the corner suddenly tightens. It is taken in 5th at 110mph.

Turn 11 is an off-camber and downhill right-left chicane which always seems to gather particles of grit, whilst a high kerb awaits the unsuspecting at

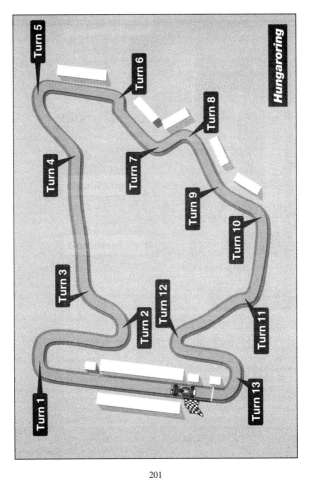

Hungaroring

Turn 1
Turn 2
Turn 3
Turn 4
Turn 5
Turn 6
Turn 7
Turn 8
Turn 9
Turn 10
Turn 11
Turn 12
Turn 13

the second apex. Taken in 3rd gear at 80mph. **Turn 12** is a hairpin-like corner directly behind the pits and taken in 2nd at 55mph. A long right-hander marks **Turn 13** – the cars first oversteer, turning to understeer by the time they exit on to the straight via the kerb. Cars take the corner at 75mph before powering up to 170mph for the straight.

5-Year Record

Year	1st	2nd	3rd	4th	5th	6th
1992	Senna (McLaren)	Mansell (Williams)	Berger (McLaren)	Hakkinen (Lotus)	Brundle (Benetton)	Capelli (Ferrari)
1993	Hill (Williams)	Patrese (Benetton)	Berger (Ferrari)	Warwick (Footwork)	Brundle (Ligier)	Wendlinger (Sauber)
1994	Schumacher (Benetton)	Hill (Williams)	Verstappen (Benetton)	Brundle (McLaren)	Blundell (Tyrrell)	Panis (Ligier)
1995	Hill (Williams)	Coulthard (Williams)	Berger (Ferrari)	Herbert (Benetton)	Frentzen (Sauber)	Panis (Ligier)
1996	Villeneuve (Williams)	Hill (Williams)	Alesi (Benetton)	Hakkinen (McLaren)	Panis (Ligier)	Barrichello (Jordan)

Qualifying

1996	1995	1994
M.Schumacher (Ferrari)	D. Hill (Williams)	M. Schumacher (Benetton)
1m 17.129s	1m 16.982	1m 18.258

Commentary

A first-second for the Williams-Renault team last year ensured them overall victory in the 1996 Constructors' Cup. It was also the fifth time their two drivers had come home one and two. Damon Hill has won twice in Hungary while Schumacher and Villeneuve will be looking to take their second victory at the circuit. Michael Schumchaer has taken pole position twice in the last three outings and a time close to or under 1m 17s should capture the position again in favourable conditions.

The stewards were busy on the Friday of last year. David Coulthard was fined US$5,000 for speeding in the pit lane, Jean Alesi was fined $10,000 and warned about his future conduct after twice passing the chequered flag, while Olivier Panis got away with a reprimand after driving his Ligier in the opposite direction to the track! In the race Giovanni Lavaggi was given a ten-second penalty for speeding in the pit lane in his Minardi.

Imola

Autodromo Enzo and Dino Ferrari
San Marino Grand Prix – April 27 1997
Lap Distance   3.132 miles/5.040 km
Race Distance   191.621 miles/308.385 km – 61 laps

Located in north-central Italy in the principality of San Marino, Imola provides one of the most atmospheric race days anywhere in the World. Major modifications have been made to the very fast circuit in the wake of the 1994 event in which Ayrton Senna and Roland Ratzenberger lost their lives. This brought revision to Tamburello, Villeneuve and Variante Bassa. It is still a long circuit with many fast straights but now much, much safer.

The Circuit

Tamburello is the first corner from the start and is a left handed S-bend which is entered in 4th gear at 75mph and exited in 4th gear at 125mph as cars power up the straight to **Villeneuve**. This is a second S-bend that slows the approach to the forthcoming hairpin and slows cars down from 165mph to 105mph in 4th gear. **Tosa** is a tight hairpin from right to left taken in 2nd gear at under 70mph. On exit cars accelerate to 165mph and climb towards **Piratella**. This is a somewhat blind left hander that is taken in 4th gear at 105mph before the driver changes quickly up to 5th gear at 160mph.

The approach to **Acque Minerali** is downhill at 75mph – a very bumpy and uncomfortable chicane negotiated in 3rd and 2nd gears. **Variante Alta** is next and coming off a short straight it is a fast chicane that can be tackled in 3rd gear and certainly requires a 3rd gear exit. Entered in 5th gear at 160mph and speeds of 85mph are maintained through it. Drivers tend to take more chance at this chicane because it does have a safe run-off area.

Out of the chicane and the track plunges downhill through some stunning countryside arriving at a double left-hander called **Rivazza** which swings the cars through 180 degrees. This requires hard braking down from 6th (180mph) to 3rd gear (80mph) shifting up briefly before changing down to tackle the final turn. Onto a slow curving right-hand line cars fly through the **Variante Bassa** at 160mph. The **Traguardo** looms up as a left-right chicane that feeds the pits straight and is taken in 2nd gear at 65mph. Cars then accelerate to 175mph across the start-finish line.

5-Year Record

Year	1st	2nd	3rd	4th	5th	6th
1992	Mansell (Williams)	Patrese (Williams)	Senna (McLaren)	Brundle (Benetton)	Alboreto (Footwork)	Martini (Dallara)
1993	Prost (Williams)	Schumacher (Benetton)	Brundle (Ligier)	Lehto (Sauber)	Alliot (Larrousse)	Barbazza (Minardi)
1994	Schumacher (Benetton)	Nannini (Ferrari)	Hakkinen (McLaren)	Wendlinger (Sauber)	Katayama (Tyrrell)	Hill (Williams)
1995	Hill (Williams)	Alesi (Ferrari)	Berger (Ferrari)	Coulthard (Williams)	Hakkinen (McLaren)	Frentzen (Sauber)
1995	Hill (Williams)	Schumacher (Ferrari)	Berger (Benetton)	Irvine (Ferrari)	Barrichello (Jordan)	Alesi (Benetton)

Qualifying

1996	1995	1994
M. Schumacher (Ferrari)	M. Schumacher (Benetton)	A.Senna (Williams)
1m 26.890	1m 27.274	1m 21.548

Commentary

Williams and Ferrari cars have come in first and second for the past two seasons and both would seem likely to be capable of similar results in 1997. Damon Hill was driving the winning car in both races.

Last year Michael Schumacher secured his first pole position for Ferrari just a couple of minutes from the finish of the one hour qualifying session at Imola. After crossing the finishing line he had a rear suspension problem and crashed, without injury, into the gravel trap at the Tamburello bend.

For the second Grand Prix in succession Frenchman Olivier Panis completed one lap too many in practice and was deducted one lap from his qualifying session.

The 80km speed limit in pit lane was constantly broken during the Imola race. Drivers who received a ten second 'stop and go' penalty included Jean Alesi, Pedro Lamy and Luca Badoer.

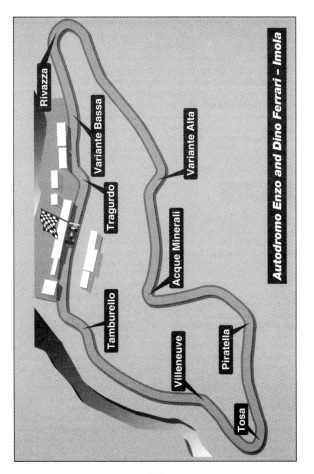

205

Interlagos

Autodromo Jose Carlos Pace
Brazilian Grand Prix – March 30 1997
Lap Distance: 2.684 miles/4.325 km
Race Distance: 190.77 miles/306.075 km – 71 laps

Located 10 miles south of central Sao Paulo the track is named after Carlos Pace who won here in 1975. It has staged the Brazilian GP since 1991. The track was resurfaced for the 1995 season but the majority of drivers complained that it was still extremely bumpy. It remains one of the most tiring circuits that taxes even the fittest of drivers.

The Circuit

At the start the cars race down to the **Descida do Sol** which drops downhill to the left. It is approached in 6th gear at about 180mph changing down approaching **S do Senna** which has a 2nd gear entry and a 3rd gear, 70mph exit. Accelerating towards and through the **Curva Do Sol** before going flat-out from along the **Reta Oposta** straight in 6th gear at 180mph.

The **Descida do Lago** is a tight left-hand corner to which there is a bumpy entrance which often throws rash drivers into a spin. Those who get through it take it in 3rd gear at 100mph. The **Ferradura** is a sweeping double apex right hander with an extremely bumpy entrance. Probably the most difficult corner on the circuit as it is approached downhill and at speed. Approached in 5th gear at 165mph. After going through the first apex in 4th gear at 90mph, the car drifts out for the second apex and, on exiting at the top in 3rd, another right hander is on top of you almost immediately as Pinheirinho approaches which is taken in 2nd gear at about 75mph.

The **Pinheirinho** is a very tight left-hander that is only taken in 2nd gear at 60mph, exited in 3rd gear and then up to 4th approaching another tight corner, this time with a right-hand turn. The **Bico de Pato** is taken in 2nd at just over 50mph, exited in 3rd gear, climbing to 5th as the car makes for a left hander prior to turning for **Mergulho**. This sweeping corner is taken in 4th gear at 145mph before accelerating along the 3rd gear **Junção**.

The final run-in to the start-finish line is fast as the circuit straightens out. **Subida do Boxes** is approached first followed by **Arquebancada**. These two left-handed corners, both banked and uphill are taken at speed before emerging onto the finishing straight.

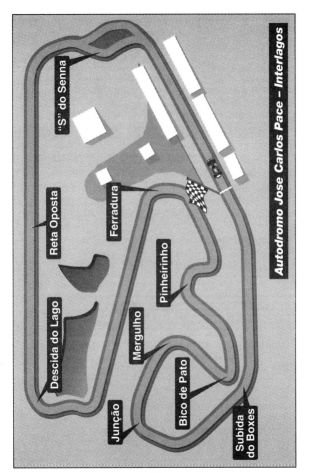

Autodromo Jose Carlos Pace – Interlagos

"S" do Senna

Reta Oposta

Ferradura

Pinheirinho

Descida do Lago

Mergulho

Junção

Bico de Pato

Subida do Boxes

5-Year Record

Year	1st	2nd	3rd	4th	5th	6th
1992	Mansell (Williams)	Patrese (Williams)	Schumacher (Benetton)	Alesi (Ferrari)	Capelli (Ferrari)	Alboreto (Footwork)
1993	Senna (McLaren)	Hill (Williams)	Schumacher (Benetton)	Herbert (Lotus)	Blundell (Ligier)	Zanardi (Lotus)
1994	Schumacher (Benetton)	Hill (Williams)	Alesi (Ferrari)	Barrichello (Jordan)	Katayama (Tyrrell)	Wendlinger (Sauber)
1995	Schumacher (Benetton)	Coulthard (Williams)	Berger (Ferrari)	Hakkinen (McLaren)	Alesi (Ferrari)	Blundell (McLaren)
1996	Hill (Williams)	Alesi (Benetton)	Schumacher (Ferrari)	Hakkinen (McLaren)	Salo (Tyrrell)	Panis (Ligier)

Qualifying

1996	1995	1994
D. Hill (Williams)	D. Hill (Williams)	A. Senna (Williams)
1m 18.111	1m 20.081	1m 15.962

Commentary

Williams have dominated pole position at Interlagos over the past three years, but only won the race from that position last year. Michael Schumacher enjoys the circuit having won twice in the past three years. Rain dominated last year's event which saw Brazilian native Rubens Barrichello qualify in second place.

Brazilian Rubens Barrichello celebrated his 50th Grand Prix race at Sao Paulo. Damon Hill clinched his 12th pole position at Sao Paulo and secured his third consecutive Grand Prix win.

German Heinz-Harald Frentzen was fined US$10,000 and warned about his future conduct by the FIA after the German driver passed the chequered flag twice after the second practice session on the Friday afternoon.

The Ligier team of Olivier Panis and Pedro Diniz were originally excluded from the qualifying times when they were adjudged to have broken the rules after Diniz had used the spare car after spinning early in the session. They were later allowed to race and both finished, with Panis scoring a World Championship point.

Jerez

Circuito de Jerez – Reserve Grand Prix
Lap Distance: 2.754 miles/4.323 km
Race Distance: 190.026 miles/298.2875 km – 69 laps

Located just north of Cadiz in southern Spain, Jerez is located in breathtaking countryside and provides outstanding facilities. As a Grand Prix circuit it is narrow and twisting and is probably more suitable to the Spanish Motorcycle Grand Prix it stages annually. Being virtually impossible to overtake, a good grid position and refuelling strategy are of utmost importance.

Jerez is the reserve Grand Prix circuit and will be called into use as substitute for any of the named circuits that, for whatever reason, are unable to host their race. Should a Grand Prix be held at Jerez it will almost certainly be classified as the European Grand Prix. The circuit last hosted a Formula 1 race in 1994 which was won by Michael Schumacher. It is used regularly for stages of the FIM World Motorcycle Championship.

The Circuit

Out of the starting grid and accelerating through to 6th gear and 180mph, **Expo 92** is approached as cars brake hard changing down to 3rd gear to negotiate this right-hand turn. A short straight run leads into **Michelin**. This is another right-hander and much tighter than Expo, requiring 2nd gear and no faster than 60mph.

Turn 3 is a sweeping turn bearing left taken in 5th gear and at speeds averaging 150mph. Coming off the gas slightly, cars enter **Sito Pons** a big right hander, at 130mph and exited at 150mph ready for the longest straight on the track which is taken flat out at 185mph, braking for the **Chicane** mid-flow. **Dry Sack** is a right-hander that takes the cars through a turn of almost 180 degrees. Approached at 130mph and exited at 90mph using 4th and 3rd gears.

Turn 6 and Turn 7 combine to bring the cars through 180 degrees. Turn 6 is a looping left-hander taken in 4th gear at 120mph. Turn 7 is slightly faster and cars can manoeuvre through it at up to 130mph. **Nieto** and **Peluqui** are two right-hand turns which follow on from one another at speeds of 90mph in 3rd gear. The final corners before the home straight is entered at **Ducodos** and finishes with a tight hairpin. This slows the cars from 6th gear down to

2nd before they turn into the finishing straight where they power through at 180mph.

5-Year Record

Year	1st	2nd	3rd	4th	5th	6th
1992	No Grand Prix staged					
1993	Senna (McLaren)	Hill (Williams)	Prost (Williams)	Herbert (Lotus)	Patrese (Benetton)	Barbazza (Minardi)
1994	Schumacher (Benetton)	Hill (Williams)	Hakkinen (McLaren)	Irvine (Jordan)	Berger (Ferrari)	Frentzen (Sauber)
1995	No Grand Prix staged					
1996	No Grand Prix staged					

1993 & 1994 events were European Grands Prix.

Qualifying

1996	1995	1994
–	–	M. Schumacher (Benetton) 1m 22.762

Commentary

If Jerez should stage a race during 1997 then Michael Schumacher is likely to be the only former winner of a Grand Prix there, lining up on the starting grid. He achieved his 1994 European Grand Prix victory in a Benetton having also won pole position.

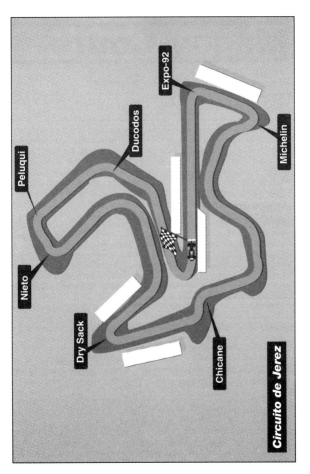

Expo-92

Ducodos

Michelin

Peluqui

Nieto

Dry Sack

Chicane

Circuito de Jerez

211

Magny-Cours

Circuit de Nevers
French Grand Prix – June 29 1997
Lap Distance   2.654 miles/4.271 km
Race Distance   180.84 miles/306 km – 72 laps

Located about half way between Paris and Lyon, Circuit de Nevers was opened to Grand Prix racing in 1991 following a massive refurbishment. This season will see the running of the 83rd Grand Prix and the seventh to be organised at Magny-Cours. Modern facilities complement a mix of slow corners, tight hairpins and quick chicanes. It's smooth surface makes it a favourite with the drivers but often difficult for teams to set the car up for, simply because there is no other circuit like it.

The Circuit

From the starting grid cars accelerate up to 165mph before entering **Grande Courbe** a long left-hand bend which is driven in 4th gear at 125mph. Drivers take great care to get the right line out of the curve into **Estoril** which is a sweeping right-hand turn that goes through 180 degrees, 4th gear is maintained at a speed in excess of 100mph. **Golf** is very nearly a straight but has a gentle curve to the right throughout its length. As such it is taken full-out in 6th gear with speeds around 180mph.

Adelaide is a 2nd gear hairpin that brings the drivers back to earth! Taken at 30mph it turns through 180 degrees and takes the vehicle back in the direction from which it has just come with the track immediately to their right. This leads straight into a fast right-left that is cleared in 4th and which leads to **Nurburgring** wriggles the cars left and right – not as tight as Adelaide but, nevertheless, is taken in 2nd gear at 50 mph despite it being long and wide. **180 Degrees** is another tight hairpin and again brings the cars through 180 degrees and back upon themselves – taken in 2nd gear at 30 mph.

From the 180 it's up quickly through the gears to 5th before changing down to meet the challenge of **Imola** at 110mph, a right-left that protects the **Chateau d'Eau** a virtual 90 degree turn entered in 4th and exited in 2nd on to a straight that allows the car to accelerate towards the 2nd gear **Chicane**. Immediately following the chicane is the sharp **Lycée** right hander taken in 2nd gear as the cars slow to 40mph before accelerating onto the finishing straight. The corner also provides the entry to the pit lane.

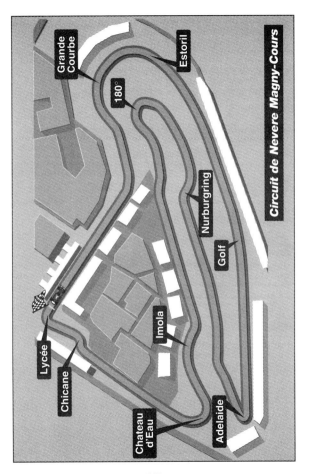

Circuit de Nevere Magny-Cours

Grande Courbe

Estoril

180°

Nurburgring

Golf

Imola

Lycée

Chicane

Chateau d'Eau

Adelaide

213

5-Year Record

Year	1st	2nd	3rd	4th	5th	6th
1992	Mansell (Williams)	Patrese (Williams)	Brundle (Benetton)	Hakkinen (Lotus)	Comas (Ligier)	Herbert (Lotus)
1993	Prost (Williams)	Hill (Williams)	Schumacher (Benetton)	Senna (McLaren)	Brundle (Ligier)	Andretti (McLaren)
1994	Schumacher (Benetton)	Hill (Williams)	Berger (Ferrari)	Frentzen (Sauber)	Martini (Minardi)	de Cesaris (Sauber)
1995	Schumacher (Benetton)	Hill (Williams)	Coulthard (Williams)	Brundle (Ligier)	Alesi (Ferrari)	Barrichello (Jordan)
1996	Hill (Williams)	Villeneuve (Williams)	Alesi (Benetton)	Berger (Benetton)	Hakkinen (McLaren)	Coulthard (McLaren)

Qualifying

1996	1995	1994
M. Schumacher (Ferrari)	D.Hill (Williams)	D.Hill (Williams)
1m 15.989	1m 17.225	1m 16.282

Commentary

Damon Hill won the 1996 French Grand Prix after finishing runner-up in the three years previous. This is another circuit where the Williams cars have done well in the past five years – they have occupied the first two places eight out of a possible ten times. Michael Schumacher, driving the Benetton in 1994 and 1995 interrupted the Williams' winning streak. In the Ferrari last year he took pole position only for the engine to blow up on the formation lap.

At last year's race British driver Johnny Herbert was disqualified from 11th place after the deflectors on his Sauber-Ford were found to be 150mm too high. Ferrari driver Eddie Irvine had to start from the back of the grid after being disqualified from the qualifying results when his car was found to have deflector panels too high by 15mm. Originally Irvine had finished 10th before the infringement was discovered when his car was weighed 22 minutes into the session.

The Benetton team were fined $10,000 for not adhering to the Race Director's instructions at least two of the team were standing in a dangerous position in pit lane.

Melbourne

Melbourne Grand Prix Circuit
Australian Grand Prix – March 9 1997
Lap Distance: 3.274 miles/5.269 km
Race Distance: 189.89 miles/305.6 km – 58 laps

Melbourne played host to its first Formula 1 World Championship Grand Prix in 1996. After 11 years in the magnificent setting of Adelaide the bid from the Victoria city was too strong to refuse. Another street circuit situated in a park, the track is a combination of fast corners and tight hairpins along with sweeping curves. The different areas on the circuit are named after the Grand Prix greats and last season's debut was another success. What a shame that a Pacific Grand Prix could not be given over to Adelaide as well.

The Circuit

Along the starting straight at 180mph past the **Fangio Stand** the cars approach two 45 degree right and left-hand turns in at the **Brabham Stand**. A change down to 3rd gear sees the first turn taken at 70mph before accelerating into 4th at 100mph and exiting in 5th at 145mph onto the 175mph straight. A sharp right-left S bend puts the cars onto a short straight to the **Whitford Stand**. Just before the stand is a sharp 90 degree right-hand turn taken in 2nd gear at 60 mph followed by a more shallow turn through 90 degrees taken in 3rd at 80mph, which sees the cars past the stand itself and accelerate onto the straight at 165mph.

A 3rd gear right-hand turn at 75mph takes the cars onto a looping right hand curve reaching 180mph which is flanked by the **Lauda Stand**. Changing down to 3rd in front of the **Clark Stand** for another tight right hander at 85mph. The **Fittipaldi Stand** marks the entrance to a long inner loop curve turning the cars left at a top speed of 175mph before they brake.

Changing down to 4th gear and 90mph the cars swing right past the **Waite Stand** and changing up to 5th and 140mph before flying past the **Hill Stand** at 175mph. Braking hard the cars change down to 3rd gear and an 80mph right-hand turn. Time to change up to 4th and 130mph past the **Stewart Stand** before another right-hander at 100mph.

The **Prost Stand** marks the most difficult section of the circuit with a near S-bend. Cars enter in 4th gear at 130mph, braking hard and changing down to

2nd to negotiate the near hair-pin at 50mph, accelerating out to a 4th gear 100mph. Onto the finishing straight and the longest section of straight on the circuit where cars can go flat out in 6th gear at 180mph passing the **Senna Stand** and across the start-finish line.

5-Year Record

Year	1st	2nd	3rd	4th	5th	6th
1992	Berger (Ferrari)	Schumacher (Benetton)	Brundle (Benetton)	Alesi (Ferrari)	Boutsen (Ligier)	Modena (Jordan)
1993	Senna (McLaren)	Prost (Williams)	Hill (Williams)	Alesi (Ferrari)	Berger (Ferrari)	Brundle (Ligier)
1994	Mansell (Williams)	Berger (Ferrari)	Brundle (McLaren)	Barrichello (Jordan)	Panis (Ligier)	Alesi (Ferrari)
1995	Hill (Williams)	Panis (Ligier)	Morbidelli (Arrows)	Blundell (McLaren)	Salo (Tyrell)	Lamy (Minardi)
1996	Hill (Williams)	Villeneuve (Williams)	Irvine (Ferrari)	Berger (Benetton)	Hakkinen (McLaren)	Salo (Tyrell)

1992-95 races at Adelaide

Qualifying

1996	1995	1994
J. Villeneuve (Williams)	–	–
1m 32.371		

Commentary

The 1996 Grand Prix threw up a number of interesting facts. Jacques Villeneuve was only the third driver in the history of Grand Prix racing to start from pole position in his debut race. The two other drivers were Carlos Reutemann and Mario Andretti. Damon Hill equalled his father Graham's record of 14 Grands Prix victories when he won in Melbourne. He also became only the fourth driver to win back to back races in the same country. Michael Schumacher, Alan Jones and Stirling Moss also achieved the feat.

The Ford Forti team were the first to suffer at the hands of the 107% rule with both their drivers, Luca Badoer and Andrea Montermini failing to qualify for the race. The race used the new starting sequence for the first time where the race is underway when all the red lights go out. Dutchman Jos Verstappen was fined US$2,500 by the FIA for abandoning his Arrows car during practice without the steering wheel in place.

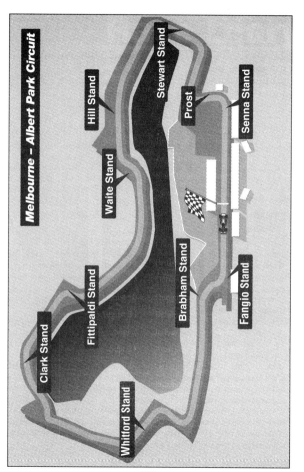

Melbourne – Albert Park Circuit

Hill Stand
Waite Stand
Stewart Stand
Prost
Senna Stand
Fittipaldi Stand
Brabham Stand
Fangio Stand
Clark Stand
Whitford Stand

Monaco

Circuit de Monaco
Monaco Grand Prix Monte Carlo – May 11 1997
Lap Distance   2.087 miles/3.328 km
Race Distance 160.68 miles/259.584 km – 78 laps

Probably the most famous Grand Prix circuit in the World, taking its macadam from the busy city streets and harbour-front of Monte Carlo in the south of France. A tight demanding circuit, there is little room on the track with over taking a near impossibility – as such pole position can be decisive. The circuit is not hard on the engines as they are never operating at full-power, it is demanding on the drivers however – a typical lap of the circuit requires 36 gear changes, that's over 2800 per race! The 1997 race will be the 55th staging of the event.

The Circuit

Approached from the start/finish line at 160mph in 6th gear then it's down into 2nd gear at 50mph for the **Virage de Sainte Devote** right hander. The **Montee du Beau Rivage** takes the cars past the world famous Rosie's Bar in 6th gear at 155mph and then it's over the crest of the hill and down to 4th gear as **Virage Massenet** beckons. A long left hander, the car must be kept close to the inside kerb in 3rd gear at 80mph. The cars come into **Virage Casino** which is a quick right hander that is taken in 3rd gear at 70mph.

Coming out of Casino the cars get a chance to accelerate briefly along a short straight before they enter one of the most complex parts of the course. The **Virage Mirabeau** is approached downhill in 4th at 130mph, requiring fast gear changes to get into 2nd gear for this bumpy right hander taken slowly at 30mph. Out of this comes the short approach to the **Virage Loews** a left-hand hairpin negotiated in 1st gear at about 20mph, the steering turned full lock, then right. The turns are ended by the **Virage du Portier** another sharp right-hander cleared in 2nd gear at 40mph.

Coming out of the turns the cars start on a long sweep through the **Tunnel**. Noise and sparks fly as the cars change up to 6th gear and 155mph. Once out of the tunnel left-right **Nouvelle Chicane** is approached at 170mph before drivers change down to 2nd gear and a sedate 30mph.

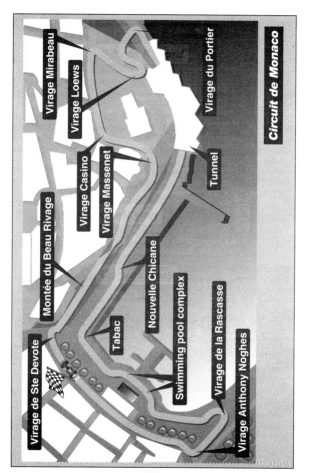

Circuit de Monaco

Virage Mirabeau
Virage Loews
Virage du Portier
Virage Casino
Virage Massenet
Tunnel
Montée du Beau Rivage
Nouvelle Chicane
Tabac
Swimming pool complex
Virage de Ste Devote
Virage de la Rascasse
Virage Anthony Noghes

The most spectacular and glamorous part of the course is **Tabac** lying as it does alongside the harbour. Driven through at 90mph in 4th gear. Piscine or the **Swimming Pool** complex provides a short kink in the circuit which push the drivers through a succession of gear changes and speeds ranging from 50mph to 100mph. For the 1997 season the corner has been slightly modified with the left-handed corner reduced in radius to about 35 degrees thus equalling the right-handed exit. The chicane has also been moved back towards Tabac using land reclaimed from the harbour. The change is to make the corner safer.

Virage de la Rascasse is the slowest part of the circuit with a very tight hairpin that is taken in 1st gear at a crawling 20mph. Along a very short straight and a faster right-hander **Virage Antony Noghes** is taken in 2nd at 45mph before accelerating and climbing upwards onto the start-finish straight.

5-Year Record

Year	1st	2nd	3rd	4th	5th	6th
1992	Senna (McLaren)	Mansell (Williams)	Patrese (Williams)	Schumacher (Benetton)	Brundle (Benetton)	Gachot (Larrousse)
1993	Senna (McLaren)	Hill (Williams)	Alesi (Ferrari)	Prost (Williams)	Fittipaldi (Minardi)	Brundle (Ligier)
1994	Schumacher (Benetton)	Brundle (McLaren)	Berger (Ferrari)	de Cesaris (Jordan)	Alesi (Ferrari)	Alboreto (Minardi)
1995	Schumacher (Benetton)	Hill (Williams)	Berger (Ferrari)	Herbert (Benetton)	Blundell (McLaren)	Frentzen (Sauber)
1996	Panis (Ligier)	Coulthard (McLaren)	Herbert (Sauber)	Frentzen (Sauber)	Salo (Tyrrell)	Hakkinen (McLaren)

Qualifying

1996	1995	1994
M. Schumacher (Ferrari)	D. Hill (Williams)	M. Schumacher (Benetton)
1m 20.356	1m 21.952	1m 18.560

Commentary

Last year produced one of the most remarkable Monaco Grands Prix of all time without one of the top three teams managing to finish. Andrea Montermini missed the race after crashing his Forti Ford during the special 15 minute wet weather practice session on Sunday. Montermini had qualified in 22nd place, driving the new car.

Montreal

Gilles Villeneuve Circuit
Canadian Grand Prix – June 15 1997
Lap Distance   2.747 miles/4.421 km
Race Distance 189.543 miles/305.049 km – 69 laps

Located on the Ile Notre Dame, the circuit is within easy reach of the Montreal city centre. It has a picturesque backdrop which includes views of the Lawrence River and the old Olympic Rowing Basin. The Canadian Grand Prix has been staged here since 1978 and the track part permanent and part street circuit. With an equal mix of slow and fast corners it has a reputation for being hard on cars. This is the only race to take place on the course each year so the roads collect a great amount of grit which the wind shifts about causing severe grip problems. As a result comparatively few cars actually finish the race.

The Circuit

From the starting grid the cars accelerate to 170mph but change down rapidly at **Turn 1** from 6th to a 50mph 2nd gear as the track swings right and turns through 180 degrees at the **Virage Senna**. The right-hand turn is taken at 40mph with cars quickly accelerating to 150mph and 6th gear as the track straightens out. A series of bends (**Turn 2-6**) see the cars down to 3rd gear and speeds averaging 60mph as the circuit sweeps left and then right.

Turn 7 marks the Pont de la Concorde occupies about a third of the track length, being a long straight which is broken up by a quick right-left turn – **Turn 8** and **Turn 9** – that can be negotiated in 3rd gear. Decelerating from 170mph the right bend is entered at 50mph and then exited at 65mph. The lead-up to the Pits Hairpin is done at full throttle with a top speed of around 170mph.

Turn 10 marks the Pits Hairpin – a long loop which often sees a lot of overtaking action as it is quite wide. It is the slowest part of the track with cars braking down to around 30mph. Patients in the Hospital get a good view of the cars accelerating up through the gears to 6th at 150mph through **Turn 11**. The Casino Straight is the final approach to the home straight. This was modified last year from the Casino Bend (**Turn 12** and **Turn 13**) which used to be a chicane slowing the cars down into the final straight; now it much shallower.

5-Year Record

Year	1st	2nd	3rd	4th	5th	6th
1992	Berger (Ferrari)	Schumacher (Benetton)	Alesi (Ferrari)	Wendlinger (March)	de Cesaris (Tyrrell)	Comas (Ligier)
1993	Prost (Williams)	Schumacher (Benetton)	Hill (Williams)	Berger (Ferrari)	Brundle (Ligier)	Wendlinger (Sauber)
1994	Schumacher (Benetton)	Hill (Williams)	Alesi (Ferrari)	Berger (Ferrari)	Coulthard (Williams)	Lehto (Benetton)
1995	Alesi (Ferrari)	Barrichello (Jordan)	Irvine (Jordan)	Panis (Ligier)	Schumacher (Benetton)	Morbidelli (Footwork)
1996	Hill (Williams)	Villeneuve (Williams)	Alesi (Benetton)	Coulthard (McLaren)	Hakkinen (McLaren)	Brundle (Jordan)

Qualifying

1996	1995	1994
D. Hill (Williams)	M. Schumacher (Benetton)	M. Schumacher (Benetton)
1m 21.059	1m 27.661	1m 26.178

Commentary

Martin Brundle celebrated his 150th Grand Prix appearance in Montreal in 1996. The British Jordan Peugeot driver made his debut at the Brazilian Grand Prix on 25 March 1984. Ukyo Katayama received a one race ban, suspended for two races, following his collision with Ricardo Rosset in the Canadian Grand Prix.

Nelson Piquet is the most successful driver at the Canadian Grand Prix. He won on three occasions: 1991, 1984, 1982. McLaren are the most successful constructors in Canada, having won the race on seven separate occasions.

Ricardo Patrese has competed in more Canadian Grands Prix than any other driver. He drove in 16 races between 1977 and 1993.

Australian Jack Brabham is the oldest winner of the Canadian Grand Prix. He was 41 years four months and 25 days old when he won the Grand Prix in 1967. Three drivers have secured their first Grand Prix victories in Canada. They are Gilles Villeneuve in 1978, Thierry Boutsen 1989 and Jean Alesi in 1995.

Three drivers have also secured their last Grand Prix victories in Canada. They were Peter Revson in 1973, Jacques Laffite in 1981 and Nelson Piquet

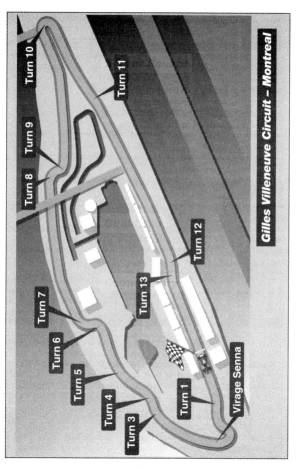

Gilles Villeneuve Circuit – Montreal

Turn 10
Turn 9
Turn 8
Turn 11
Turn 7
Turn 6
Turn 5
Turn 4
Turn 3
Turn 13
Turn 12
Turn 1
Virage Senna

Monza

Autodromo Nationale di Monza
Italian Grand Prix – September 7 1997
Lap Distance   3.604 miles/5.80 km
Race Distance   191.01 miles/307.50 km – 53 laps

Fifteen miles north-east of Milan, Monza was built in 1922. The modern day autodromo combines fast sweeping corners and long straights with Parabolica and Lesmo two of the more famous. The Italian Grand Prix has been staged here for all but one year since the World Championship was introduced in 1950.

The Circuit

The **Rettifilio Tribune** is the long start straight and leads to the **Variante Goodyear**. This is approached at some 190mph due to the long, wide pit straight that precedes it. A very fast but bumpy left-right-left-right second gear chicane that's entered in 2nd at 55mph and exited in 3rd at 110mph. Almost immediatley is **Curva Grande** which is a very bumpy longish right hander that is hard work on the steering. Drivers invariably use the kerb at its exit at 185mph along the straight.

The **Variante della Roggia** is also known as 2A Variante; the braking area prior to entering this left-right chicane is both bumpy and slippy. Approached in 6th gear at 190mph, it is negotiated in 2nd at 60mph and exited in 3rd at 85mph. **Curvo di Lesmos** is a contentious sharp right handers. Invariably taken at speed shifting between 4th and 3rd gears with speeds ranging between 150mph and 95mph. Coming out of the turn the cars rocket down **Curva del Serraglio**, a long straight that means the driver approaches the next chicane at speeds approaching 200mph.

Drivers hope their brakes are in good order as they approach Curva del Vialone, this left hander braking from 200 mph in 6th gear to 4th gear at the 100 metre board. Then onto **Variante Ascari** the second part of the chicane quickly flicking right, then left. Exited in fifth on to the **Rettifilio Centro** straight.

The **Curva Parabolica** is a long, looping right hander that is entered from the Rettifilio straight in 4th gear at 100mph before moving into a 160mph 5th gear as the bend begins to open up and is exited in 6th. This corner is known for generating a great deal of understeer. Cars head towards the finishing line at up to 200mph in 6th gear.

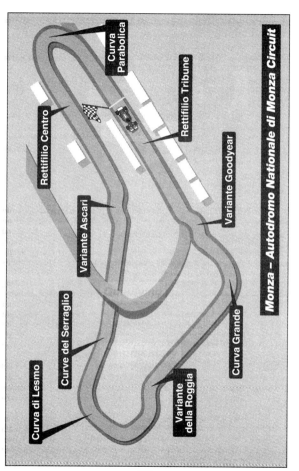

Monza – Autodromo Nationale di Monza Circuit

Curva Parabolica

Rettifilio Tribune

Rettifilio Centro

Variante Goodyear

Variante Ascari

Curve del Serraglio

Curva Grande

Curva di Lesmo

Variante della Roggia

5-Year Record

Year	1st	2nd	3rd	4th	5th	6th
1992	Senna (McLaren)	Brundle (Benetton)	Schumacher (Benetton)	Berger (McLaren)	Patrese (Williams)	de Cesaris (Tyrrell)
1993	Hill (Williams)	Alesi (Ferrari)	Andretti (McLaren)	Wendlinger (Sauber)	Patrese (Benetton)	Comas (Larrousse)
1994	Hill (Williams)	Berger (Ferrari)	Verstappen (Benetton)	Barrichello (Jordan)	Brundle (McLaren)	Coulthard (Williams)
1995	Herbert (Benetton)	Hakkinen (McLaren)	Frentzen (Sauber)	Blundell (McLaren)	Salo (Tyrell)	Boullion (Sauber)
1996	Schumacher (Ferrari)	Alesi (Benetton)	Hakkinen (McLaren)	Brundle (Jordan)	Barrichello (Jordan)	Diniz (Ligier)

Qualifying

1996	1995	1994
D. Hill (Williams)	D. Coulthard (Williams)	J. Alesi (Ferrari)
1m 24.204	1m 24.462	1m 23.844

Commentary

Michael Schumacher delighted the *tifosi* at last year's Italian Grand Prix by coming home first after Damon Hill, who secured pole position, spun out early on. Being the home race for Ferrari the fans poured into the circuit. Michael Schumacher's test at Monza in the week prior to the race attracted 13,000 fans alone.

After drivers had been constantly warned about driving across the kerbs at the chicanes at Monza, stacks of tyres were placed at the exit of two chicanes for qualifying and the race last year. They created a lot of problems for drivers and it will be interesting to see if they are retained in 1997.

Nurburgring

Nurburgring (Germany)
Luxembourg Grand Prix – September 28 1997
Lap Distance   2.822 miles/4.542 kms
Race Distance   189.683 miles/304.314 kms – 67 laps

Despite being situated in Germany, about 55 miles south-west of Cologne, the Nurburgring is staging the first ever Luxembourg Grand Prix. The circuit was opened for Grand Prix action in 1984, when Alain Prost won the European event. This was followed by the German Grand Prix which was the last for some time. Then after 10 years of Grand Prix inactivity the circuit was used for the European Grand Prix in 1996 which gave Jacques Villeneuve his first win in Formula One.

Situated in beautiful countryside, the Nurburgring is both fast and forgiving with wide run-off areas and large gravel traps. Its twelve corners and curves make for an exciting race.

The Circuit

Out of the blocks and into 6th gear at 180mph towards the **Castrol 'S'** bend which is entered at 75mph in 2nd gear. The curve is exited in 4th gear at 130mph as drivers change up. Quickly up to 6th gear and accelerating to 165mph for the approach to **Ford Kurve**. This is a tight right-handed curve of an almost hairpin nature taken at 65mph in 2nd gear before accelerating up to 170mph in 6th gear.

The **Dunlop Kehre** is a right-hand 180 degree loop making it the second slowest part of the circuit at under 65 mph in 2nd gear. Out of here the approach to the **Yokohama Kurve** sees the cars in top gear at 180mph which is halved to 3rd gear at 95mph through the near 90 degree left-hand turn. Having swept left, the **Bit Kurve** sweeps another 90 degrees through a right-hand turn again in 3rd gear at 95mph.

Onto the straight taken full-out in 6th gear at 180mph, cars brake to the **Veedol Chicane** which is the slowest part of the course as cars brake down to 60mph and sweep left and then right in 2nd gear, before accelerating to 135mph in 4th gear. Out of here comes the sharp left-hand turn through 160 degrees which marks the **Valvoline Kurve.** This is taken in 2nd gear at 75mph before accelerating out onto the finishing straight at top speed.

5-Year Record

Year	1st	2nd	3rd	4th	5th	6th
1996	Villeneuve	Schumacher	Coulthard	Hill	Barrichello	Brundle
	(Williams)	(Ferrari)	(McLaren)	(Williams)	(Jordan)	(Jordan)

1992-95 – No Grand Prix on this circuit. 1996 – European Grand Prix.

Qualifying

1996	1995	1994
D. Hill (Williams)	–	–
1m 18.941		

Commentary

The Nurburgring celebrates its 70th birthday this year. The old circuit was opened on 18 June 1927.

At last year's European Grand Prix, Finnish driver Mika Hakkinen equalled the record of having two ten second 'stop go' penalties imposed on him during a race, after speeding in the pit lane. Both Tyrrell Yamaha drivers were excluded from the results after the race at the Nurburgring. Mika Salo, who originally finished tenth, was excluded because his car was underweight. Ukyo Katayama was excluded from 12th because he received a push start.

The European Grand Prix turned into an expensive race for the Benetton Renault team, and their French driver Jean Alesi in particular. In all they were fined US$22,500 after Alesi crashed on the second lap of the race at the chicane. Alesi was fined US$2,500 for crossing the track during the race. He was fined a further $10,000 for leaving the circuit without their permission and the Benetton team were fined a similar amount for letting him break the rules!

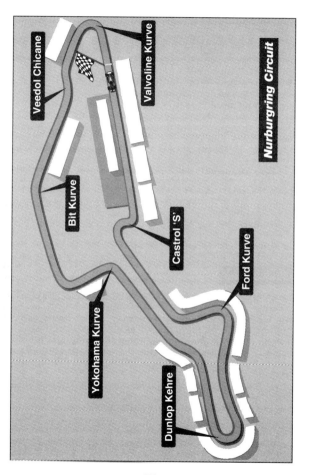

Nurburgring Circuit

Veedol Chicane

Valvoline Kurve

Bit Kurve

Castrol 'S'

Ford Kurve

Yokohama Kurve

Dunlop Kehre

229

Silverstone

Silverstone Circuit
British Grand Prix – July 13 1997
Lap Distance   3.196 miles/5.143 km
Race Distance   194.956 miles/313.723 km – 61 laps

Silverstone is Britain's longest continually used race circuit and staged the first ever British Grand Prix in 1926. Although not used for all British Grand Prix, it has held the event since 1987. The circuit is located in the Northamptonshire countryside near the village of the same name.

Operated and owned by the British Racing Drivers' Club, Silverstone held the first ever round of the World Championship in 1950, and this season will be the 31st held at the circuit where a near 100,000 crowd is expected. Most drivers feel that the Becketts complex of turns is one of the best sections of race track in the world.

During the lead up to the 1997 season the circuit underwent several changes with Priory, Brooklands, Luffield and Copse either re-shaped or re-profiled. The changes will allow increased speed and added safety and also increase the lap distance slightly.

The Circuit

From the grid, cars pull away and the straight allows speeds of 175mph to be reached on the approach to **Copse**. The shallow right handed double-turn has now been replaced by a single corner, opening out onto the approach to Maggots. Taken in 4th gear at speeds in excess of 100mph, the Maggotts-Becketts complex is approached in 6th gear **Maggots** is taken in 5th at 135mph leading to **Becketts**, a left hander entered in 4th at 125mph and completed in 4th. **Chapel** ends the series of left-right bends which maintains 4th gear.

The **Hanger Straight** is the fastest part of the circuit at 180mph before braking hard into **Stowe**, a right-hand turn that can be taken in 3rd gear and speeds of 70mph maintained. **Vale** is a quick straight in which the cars go through at something like 170mph with a 3rd gear, sharp left into **Club**, a right-hand corner. Both Vale and Club present good overtaking opportunities.

Abbey is a 3rd gear, 75mph left-right bend leading into **Farm Straight** and the right-turning **Bridge** the corner entered out of Farm at 150mph. Priory and Brooklands are two corners which steer the car through 180

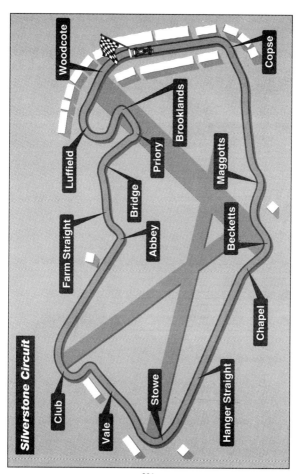

Silverstone Circuit

Woodcote · Copse · Brooklands · Luffield · Priory · Maggotts · Bridge · Abbey · Farm Straight · Becketts · Chapel · Club · Stowe · Vale · Hanger Straight

degrees. These have both been re-developed in the run up to the 1997 season. **Priory** has been re-shaped to provide a longer following straight for safety. It is negotiated in 3rd at 90mph and the approach to **Brooklands**, which used to be quite tight, has been moved back to provide a more open curve that allows cars to maintain 3rd gear through it.

Luffield used to be two corners called Luffield 1 and Luffield 2. Now it has been re-profiled with a camber to provide a single, faster corner which takes the cars through 180 degrees for a quick dash through **Woodcote** to the finishing straight at 175mph.

5-Year Record

Year	1st	2nd	3rd	4th	5th	6th
1992	Mansell (Williams)	Patrese (Williams)	Brundle (Benetton)	Schumacher (Benetton)	Berger (McLaren)	Hakkinen (Lotus)
1993	Prost (Williams)	Schumacher (Benetton)	Patrese (Benetton)	Herbert (Lotus)	Senna (McLaren)	Warwick (Footwork)
1994	Hill (Williams)	Alesi (Ferrari)	Hakkinen (McLaren)	Barrichello (Jordan)	Coulthard (Williams)	Katayama (Tyrrell)
1995	Herbert (Benetton)	Alesi (Ferrari)	Coulthard (Williams)	Panis (Ligier)	Blundell (McLaren)	Frentzen (Sauber)
1996	Villeneuve (Williams)	Alesi (Benetton)	Hakkinen (McLaren)	Barrichello (Jordan)	Coulthard (McLaren)	Brundle (Jordan)

Qualifying

1996	*1995*	*1994*
D. Hill (Williams)	D. Hill (Williams)	D. Hill (Williams)
1m 26.875	1m 28.124	1m 24.960

Commentary

Damon Hill has dominated qualifying at Silverstone in the past three years, but only won once. Hill was awarded the Mike Hawthorn Trophy for the third year running before the race last year. The trophy is given to the British or Commonwealth driver who has scored the most points in the Formula One World Championship. Hill has won it in 1993, 1994 and 1995.

The Jordan team were fined US$10,000 for not having a team member with a fire extinguisher when they refuelled one of their cars during qualifying. Ligier were fined US$10,000, with US$5,000 suspended for the next four races, for pit lane safety offences.

Spa

Circuit de Spa-Francorchamps
Belgian Grand Prix – August 24 1997
Lap Distance   4.334 miles/6.974 km
Race Distance   190.4 miles/306.865 km – 44 laps

Lying 30 miles south-east of Liege, Spa-Francorchamps is located in central Belgium. First used in 1985, at 4.334 miles in length it is the longest circuit in use in the World Championship. A temporary circuit that makes use of public roads, it remains a firm favourite with most drivers not least because of its picturesque setting, and because it is demanding enough to present a difficult challenge to those racing.

The Circuit

From the start, the corner at **La Source** comes very quickly after the beginning of the race and is a sharp right hander taken in 2nd gear at 40mph before accelerating along the straight to 180mph. Next up comes **Eau Rouge**, entered in 5th gear; this 'kink' in the track goes sharply downhill and then uphill left, right, and left. Cars exit at **Raidillon** and then encounter the fastest part of the course along the Kemmel straight at 190mph.

As the track bears round slowly to the right, there exists good overtaking possibilities at **Les Combes** due to the good run-off areas. The right-left combination chicane is taken in 3rd gear and 80mph and is exited at **Malmedy**.

Rivage is a virtual hairpin which, due to being off camber and downhill, causes cars all sorts of steering problems. It is approached in 4th gear at 155mph, taken in 2nd at 70mph and exited in 3rd at 110mph. Out of Rivage the cars sweep through **Pouhon** at 100mph towards the double-left hander called Le Pouhon (6). Also off camber, it is entered and exited in 5th at 160mph, with a change down to 4th mid-way through. On exit cars power through the gears to 175mph before slowing at **Fanges** – a right-left chicane which is taken in 3rd gear at 95mph.

Stavelot is a double right-hand loop turning the cars through 180 degrees as they go downhill. Entered in 3rd with 4th (135mph) being engaged in the middle, but it is bumpy and cars tend to skip about a bit. **Blanchimont** is a long sweeping left hander taken full-out in 6th gear at 185mph. With the start-finish line almost in sight, **Bus Stop Chicane** appears, a sharp right-left-right chicane that slows the cars right down to a 2nd gear 50mph before they emerge on to the pit straight at 170mph.

5-Year Record

Year	1st	2nd	3rd	4th	5th	6th
1992	Schumacher (Benetton)	Mansell (Williams)	Patrese (Williams)	Brundle (Benetton)	Senna (McLaren)	Hakkinen (Lotus)
1993	Hill (Williams)	Schumacher (Benetton)	Prost (Williams)	Senna (McLaren)	Herbert (Lotus)	Patrese (Benetton)
1994	Hill (Williams)	Hakkinen (McLaren)	Verstappen (Benetton)	Coulthard (Williams)	Blundell (Tyrrell)	Morbidelli (Arrows)
1995	Schumacher (Benetton)	Hill (Williams)	Brundle (Ligier)	Frentzen (Sauber)	Blundell (McLaren)	Barrichello (Jordan)
1996	Schumacher (Ferrari)	Villeneuve (Williams)	Hakkinen (McLaren)	Alesi (Benetton)	Hill (Williams)	Berger (Benetton)

Qualifying

1996	1995	1994
J. Villeneuve (Williams)	G. Berger (Benetton)	R. Barrichello (Jordan)
1m 50.574	1m 54.392	2m 21.163

Commentary

The Belgian Grand Prix has been dominated by Michael Schumacher and Damon Hill in the past five years. The German will be going for a third successive, and fourth victory in all, this year.

In 1994 Rubens Barrichello secured what at the start of the 1997 season was Jordan's first and only pole position to date. It remains the Brazilian's only pole as well.

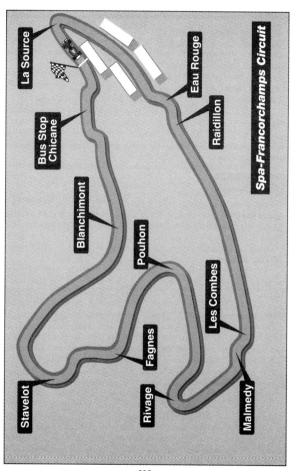

Spa-Francorchamps Circuit

La Source
Eau Rouge
Raidillon
Bus Stop Chicane
Blanchimont
Pouhon
Les Combes
Fagnes
Stavelot
Rivage
Malmedy

235

Suzuka

Suzuka International Racing Course
Japanese Grand Prix – October 12 1997
Lap Distance   3.64 miles/5.864km
Race Distance   193.126 miles/310.792km – 53 laps

Located between Osaka and Nagoya south-west of Tokyo, Suzuka has been a regular date on the Grand Prix calendar since 1987. The circuit is unique to the Championship in that it follows a 'figure of eight' pattern with numerous turns and straights.

The Circuit

The start is downhill and this can help cars get away. Indeed in 1988 it helped Ayrton Senna get away after he stalled just before the go signal. Once away the cars approach **First Curve** flat out in 6th gear at speeds of up to 190mph with a change down to 5th into the bend and into a second curve which is much tighter than the first corner and can only be negotiated in 4th with speed dropping to 95mph.

The **S Curve** is a left-right-left-right combination that severely taxes any car that is not well balanced. It can usually be taken in 4th. The sequence is entered at 130mph dropping to 90mph on exit. On exiting, the S Curve's 4th gear is maintained for the approach to the **Dunlop Curve**. This long left hander is extremely bumpy with plenty of understeer at 140mph.

The **Degner Curve** is a tight right hander that is entered in 4th gear at 120mph, down to 3rd as the second part of the corner becomes tighter still, and then generally exited with the use of the kerb. Then it is up to 4th and 5th to go under the bridge where the course crosses itself to the **Hairpin Curve**. This is guarded by a short right hander which slows the cars, but then they have to get down very quickly to 2nd gear for the 40mph hairpin.

Spoon Curve is approached via a long looping right hander in 6th gear at 170mph before entering the actual left hander in 4th. It tightens up forcing the cars to brake from 110mph to 80mph as they drift to the outside. From here its a 185mph straight-screamer to **130R**, a very fast left hander which forces a slight deceleration to 165mph as it crosses over the track below. The **Casino Chicane** (Triangle Chicane) guards the entrance to the finishing straight. The

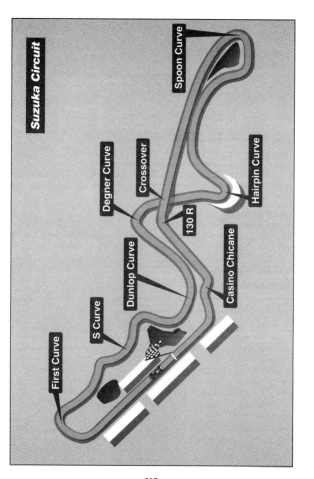

Suzuka Circuit

First Curve
S Curve
Dunlop Curve
Degner Curve
Crossover
130 R
Spoon Curve
Casino Chicane
Hairpin Curve

right-left combination is taken in 1st at 40mph with the cars having to break hard from 175mph as they approach it.

5-Year Record

Year	1st	2nd	3rd	4th	5th	6th
1992	Patrese (Williams)	Berger (McLaren)	Brundle (Benetton)	de Cesaris (Tyrrell)	Alesi (Ferrari)	Fittipaldi (Minardi)
1993	Senna (McLaren)	Prost (Williams)	Hakkinen (McLaren)	Hill (Williams)	Barrichello (Jordan)	Irvine (Jordan)
1994	Hill (Williams)	Schumacher (Benetton)	Alesi (Ferrari)	Mansell (Williams)	Irvine (Jordan)	Frentzen (Sauber)
1995	Schumacher (Benetton)	Hakkinen (McLaren)	Herbert (Benetton)	Irvine (Jordan)	Panis (Ligier)	Salo (Tyrell)
1996	Hill (Williams)	Schumacher (Ferrari)	Hakkinen (McLaren)	Berger (Benetton)	Brundle (Jordan)	Frentzen (Sauber)

Qualifying

1996	1995	1994
J. Villeneuve (Williams) 1m 38.909	M.Schumacher (Benetton) 1m 38.023	M.Schumacher (Benetton) 1m 37.209

Commentary

Damon Hill's victory last year secured his first Drivers' World Championship. It was the first time in the history of the sport that a father and son have won the Drivers' World Championship.

Jacques Villeneuve gave the Williams team their 100th fastest lap at Suzuka. It was the 50th all-Williams front row on the grid at Suzuka.

Jacques Villeneuve was in pole position for the third time this season at Suzuka.

Gerhard Berger (1987, 1991). Damon Hill (1994) and Michael Schumacher (1995) were the previous winners of the Japanese Grand Prix on the Suzuka track.

107% Times

To qualify for the starting grid, cars must finish within 107% of the pole position qualifying time. The simple table below provides a rough 107% guide for potential qualifying times.

Qualifying Time	107% Time	Qualifying Time	107% Time
1m 15.00s	1m 20.25s	1m 53.00s	1m 60.91s
1m 16.00s	1m 21.32s	1m 54.00s	1m 61.98s
1m 17.00s	1m 22.39s	1m 55.00s	1m 63.05s
1m 18.00s	1m 23.46s	1m 56.00s	1m 64.12s
1m 19.00s	1m 24.53s	1m 57.00s	1m 65.19s
1m 20.00s	1m 25.60s	1m 58.00s	1m 66.26s
1m 21.00s	1m 26.67s	1m 59.00s	1m 67.33s
1m 22.00s	1m 27.74s	2m 00.00s	2m 08.40s
1m 23.00s	1m 28.81s	2m 01.00s	2m 09.47s
1m 24.00s	1m 29.88s	2m 02.00s	2m 10.54s
1m 25.00s	1m 30.95s	2m 03.00s	2m 11.61s
1m 26.00s	1m 32.02s	2m 04.00s	2m 12.68s
1m 27.00s	1m 33.09s	2m 05.00s	2m 13.75s
1m 28.00s	1m 34.16s	2m 06.00s	2m 14.82s
1m 29.00s	1m 35.23s	2m 07.00s	2m 15.89s
1m 30.00s	1m 36.30s	2m 08.00s	2m 16.96s
1m 31.00s	1m 37.37s	2m 09.00s	2m 18.03s
1m 32.00s	1m 38.44s	2m 10.00s	2m 19.10s
1m 33.00s	1m 39.51s	2m 11.00s	2m 20.17s
1m 34.00s	1m 40.58s	2m 12.00s	2m 21.24s
1m 35.00s	1m 41.65s	2m 13.00s	2m 22.31s
1m 36.00s	1m 42.72s	2m 14.00s	2m 23.38s
1m 37.00s	1m 43.79s	2m 15.00s	2m 24.45s
1m 38.00s	1m 44.86s	2m 16.00s	2m 25.52s
1m 39.00s	1m 45.93s	2m 17.00s	2m 26.59s
1m 40.00s	1m 47.00s	2m 18.00s	2m 27.66s
1m 41.00s	1m 48.07s	2m 19.00s	2m 28.73s
1m 42.00s	1m 49.14s	2m 20.00s	2m 29.80s
1m 43.00s	1m 50.21s	2m 21.00s	2m 30.87s
1m 44.00s	1m 51.28s	2m 22.00s	2m 31.94s
1m 45.00s	1m 52.35s	2m 23.00s	2m 33.01s
1m 46.00s	1m 53.42s	2m 24.00s	2m 34.08s
1m 47.00s	1m 54.49s	2m 25.00s	2m 35.15s
1m 48.00s	1m 55.56s	2m 26.00s	2m 36.22s
1m 49.00s	1m 56.63s	2m 27.00s	2m 37.29s
1m 50.00s	1m 57.70s	2m 28.00s	2m 38.36s
1m 51.00s	1m 58.77s	2m 29.00s	2m 39.43s
1m 52.00s	1m 59.84s	2m 30.00s	2m 40.50s

Race Diary '97

Listed below are dates and venues for the 1997 Formula One season which consists of 16 races. Although the dates and venues of these races were correct at the time of writing they are subject to change and alteration.

Date	Grand Prix	Circuit	Laps	Start GMT
March 9	Australian	Melbourne	58	04.00 hours
March 30	Brazilian	Interlagos	71	16.00 hours
April 13	Argentinian	Buenos Aires	72	16.00 hours
April 27	San Marino	Imola	63	12.00 hours
May 11	Monaco	Monte Carlo	78	13.30 hours
May 25	Spanish	Catalunya	65	12.00 hours
June 15	Canadian	Montreal	69	18.00 hours
June 29	French	Magny-Cours	72	12.00 hours
July 13	British	Silverstone	61	13.00 hours
July 27	German	Hockenheim	45	12.00 hours
August 10	Hungarian	Hungaroring	77	12.00 hours
August 24	Belgian	Spa	44	12.00 hours
Sept 7	Italian	Monza	53	12.00 hours
Sept 21	Austrian	A1-Ring	71	12,00 hours
Sept 28	Luxembourg	Nurburgring	67	12.00 hours
October 12	Japanese	Suzuka	52	04.00 hours
October 26	Portuguese	Estoril	70	13.00 hours
Reserve	Spain	Jerez		